For my own father,
Andrew,
who carried me all of the way here,

and for Simon, Nancy and Esther,
who make every single day brighter.

Jewish Masculinity in the Holocaust

Jewish Masculinity in the Holocaust

Between Destruction and Construction

Maddy Carey

BLOOMSBURY ACADEMIC
LONDON • NEW YORK • OXFORD • NEW DELHI • SYDNEY

BLOOMSBURY ACADEMIC
Bloomsbury Publishing Plc
50 Bedford Square, London, WC1B 3DP, UK
1385 Broadway, New York, NY 10018, USA

BLOOMSBURY, BLOOMSBURY ACADEMIC and the Diana logo are
trademarks of Bloomsbury Publishing Plc

First published 2017
Paperback edition published 2019

A catalogue record for this book is available from the British Library.

ISBN: HB: 978-1-3500-0806-9
PB: 978-1-3501-0848-6
ePDF: 978-1-3500-0808-3
eBook: 978-1-3500-0809-0

Names: Carey, Maddy, author.
Title: Jewish masculinity in the Holocaust: between destruction and
construction/Maddy Carey.
Description: New York: Bloomsbury Academic, 2017.
Identifiers: LCCN 2017009971 | ISBN 9781350008069 (hardback) |
ISBN 9781350008090 (eBook)
Subjects: LCSH: Masculinity. | Sex role–Psychological aspects |
Jewish men–Psychology. | Holocaust survivors–Psychology. |
Holocaust, Jewish (1939–1945)–Psychological aspects
Classification: LCC BF692.5.C37 2017 | DDC 305.38/8924–dc23
LC record available at https://lccn.loc.gov/2017009971

Typeset by Integra Software Services Pvt. Ltd.

To find out more about our authors and books visit
www.bloomsbury.com and sign up for our newsletters.

Contents

Acknowledgement

First, I owe my sincere thanks to Dan Stone, who taught and supervised me for over 9 years, who kept encouraging me to publish when my life had wandered and who offered me the ongoing advice and support which made this book possible. To many others who taught and inspired me throughout my time as a history student, perhaps most importantly, Jinty Nelson, Stephen Lovell, Ian Wood and John Seabrook, I am also truly grateful.

Secondly, I offer thanks to the Holocaust Research Centre at Royal Holloway, the Friendly Hand Society and the Rothschild Foundation whose generous funding allowed me to complete the research which underpins this book. Also a financial support, but very much more than that, Vilnius Yiddish Institute, shaped my understanding of the life and culture destroyed by the Holocaust in a way that no library or book ever could, and enabled me to spend a month of sun, potato pancakes and diphthongs in Lithuania learning Yiddish with the incredible and humbling Jewish community of Vilna and their songs.

To my friends I owe a great deal more than I can repay. Alex Fairfax and his family without whom I would never have completed my PhD, and therefore this book, big Nancy who, even when carrying her own weights with such grace, has never, ever not been there, Annik and Kate who make me belly laugh, Britta who makes me pause and Rebecca who took me for cocktails when I was looking grey. And to our family, the Jessops whose joy and positivity shine into our lives and my complicated lot who offer endless doses of wisdom, laughter and love, too many to mention individually but more important that I can say.

And so to the final few. Alan, my father-in-law and a man of strength, pride and love, exactly like the fathers in this book. Matthew, my theoretical support when my brain baulked. My incredible father, the inspiration of this book as a man and parent and my tireless proofreader, to whom I owe so much. My amazing girls, Nancy and Esther, who make me smile everywhere, forever. And very finally Simon. Thanks continue to feel meagre compared with the ceaseless support, belief, encouragement, comfort and love which you have offered throughout this often gritty time, but I humbly offer them, nonetheless.

Introduction

The Holocaust resulted in the deaths of around ninety per cent of Polish Jewry, including 254,000 Jews from the Warsaw ghetto in two months of 1942, eighty per cent of Dutch Jewry and nearly fifty per cent of Belgian Jewry; yet as historians we know little or nothing about the impact that this had on the gender identities of half of these people: the men. Instead, and in spite of a burgeoning academic interest in the history of modern masculinity, a small but detailed understanding of Jewish masculinity more generally, and an established body of work relating to gender in the Holocaust, the question of Jewish masculinity during the Holocaust is one that has barely been considered, and no systematic attempt has been made to analyse the impact of humiliation, ghettoization and genocide on the gender identities of the Jewish men whose lives they so clearly impacted. More specifically, beyond a series of assumptions and some limited research, historians have paid little attention to the detail of these lives including the role of men in the home and in public, the significance of fatherhood and parenting and the multiple and diverse masculinities practised by Jewish men in this period.

Why then do we know so little about the gender identities of men in this period and why does it matter? One response might be that a lack of knowledge can be explained by the conditions experienced by Jewish communities during this period: any study of the gender implications of the Holocaust is irrelevant when, for those involved, a focus on basic survival, to the exclusion of all else, was so clearly paramount. Perhaps the conditions faced by European Jewry from 1939, and earlier, were so dire that to consider them in the context of gender is to misrepresent them completely: in their struggle simply to survive and in light of the primacy of the paradigm of race fostered by Nazi Germany as it occupied Europe, questions of gender became redundant for Jewish populations and therefore should also be redundant in its scholarship. This approach, however, does not hold water, if for no reason other than its inherent and highly problematic teleology. From the late 1930s onwards, the lives of Jews in occupied

Europe became gradually harder but it was not until significantly later, if at all, that they came to realize the likelihood of their ultimate deaths. For most of the period between 1939 and 1941 or 1942 (depending on their circumstances and the country in which they lived), most Jewish people hoped, however hard life might be in the short term, to survive – they continued their lives, their marriages, bringing up children, earning money and socializing and, in doing so, practised their gender identities on a daily basis.

If we accept then that this period, despite being one of unimaginable hardship, was also one in which Jewish people continued to develop their identities influenced by gender, class and race, then it is clear that understanding the detail of those lives constitutes a valuable historical study. It enhances our knowledge of the victims of the Holocaust, our understanding of Jewish identity and, more broadly, the role of gender in managing extreme and catastrophic experiences, providing more of Marion Kaplan's 'little picture' of Jewish life in order to 'cast new light on the big picture'.[1] As Dalia Ofer and Leonore Weitzman have eloquently argued, 'questions of gender lead us to a richer and more finely nuanced understanding of the Holocaust. They help us envision the specificity of everyday life and the different ways in which men and women responded to the Nazi onslaught'.[2] Yet these accepted explanations for the relevance and importance of a gendered approach to history almost invariably relate uniquely to a study of women, and some might argue that a gendered study of men requires more skilful gymnastics of reason. Those who pioneered the study of women in the Holocaust certainly argued that the history which had previously been written was de facto a history of men.[3] Written by men and about men, it was argued that, although such works purported to be general studies of the Holocaust, they in fact documented only the lives of men during the Holocaust and failed to recognize conditions and experiences specific to women, of which menstruation and sexual assault are but two of the most obvious examples.[4]

Far from securing the argument that men's history has already been written, however, nothing shows the value of an historical study of male gender identity so well as the wealth of brilliant work which exists on the subject of women in the Holocaust. In attempting to redress an imbalance in historical writing, Joan Ringelheim looked not only at women's experiences but also beyond them to attempt to understand women's responses to those experiences: the emotional and physical impact of the Holocaust, the coping mechanisms used and, most importantly, the social conditioning that allowed/enabled/forced women to respond as they did.[5] Effectively, Ringelheim sought to understand both the impact of the Holocaust on the gender identities of the women who lived it and the impact of their gender identities on those women's behaviour. Whilst our understanding of the Holocaust was greatly in need of such a gendered approach to women's lives and Ringelheim, and those who followed her, did a great deal to add nuance to our history, it is precisely the depth of their study that justifies applying that same approach to men in the Holocaust. The early histories of the Holocaust may have been written predominantly by men (which ought anyway to be as irrelevant as my own status as a gentile woman) and about men, but they do not consider men *as* men, or as Jane Caplan explains it, 'the unmarked male ostensibly escapes gender altogether'.[6] Indeed, they say no more about the gender identities of men than they do of women. In presenting men's experiences as universal, such histories fail either to understand the impact of the Holocaust on male gender identities or to analyse the important influence of these gender identities on men's behaviour and experiences; traditional histories may present the Holocaust according to men, but they do not acknowledge those men as gendered. As a result, the arguments used to justify the need for a gendered history of women are equally applicable in the case of men – to quote Ofer and Weitzman again, '[t]he discussion of women's unique experiences provides a missing element of what we must now see as an incomplete picture of Jewish life during the Holocaust'.[7]

Beyond simply making the case for a study of male gender identities (which I shall usually call masculinity hereafter) in the Holocaust, the development of a history of women in the same period over the last twenty years has taught us valuable lessons which should inform any study of masculinity. Most importantly, women's history, and especially the impressive self-reflection of Joan Ringelheim, illustrates the clear dangers of combining a historical study of gender with gender politics – a particular concern since an interest in gender very often extends outside the confines of history for those in the field. In a radical rethinking of her original, groundbreaking work on gender, Ringelheim, in her article 'Women and the Holocaust: A Reconsideration of Research', questions the impact of her 'cultural feminism' upon her historical study.[8] This work, which sought to find value in – and celebrate women performing – traditional female roles (in contrast to more radical feminism based around overturning the power imbalance), Ringelheim suggests, led her to seek out examples of women performing positive female roles during the Holocaust rather than questioning their position on a more fundamental level. Moreover, she observes, her 'cultural feminism' led her to attempt to prove that women were better than men, rather than asserting the argument that the sexes were fundamentally the same and should be treated as equals. According to Ringelheim, the ultimate impact of this process was that '[m]y use of cultural feminism as a frame (albeit unconsciously) changed respect for the stories of the Jewish women into some sort of glorification and led to the conclusion that these women transformed "a world of death and inhumanity into one more act of human life".[9] Writing some time later, Zoë Waxman identified an approach to gender similar to that of Ringelheim, commenting, '[s]uch studies … [focus] on women's testimonies to show how it was women and not men who mostly acted in moral, heroic or noble ways'.[10]

Ringelheim's auto-review illustrates clearly the pitfalls of combining gender history with personal gender politics,[11] which is worth considering in the particular context of men's history. Perhaps a study of masculinity raises less obvious questions in this regard due to the largely uncontested nature of male power and the resultant weaker gender politics which attach to it. Yet two existing themes in studies of masculinity suggest that they remain susceptible to the politicization that Ringelheim identifies; her work, therefore, should be taken equally seriously in approaching any study of masculinity. In the first place, contemporary sociology shows a clear corrective tendency in studies of masculinity, a tendency that is aimed at defining masculinity in such a way as to necessarily 'improve' its practise.[12] Equally problematic is the, politically influenced, representation of men that we find in the conclusions often drawn about masculinity in the Holocaust, which show men as failing to perform the strong, positive roles expected (by historians) and therefore becoming weak and depressed. I shall go on to consider the implications of this telling of history in Chapter 2, but in essence, and in a reflection of Ringelheim, this approach risks provoking the historian into attempting to disprove this image of masculinity by providing examples of men successfully performing these positive roles, rather than questioning the accuracy of a representation of gender identity, which fundamentally links masculinity with positive behaviour.

Whilst historians have predominantly defined female gender identity through positive behaviours around nurturing, caring and bonding (although this too is now being reconsidered and refined),[13] any definition of masculinity must necessarily include a consideration of a number of traits, which might be considered as fundamentally negative, perhaps including violence, distance and domination. One example illustrates this point well: in more than one case historians have suggested that men in the ghettos stole food from their children, an action often cited in stark contrast to reports of women giving up food for their children and offered as an example of the compromising of men's gender identities that occurred in response to the Holocaust.[14] It is possible to argue, however, following Evelyn Waugh and the bananas, that far from this being an action that demonstrates the erosion of a man's gender identity, such behaviour might, on the contrary, be an active display of masculinity.[15] For a man, as head of the family and perhaps used to being fed more and better food than his children, to prioritize his own hunger over that of his family might not be seen as a collapse of manhood but an exercise thereof. That Dawid Sierakowiak, the sole cited recorder of this phenomenon, finds such behaviour from his father objectionable is not surprising, but it does not necessarily mean his father, or indeed Dawid himself, didn't also consider it masculine.[16] Likewise, when Sara Zyskind's uncle and guardian offered her bread in the Łódź ghetto and she refused it, she records him becoming angry and shouting, '[y]ou little upstart! Who's asking your opinion? It's still mine that counts around here!'.[17] Whilst this response was clearly objectionable, in his outburst Zyskind's uncle showed a strong sense of masculinity through a display of patriarchy and dominance. In order to attempt to fully understand the impact of the Holocaust on masculinity, therefore, it is important to avoid some of the politics around gender history by acknowledging not only the positive attributes of masculinity which we might hope to find, but also the less admirable traits that might be equally important.

Gender historians of the Holocaust working on women's history, however, whilst offering the lessons needed for a history of masculinity to be developed, have also penned some of the existing, highly problematic, minimal history of Jewish masculinity during Holocaust, which it is necessary to discuss in some detail before any further study can take place. The approach which this history takes predominantly stresses the impact on Jewish male gender identities of the loss of work, the problems of supporting one's family, and the consequent slide into depression. It is often perfunctory and reliant on limited research, but, perhaps of most concern, they have been drawn in the service of another master. Written predominantly by historians whose primary interest lies in understanding the impact of the Holocaust on Jewish female gender identity, much of what we know about Jewish masculinity is effectively a corollary of successful attempts to show the significant role that Jewish women played in enabling families and communities to endure and survive the Holocaust. And whilst book titles sometimes suggest a more balanced approach to the study of gender in the Holocaust, in most cases for 'gender' it would be fair to read 'women'.[18]

The outcomes of this relative neglect of male gender history in the Holocaust have been wide-ranging, but I shall focus here on three key concerns and their impact on the way in which we currently understand Jewish masculinity in this period: the marginalization of the male experience, the malformation of conclusions about male history and the narrowing of our understanding of the spheres in which masculinity is formed and practised. In the first case, seen in Marlene Heinemann's references to women as being 'doubly damned'[19] – since they were attacked both as Jews and as women – we see gendered explanations applied to experience without serious thought given to their impact on the other sex and therein the marginalization of the male experience. Were men not in fact equally 'doubly damned' – most notably, perhaps, in the gendered imagery of antisemitic rhetoric, which targeted men both for their race and for their gender?[20] In the same vein, Nechama Tec, who has more to say than most about the male experience of the Holocaust, writes that 'Jewish mothers had often to experience the unimaginable pain of watching their children starve to death'[21] – that she seems to consider this pain specific to women not only directly contradicts the research of Raul Hilberg, who suggests that in general men took the deaths of children and family harder than women, but perhaps more problematically, it does not seem to be based on any particular research.[22]

This tendency to sideline the gendered experiences of men is not recent, however, and importantly reflects a gender discourse which was already evident during the Holocaust and is present in the contemporary sources. In the archives of the Warsaw ghetto, *Oneg Shabbat*, we find Emmanuel Ringelblum, its founder and director and also a noted historian, writing in his diary of the role of women in the Holocaust: 'The historians of the future will have to devote a fitting chapter to the role of the Jewish woman during the war. It is thanks to the courage and endurance of our women that thousands of families have been able to endure these bitter times.' Later in his diary, Ringelblum records an entry about how tirelessly women work in taking over from the exhausted and depressed men who were previously running the housing committees.[23] Whilst Ringelblum is right to emphasize the role of women in the daily functioning of the ghettos, that men also worked tirelessly in the housing committees, until women took over later, goes unreferenced both by Ringelblum himself, because it is an assumed part of men's gender roles, and by the historians who rely on him, because their focus is on women.

The second result of the limited attention paid to men and masculinities by historians of the Holocaust to date has been the way in which some conclusions rest on incorrect or undemonstrated assumptions. Most particularly, this relates to the assertion that Jewish men were left depressed and diminished by the Holocaust, with only limited evidence for this having in fact been the case. Historians of women and the Holocaust have particularly stressed that, in the face of persecution, Jewish women found reserves of strength to fight for themselves, their families and their communities and that they rose to the challenge of the assault they faced, taking on whatever roles and tasks were required of them. In many cases this is described as an assumption of the male role, citing women retraining, working to provide for their families, petitioning public bodies for support and taking the lead in researching and organizing emigration opportunities as examples of this role reversal. As women assumed men's roles (or, more correctly, performed tasks usually performed by men), the argument follows, they became masculinized and the men who were, for whatever reason, failing to perform their gender roles, became feminized. Taking exactly this seemingly logical step, Tec writes, '[t]he majority of the adult men who survived the initial Nazi onslaughts were prevented from fulfilling their main traditional roles of provider and protector. Equating these roles with masculinity, many men became depressed and apathetic when they found themselves unable to meet these obligations'.[24] Crucially, however, these conclusions rest on a finite or zero-sum approach to gender identity where the 'masculinization' of the woman must necessarily lead to the 'feminization' of the man, not because evidence shows this, but because one is thought to be a necessary corollary of the other, an assumption which this study will challenge.

Finally, these trends in historical analysis have resulted in a tendency to consider male behaviour and identity principally in the spheres of society in which women have traditionally been understood to function. This has led to an over-reliance upon the domestic sphere in discussions of male gender identity, with a particular emphasis on men's depression and decision-making limitations within the home, whilst the role of men in the community, particularly in collective decision-making, and the importance of public space and the workplace as spheres in which men form and reinforce their masculine identities, have been partially overlooked. In contrast, a more wide-ranging approach to the study of men in multiple social spheres, looking at the roles of men throughout society, including their work, public and private lives, enables one to understand not only the ways in which masculinity is undermined but also how it can be strengthened and reinforced.

None of this should be seen by any means as an attempt to diminish the brilliant work done by numerous historians on women and gender in the Holocaust. This work was overdue when it was first begun by Joan Ringelheim, and has since made an immensely important contribution to our understanding of the history of the Holocaust and to the historical study of gender.[25] Nevertheless, it becomes clear that research into Jewish masculinity in the Holocaust should be conducted not as a by-product of the study of Jewish women but in its own right and on terms which are relevant to the lives and gender identities of those it sets out to study. In beginning to address these lacunae, by focusing on the evidence we have about men and their behaviour and by interrogating sources like *Oneg Shabbat* not for what they say about women but for what they do, and do not, say about men, we can begin to understand the resulting impact that these experiences would have had upon the gender identities, the masculinities, of those men.

In attempting to redress this imbalance, this book is clearly framed in both time and place. It will focus entirely on the lives of Jews living in Poland, France, Belgium and Holland, a cross section of countries which offers a broad range of experiences, encompassing different religious backgrounds in the obvious contrasts between orthodox and atheist Jews, social contrasts in the degree of separation and assimilation different communities experienced and political contrasts in the nature and practise of German occupation and discrimination. This approach provides the chance to consider whether changes in the practice of masculinity were provoked by the specific circumstances of individuals and their experience of persecution or whether more general changes can be identified which seem to arise from the forms of gendered persecution that affected most Jewish men in similar ways, despite the very different settings and situations in which the Holocaust took place.[26] Quite particularly, this book avoids the inclusion of Germany, which experienced a very different Holocaust from other European countries, with a much slower introduction of persecution and marginalization than most. It also does not consider the events of the Holocaust in the Soviet Union which, in contrast, experienced the extremes of the Holocaust in the actions of the Einsatzgruppen but far fewer of the daily occurrences that combined to create lives lived under occupation and which help to complete our understanding of masculinities in the period. I have also expressly avoided any analysis of both the death camps and the concentration camps. Beginning with the origins of Nazi persecution in each of the countries in question, this book will end at the point when Jewish communities began to be systematically destroyed by incarceration and murder in camps. The nature of the camps, lacking the traditional social units, families and communities which comprised both men and women, and with their own very particular form of gendered practice, I shall leave to other historians.[27]

One final and clear limitation placed on my research is that it does not purport to represent those Jewish men who might be described as ultra-orthodox or haredi. This is not an academic choice like those of time and place but rather a qualification of necessity; for reasons of circumstance, adaptability and targeted persecution, ultra-orthodox men seem to have been less likely than others to survive the Holocaust and therefore to record their testimonies, making any study of their likely very different masculinity almost impossible in the scope of this book. Whilst this is regrettable, however, I would argue that the loss of this perspective is not significantly damaging to my overall conclusions, since the importance of such representations have often been overemphasized for two main reasons. First, historians are keen not to be seen to be prioritizing the experiences of assimilated, Westernized Jews and thereby seeming to ignore the 'Jewishness' of the Holocaust – this, however, is a largely political problem which I intend to avoid by using as broad a range of sources as possible including a number written by Orthodox Jews and by highlighting the Jewish, religious or cultural, masculinities. Second, I would suggest that this sense of the importance of the sources arises from misconceptions regarding the religious affiliation of the Jews of Poland in this period. Attempting to rank the religious commitment, not in any case a static or definable concept, of those about whom one is writing is impossible, however, it was orthodox Jewry which comprised the large majority of Polish Jewry in this period, and they are considered throughout the study. Finally, outside Poland the question of ultra-orthodox Jews is even less numerically significant than within Poland. A tiny proportion of Jews in Holland, Belgium or France would have been ultra-orthodox and, as such, an inability to consider them as a valid exception to my ideas on masculinity does not amount to a theoretical failing, much as it is regrettable. Nevertheless, without a study of the ultra-orthodox I am clear that this book cannot, and will not try to, offer a detailed analysis of those elements of religious Polish Jewish heritage relating to masculinity.

* * *

A background study of masculinity is central to the credibility of this book, as only through a detailed definition of what masculinity is and how it can be inferred from sources in which it is never explicitly mentioned, can it be possible to begin to draw meaningful conclusions. This book, therefore, will open with an analysis of three central bodies of theory and research: the primarily sociological study of masculinity, the historical application of masculinity theory and the history of Jewish masculinity. The first of these not only defines what masculinity is, what it comprises and how it is formed and adapted but also discusses the capacity for writing on this subject to be compromised by currents in gender studies. Central to writing meaningfully about masculinity will be the ability to avoid these currents and to embrace all the characteristics of male gender identity, even those that might be seen as more morally compromised – something I have touched on briefly already. The second body of theory covered here is that relating to the historical studies of masculinity, the ways in which the theory of masculinity has been applied and the conclusions that historians have drawn. Unrelated to Jews in the Holocaust, this research, drawn from a range of historical periods and approaches, illustrates the different ways of tackling the core questions of masculinity from a historical perspective and offers an opportunity to consider what might work in this case. Finally, this book will be underpinned by an analysis of the theoretical study, both in sociology and history, of Jewish masculinity (very little of which, as we have seen, relates specifically to the period covered by this book). An analysis of this body of work, which includes such broad themes as the Jewish body, the Diaspora and gender, what some would see as the inherent femininity of Jewish religious masculinity and the impact of *Aliyah*[28] and Zionism, is central to understanding the often diverse nature of Jewish masculinity in the years before the Holocaust. Since masculinity, depending on an inexhaustible range of factors including culture, location and age, can include almost any element of behaviour and identity, in order to discuss the impact of the Holocaust on these identities it is important that we understand, necessarily broadly speaking, those elements of identity which most strongly impacted upon masculinity for Jewish men before the Holocaust.

This rigorous theoretical underpinning, which forms the basis of Chapter 1, is necessary precisely because of the limited research that exists in the field of masculinity in the Holocaust and because of the degree of extrapolation often required to understand the impact of gender on sources in which it is never specifically referenced. Having established this framework for study, Chapters 2, 3 and 4 lay out the substance of the book, analysing and understanding a wide range of sources relating to Jewish masculinity in the Holocaust, looking not only at diaries written during the Holocaust and preserved often in extreme circumstances, but also at testimonies written and recorded in the years since the war, either as published books and unpublished manuscripts or as oral interviews, and collective sources such as *Oneg Shabbat* and the Łódź Ghetto Chronicle.[29]

Importantly, in these chapters I take the approach of dividing the Holocaust into two distinct periods, which I have called 'deconstruction' and 'enclosure'. Considered chronologically, for any individual the experiences of the deconstruction would have preceded those of enclosure. However, there is no single date, or even year, in which the first period ends and the second begins; the distinction is instead one of circumstance. Explained later in more detail, Chapter 2 discusses the period that I call the deconstruction, and focuses on the initial stages of persecution, where Jewish men lost their jobs and their places in society as their lives were deconstructed piecemeal, but for the most part retained a certain freedom of movement and continued to live with their families and communities. In contrast, Chapter 3 focuses on the period which followed in which Jewish men and families were enclosed: enclosure being here defined loosely as a period spent by an individual, family or community in a space which they were not free to leave, either owing to German regulations or for their own safety and security. Necessarily, Chapter 3 will concentrate largely on ghettoization and the experiences of Jewish men living in Poland but will also include examples from Belgium, Holland and France of families who spent periods in hiding. Whilst these two chapters, covering the deconstruction and enclosure, are broadly chronological, neither period has a fixed beginning or end and what divides them is not a point in time, a date or an event, but a shift in circumstances, which came to different families and communities, for various reasons, at very different times. The German invasion which would begin the deconstruction in each country occurred at different times, progressed at different speeds, and involved very different forms of occupation and experiences. The point at which lives passed from the painful deconstruction to the petrified stability of enclosure also varied across Europe and, finally, the point at which enclosure ended, occasionally in liberation but for most in internment or death, also varied drastically. But for most Jews who lived through the Holocaust, the former preceded the latter and it is to this chronology that my chapters relate. This not only provides periodization which Jane Caplan and Nikolaus Wachsmann argue is the most useful tool for 'intervening in the meaningless flow of time and imposing interpretative and explanatory clarity'[30] but allows for a consideration of how different experiences raised questions for male gender identities, highlighting the contrast between the instability of deconstruction and what I shall argue was the relative stability of enclosure – a contrast which, I believe, ultimately had a greater impact on gender identities than the degrees of horror involved in people's daily existence.

Finally, Chapter 4 is a study of Jewish fatherhood during the Holocaust. It considers whether Jewish fathers understood and managed their masculinity in the same way as Jewish men more broadly, or whether the effect of children, questions of paternal respect and the often enhanced importance of providing and protecting changed male gender identities and practices. Many sources pertaining to fatherhood are written by children about their fathers, often those who were teenagers during the Holocaust. Whilst this presents some theoretical questions for a study of fatherhood, it also highlights interesting conclusions concerning the masculinity of youth and its formation, as well as the transmission of masculinity from father to son. Together, these offer an interesting addendum to the central conclusions of earlier chapters. Ultimately, as my research begins to show how, across the deconstruction and enclosure, a trajectory of collapse and rejuvenation can be charted for Jewish masculinity, these nuances of fatherhood will illustrate some important exceptions and reflections.

* * *

A number of issues present themselves when attempting to write about Jewish masculinity in the Holocaust, from questions of source selection and language to theoretical approaches to collective analysis.[31] Many of these are explored throughout this book as they become relevant, and, in certain cases, most obviously limitations set by source availability, the most I can do is to acknowledge an issue and thereby hope to limit its impact upon my work. Nevertheless, underpinning the whole, and therefore worthy of direct consideration, is the nature and scope of the available sources, the related analysis and conclusions and the question, '[h]ow may a historian of the Holocaust use a variety of different, often conflicting and contradictory, in some cases clearly mistaken, memories and testimonies of individual survivors as evidence to construct a history that otherwise, for lack of evidence, would not exist?'.[32] My response to this – to acknowledge that one is fundamentally writing an 'imperfect' history whilst forming an important starting point for more detailed work to follow – and the conclusions that follow will, if they are doing their job, ultimately provoke as many questions as they answers.

Attempting a study of such breadth as to adequately address the nascent debate on masculinity in the Holocaust means facing a staggering range of sources – Kushner estimates the number of accounts of the Holocaust including diaries, written testimonies and interviews to be around 100,000.[33] To be added to this number are sources ranging from clandestine newspapers and archives such as the Łódź Ghetto Chronicle or *Oneg Shabbat* to 'non-factual' works of memory such as Maus,[34] all of which potentially have something to offer our understanding of masculinity in the period. On this basis some distinction between types of source is necessary, and yet source selection in this way presents a significant problem for the historian. Perhaps considered the least problematic source type to focus on, were one to limit oneself, would be diaries written during the Holocaust. Our only access to the voices of many of the victims, often clearly dated and thus easily confirmed as genuine and largely accurate (both strong bulwarks against the criticisms of Holocaust deniers and historians alike), diaries are respected as perhaps the most 'authentic' sources. Yet diaries are not without significant methodological problems; often written not just for personal record but with the intention of recording for posterity, and therefore perhaps with the idea of publication or dissemination in mind, many diaries comprise a selective recording of those things that the author considers meaningful, and therefore perhaps blur the distinction between 'intentional' and 'non-intentional' documents upon which historians rely.[35] One clear example of this tendency is Anne Frank who, writing whilst in hiding with her family in Amsterdam, began to edit her own diary in preparation for its later publication,[36] but many writers who did not get this far still reference a need to testify in their reasons for writing, suggesting that a process of personal editing might have been in existence throughout.

A further concern, voiced by some historians, is that, only with hindsight can one even begin to 'witness' the Holocaust, so great was its impact – an approach which effectively renders these testimonies unreliable since they lack the reflective qualities of post-war records. In exactly this vein Dori Laub comments, 'the degree to which bearing witness was required entailed such an outstanding measure of awareness and comprehension of the event … of its radical otherness to all known frames of reference … that it was beyond the limits of human ability (and willingness) to grasp, to transmit, or to imagine'.[37] However, despite the other limitations of such sources, this is an approach I strongly reject; in understanding gender one cannot look for comprehension of the totality of the Holocaust, but rather one should actively seek the reverse — to reconstruct the daily lives of those who lived it. And diaries, exactly because of this lack of hindsight, provide an understanding of how men managed on a daily basis before they fully understood their likely fate. To rely only on those sources recorded after the war would be, therefore, to ignore the detail of the life in lieu of the totality of the death.

Equally problematic is the approach that sees some historians elevate testimony to a status above that of a normal source as Annette Wieviorka does in describing them as the 'ethereal representation of a mood', writing that 'testimony contains extraordinary riches: … not factual truth but the more subtle and also indispensable truth of an epoch and of an experience'.[38] Whilst testimony is a particularly rich source exactly because it offers something beyond factual truth – indeed gender relies on such a reading – to suggest that fact is lacking altogether both patronizes those who experienced the Holocaust and undermines the historian who reasonably attempts to use such sources. This approach is further brought into question by the accompanying reverence that can often be found toward such sources. This can be found, for example, in the approach of Saul Friedländer, a survivor and historian, still a child during the war and hidden in a Catholic boarding school in France from 1942 to 1946, who argues that sources are there to 'tear through seamless interpretation and pierce the (mostly involuntary) smugness of scholarly detachment and "objectivity"' – something which he sees as relevant not in all historical study but specifically for those writing about 'mass suffering'.[39] Most problematically, this approach often leads to a questioning of the vigour with which one could or should analyse, or perhaps challenge, a Holocaust testimony, the answer to which ought to be simple – '[s]urvivor testimony cannot be accorded a privileged status, immune from the same careful examination of evidence to which our profession routinely subjects other sources'.[40] To do so would be to render these sources unusable. It is exactly because they are historical sources to be rigorously analysed in the same way as any other source type that they are useful to us. For the rest, although these sources are not perfect, and cannot be made so even with clever analysis, perhaps Christopher Browning was on the right lines when he wrote of two of his monographs which rely primarily on testimony, one perpetrator and one victim, 'if one can attempt to write a history from sources in which the witnesses are mostly trying to lie, surely... I can try to write a history from sources in which the witnesses are mostly trying to tell the truth'.[41]

Other contemporary sources, including archives and newspapers, whilst possessing the same stamp of 'authenticity' as diaries, have a perceived added level of objectivity which might be beneficial to the historian.[42] Yet, as sources, these too have their drawbacks, the most significant of which – fear of discovery – limited the range of topics such sources covered, the information they were willing to record and the opinions they presented. Most notable in this regard is the Łódź Ghetto Chronicle, which seems to have used code words and perhaps even written in praise of ideas which logic suggests it would have opposed. Whilst some of these feints have been identified, we have to assume that others have not, making such sources problematic to handle. Moreover, these sources often privilege the experiences of the collective over those of the individual, recording broad changes in ghetto conditions, whether it be laws, illness, work or round-ups, rather than personal experiences. Again, this tendency is particularly problematic for a study of masculinity since records of collective experience can tell us a good deal about the gendered treatment of Jews, but much less about Jewish gender. In spite of these limitations, however, collective sources offer a good compromise between the authenticity of contemporary sources and the distance and reflection of post-war writing.

This study will also rely on post-war testimony, which is certainly the most abundant source for studies of the Holocaust and includes some of the most revealing accounts of masculinity in the Holocaust and yet is also perhaps the most problematic source for the historian. The way in which historians approach post-war testimony as a source has been refined and developed since the war ended, and early scepticism, strongly favouring the voice of perpetrators over that of victims, has turned into a more grudging respect for the irreplaceable detail that such sources can provide when used correctly.[43] Nonetheless, an ongoing cautious treatment of testimony hinges on two central concerns: factual inaccuracy, particularly stemming from confusions around time and space, and inaccuracy of perception due to vested emotional interests and lapse of time. The question then is whether a suitable methodology can be found to allow the use of such sources in historical writing in spite of these perceived failings.

The question of factual accuracy hinges on the concerns expressed by Primo Levi when he wrote, '[t]he memories which lie within us are not carved in stone; not only do they tend to become erased as the years go by, but often they change, or even increase by incorporating extraneous features'.[44] And yet whilst this is undeniable, to discount them as sources on this basis would be to suggest that other types of source were without their own questions of accuracy. Instead, this concern should be met, exactly as one would with any other source, by placing the responsibility for rigorous analysis, including understanding potential inaccuracies of fact or interpretation, squarely with the historian and insisting that these concerns form a part of the conclusions they draw. A further burden of factual accuracy, provoked by the claims of Holocaust deniers, has, however, been imposed on post-war testimonies. Invariably citing Wilkomirski as a cautionary tale[45] (although this is to miss the point entirely since his was not a genuine testimony), this approach blames testimony and its inaccuracies for exposing the entire field of Holocaust history to the challenges of deniers. For some, this threat effectively renders these sources unusable unless they can be proved to be unimpeachable, and yet I would argue that this approach employs faulty logic. Holocaust deniers will always find fodder for their claims, and, if testimony did not exist, something else would take its place. Moreover, where errors do open the source to challenge, the fault is not with the source but any analysis which presents it as anything other than fallible.

Finally, it is worth considering to what extent notions of factual accuracy are even a relevant or useful frame of analysis for studies of gender identity. Gender identities do not rely on a chronological thread or even, in many cases, on events or anything which can be factually verified. Unless inaccuracies are so great as to question the veracity of the source altogether (as with Wilkomirski), conclusions concerning identity are not necessarily undermined by what might appear to be relatively superficial errors. Writing during the Holocaust, Chaim Kaplan summarized exactly this approach when he noted,

> I risk my life with my writing, but my abilities are limited; I don't know all the facts; those that I do know may not be sufficiently clear, and many of them I write on the basis of rumors whose accuracy I cannot guarantee... But for the sake of truthfulness, I do not require individual facts, but rather manifestations of the fruits of a great many facts that leave their impressions on the people's opinions, on their mood and morale. And I can guarantee the factualness of these manifestations because I dwell among my people and behold their misery and their soul's torment.[46]

In contrast to concerns around fact, however, the potential for inaccuracy of perception in sources offers a more fundamental challenge to the historian. Not only can an accusation of this type be effectively levelled at almost any source but also, even with careful analysis, these inaccuracies are less easily identified or refuted than factual errors. Moreover, inaccuracy of perception arguably has a far greater impact on our understanding of gender identity than does any factual inaccuracy, since it relies more heavily on interpretation than on more easily corroborated data. In a study of nutrition in the ghettos, for example, it would be possible, having consulted relevant testimonies and diaries, to attempt to confirm one's findings using alternative documents from both the Germans and the *Judenräte* regarding the quality and quantity of food available in the ghettos and its distribution.[47] This type of standard historical corroboration of evidence is here impossible; there are no facts to be confirmed and no statistical realities. Amongst post-war testimonies one can note several tendencies in representation which encapsulate this challenge – from idealizing one's pre-war childhood to idolizing one parent whilst diminishing the efforts of the other or, in the case of those who were already parents in the period they discuss, diminishing the coping abilities of a spouse whilst vaunting one's own achievements. Many of these tendencies provoke questions including whether so many people can really have had halcyon childhoods in spite of often back-breaking poverty and overt antisemitism? And in many cases there is little one can do to comprehensively confirm or dismiss a challenge of inaccuracy of perception. For every person who idolizes their father the criticism might be levelled that they are only saying that because their father died during the Holocaust – and yet it is equally likely that their father did in fact behave in the way in which they describe. Ultimately these cases can only be managed by treating them, as a historian might any source, with a balance of belief and healthy scepticism. Moreover, one can argue that these misperceptions, of which everyone is guilty, are a part of the individual's world view and, as such, even central to understanding his masculinity.

In a few cases, however, it has been possible to apply close analysis to confirm or deny the gendered reading of a source. In a few cases men have recorded numerous testimonies, which provide the opportunity to study their, often highly illustrative, differences and similarities. Roman Halter is a good example of this, recording multiple different testimonies throughout his life, oral and written, which seem to show a consistent balance between respect for his father's masculinity, evidenced by his ongoing protection of his family and strong patriarchal role at various times, and often overt criticism of his father's behaviour.[48] This balance, particularly over time, makes Halter's praise seem more believable and undermines any suggestion that he might have idolized his father. In other cases, relatives, including brothers and sisters or fathers and daughters, have survived to record overlapping testimonies, allowing one to cross-check their impression of events and their understanding of gender. One example of this is Ben Helfgott, a Polish Jew from Łódź who was ten when the Germans invaded in 1939, who has been particularly effusive in interviews when speaking about his father.[49] Helfgott's sister, Mala Tribich, also survived the Holocaust and her interviews, despite her being younger than Ben, and therefore providing vaguer descriptions, confirm many of Helfgott's impressions.[50] Of course this approach is not definitive; the siblings have had many years since the Holocaust to merge their memories and to form a family narrative; nonetheless their similar testimonies do offer limited corroboration of their individual impressions of their father and confirmation of events and actions which speak to their father's masculinity. In contrast, the testimony of Halina Sand seems to contradict that of her father, Martin Parker, and the way in which he writes about the behaviour of his wife. Parker, a Polish Jew from Warsaw who spent three years in the ghetto with his wife and daughter before they all escaped into hiding in 1943 where they lived out the war, tends to describe his wife as overly emotional and even hysterical, thereby promoting his own role in protecting the family, Sand, only four in 1940 when she entered the ghetto, offers a much more positive portrayal of her indefatigable mother.[51] Neither impression is definitive, making the question of Parker's masculinity during the Holocaust problematic; nonetheless, such confirmation is all that is available and, as such, treated carefully, constitutes a valuable check to one's analysis.[52]

Since this type of corroboration is possible in only a few cases, however, in order to form a general picture of gendered identities, it is important that a sceptical approach to analysing individual sources be combined with some form of collective corroboration. Having interrogated individual sources for evidence of male gender identity, but still being largely unable to objectively confirm any impressions derived from them, the historian is left with a group of discrete results. No individual's experience of gender can tell us anything definite, or even probable, about the gender identity of another, and there are few collective sources upon which to fall back. My approach to turning this data into meaningful analysis of gender, therefore, relies on two methodological keys: first, that branch of gender theory relating to normative and individual constructions of masculinity and, second, Christopher Browning's work on the 'individual plural'. In the first case, explained in more detail in Chapter 1, it is my contention that gender identity during the Holocaust adhered to a more rigid frame than modern sociological approaches allow. Whilst acknowledging Raewyn Connell's arguments concerning contrasting masculinities as developed in counterpoint to, and often in conflict with, one another, I contend that, as a basis for developing their own, individual masculinities, men in this period largely conformed to one of several socially constructed masculinities.[53] On this basis the capacity of several men to speak for the collective becomes clearer. For example, if through the biographies and testimonies of several intellectuals one can detect a thread which seems to unite them, then this can be used to discuss the existence of an 'intellectual masculinity' significant to men with certain class and social identities during the Holocaust. Of course the approach is not conclusive and there are exceptions to every socially constructed idea of masculinity; nonetheless, it presents what I consider a valid generalization that can be used to draw on individual sources to provide collective answers.

The second methodological key that I shall use to counter these questions of inaccuracy and the necessarily individual nature of all sources is found in Christopher Browning's work on the Starachowice labour camp. In his book *Collected Memories: Holocaust History and Postwar Testimony*, Browning offers a way of managing collected data, using a finite number of testimonies from the post-war period recorded in different times and places, by 'looking at memory not in the collective singular but rather in the individual plural, not collective memory but rather collected memories'.[54] In applying this theory, Browning looks not for repetition from the sources but corroboration, such that together they make up something more than their individual parts. Browning applies this process in attempting, predominantly, to reconstruct factual events, dates, time-lines and actions, where the capacity for sources to corroborate one another can be quite apparent. And whilst such clarity is perhaps harder with questions of identity than events, the approach can, nevertheless, serve as a model for allowing sources to collectively represent experiences and perceptions of gendered identities. In both my own and Browning's work, similar trends can be found: where several men mention the same thing, for example doffing their hats to Germans as a source of intense shame, this suggests that it may have had collective significance; however, where this tips over into repetition, most obviously individuals recounting seeing Mengele on the ramp at Auschwitz, it can appear suspicious. Here it is worth noting the interesting and encouraging phenomenon that there seems often to be more corroboration across several sources, than internally within one. Whilst one man might quite differently describe the impact of one event in several accounts, or very similar events in one account, across several testimonies it becomes easy to identify clear and consistent gendered responses, for example to the physical assault of Jewish men in the street. It is this phenomenon that allows me to apply Browning's theory to my work, suggesting that whilst individual sources provide only limited proof of a given thing, collectively they can paint a relatively clear picture.

* * *

In order to begin to understand the impact of the Holocaust on the gender identities of Jewish men, we must accept first that we are reading sources for a gender which is never clearly defined or acknowledged and that those sources do not evenly represent the Jewish men who experienced the Holocaust. The conclusions of this book are not universal and do not purport to be; there are numerous sources I did not consider and countless men who did not survive or who did not record their testimonies, any and many of whom may have experienced their masculinity in the Holocaust very differently from the masculinities I have studied, analysed and attempted to define. Nonetheless, by beginning the work of understanding the normative Jewish identities of this period and the ways in which men enacted them, by analysing some of the individual elements of these masculinities and by forming a picture of how men during the Holocaust succeeded and failed in performing their masculinities on a daily basis, we begin to be able to say something about the way in which the gender identities of Jewish men met and responded to the horrors of the Holocaust. If it is not enough that this is historically interesting, then we should once again turn to Ofer and Weitzman – '[t]he discussion of women's unique experiences provides a missing element of what we must now see as an incomplete picture of Jewish life during the Holocaust'. The same must surely be true for men.

Jewish Masculinity in Theory and Practice

Masculinity in theory

At the core of this book lies the question of how we define *masculinity* and how one interrogates sources, contemporary or otherwise, for gender when use of the word *masculinity*, or any direct comparator, is so rare. To complicate the matter, however, the answer to the former must be properly historicized if it is to be meaningful: understanding not only what masculinity is but how it was constructed, negotiated and practised specifically in the interwar period in Europe, both in Jewish communities and more generally in the societies in which those communities lived.

Existing analysis of both of these questions has for many historians of Holocaust studies, however, as already alluded to, been blighted by personal gender politics which potentially confuse the masculinity we would wish men had with the, often less positive, manifestations that we find in history. Many sociologists argue, not incorrectly, that masculinity is heavily dependent upon a patriarchal structure which oppresses women, but many have also, perhaps as a result, attempted to use their research to begin to redress this imbalance in male–female power relations, a point which Stephen Whitehead and Frank Barrett clearly make when they comment, '[w]riters within this genre [the sociology of masculinity] are understood to be personally/politically aligned with feminist agendas and to have a desire for gender justice'.[1] Significantly, this agenda has not been entirely eschewed by historians working on the subject of masculinity, and can be seen in, amongst others, Michael Roper and John Tosh's *Manful Assertions*, which optimistically notes that 'in our assertion that both male dominance and masculinity have shifted over time lies the possibility that they will not always be entirely fused'.[2] It should be clear, however, that, whilst questions of power and domination are relevant to historical research, the attempt to rectify or alter them is not. Well-researched history may have the capacity to impact upon the way in which gender identity is understood and therefore practised, but either an uncritical reliance on corrective sociological theory which potentially confuses actual gender identity with desired identities or a reversal of cause and effect where the historian chooses their gendered outcome and writes their history to that end renders the resulting history fundamentally flawed.

* * *

Key protagonists of the drive toward corrective sociological theories in this field were the sociologists of the 1930s who first defined *masculinity* using a theory called Sex Role Identity (SRI) which posited the idea that there existed a single, socially agreed notion of what it was to be masculine, with which all men attempted to conform. However, formed in the United States in the aftermath of the Wall Street Crash and the ensuing depression, it did not so much consider the realities of male gender identities as impose its own, and whilst the theory seemed to promise that those men who could conform to the norm presented would be fulfilled and content, to many of its contemporaries this was demonstrably untrue. Established to correct this tendency, the theory of Sex Role Strain (SRS) followed, arguing that, whilst there was indeed a single normative notion of masculinity, its impact could be extremely damaging, condemning as unmasculine those who tried to conform but, for whatever reason, could not.[3] There are numerous reasons for the ultimate rejection of both SRI and SRS, however, principally they were challenged for their reliance upon a singular notion of masculinity and the lack of attention paid to the capacity of the individual to influence his own gender identity. If we assume, as SRI and SRS both do, that society allows for only one normative masculinity, we would have to conclude that it is that of white, Christian, middle-class heterosexual men and that those who cannot fulfil its requirements – gay men, old men and black men to name a few – would be, as Michael Kimmel and Michael Messner put it in their attack on such theories, 'enacting "problematic" or "deviant" versions of masculinity'.[4]

Several more recent theories of masculinity align broadly with this approach whilst presenting multiple potential masculinities, allowing for the individual to orient themselves toward one of several masculine identities – effectively allowing men to behave in a variety of ways and still to consider themselves masculine. Yet, whilst these theories offer an approach to gender identity which seems to better reflect reality than that of a single normative masculinity, the way in which these multiple identities interact with one another remains contested and sociologists are divided between those who suggest a series of related but parallel masculinities and those who argue for a hierarchical approach.

Frameworks which offer theories of 'parallel masculinities', for example Kimmel and Messner's 'matrix of masculinities'[5] which posits the idea of a web of gender identities related through ideas and values rather than linked by power or dependence, present a number of problems for anyone attempting to apply those theories to historical research. In particular, these approaches tend to disassociate the formation and reinforcement of normative identities from questions of power, thereby leaving little space to understand the complex formation of gender identities amongst repressed minorities. For many, Jewish men and homosexuals for example, the association between identity and power is incontrovertible, and gender is better represented by an approach which recognizes this hierarchical structure of identities. One key example of such an approach is Connell's theory of 'hegemonic masculinities' which argues that at any given time in a society there is a dominant, or hegemonic, idea of masculinity, that which is 'culturally exalted', and which 'embodies the currently accepted answer to the problem of the legitimacy of patriarchy, which guarantees (or is taken to guarantee) the dominant position of men and the subordination of women'.[6]

Whilst the basis of this hegemonic structure is domination of women, Connell, who relies on a Gramscian approach to the exercise of power, defines a number of alternative masculinities created by, and designed to reinforce, the dominant masculinity. These alternative masculinities fall into the categories of complicit and subordinate masculinities, the first of which refers to those men who do not embody the dominant masculinity but nonetheless benefit from a tacit acceptance of its relations of gender hegemony and power; in Connell's words, they reap the 'patriarchal dividend'. In contrast, subordinate masculinity, according to this theory, refers to those men who have been rejected by the dominant masculinity as inherently 'unmasculine' or 'expelled from the circle of legitimacy'.[7] Connell develops this theory using the example of gay men, arguing that they are established as a feminine other by a dominant masculinity seeking to reinforce its own gender identity, as she describes it: 'gayness, in patriarchal ideology, is the repository of whatever is symbolically expelled from hegemonic masculinity'.[8]

Several historians have relied on Connell's theories to foreground work on masculinity, and John Tosh particularly has applauded Connell's theory of hierarchy and the way in which it views alternative masculinities through the prism of the dominant gender. However, the sidelining of theories of parallel dependent masculinities, like that of Kimmel and Messner, comes at a cost, and Connell's theory struggles as a comprehensive approach to normative gender identities exactly because it too completely rejects such theories. For some minorities, in different times and circumstances, it has been possible to create gender identities which, although built around the same social influences as dominant gender identities, should not be principally defined through their subordination. It is these masculinities to which Alexandra Shepard alludes in her division of masculinities into patriarchal, anti-patriarchal and alternative. Shepard's tripartite division, which is aimed at the intent behind the masculinities rather than at the structures of power that created them, is accompanied by an analysis of the 'internal inconsistencies and contradictions' of patriarchal manhood and the resulting influence that might be exerted by alternative masculinities.[9] Although Shepard is writing about early modern England, nonetheless, the emphasis that she places on the role played by alternative gender identities, when combined with the hierarchical, power-based approach of Connell, creates a means of attempting to understand masculinity that might well be applied to Jewish men in the period in question here.

Beyond simply acknowledging the existence of multiple masculine identities, however, one must consider how men engage with normative identities in the performance of their own masculinity. Theories exist which explain normative identities as the conscious impositions of the state or certain strata of society.[10] However, although there are periods of history in which such an approach might be shown to exist, normative identities in the early twentieth century are a more complex concept than a theory of mere imposition allows. Instead, this period should be understood as one in which masculinities were formed and reinforced through engagement by the individual with society, a process which established the subjecthood of those individuals. As Alan Petersen writes, '[a]s Foucault's concept of practices of the self suggests, identity is never simply imposed on (pre-social) subjects but involves a process of self-constitution within specific socio-cultural contexts. Through engaging with culturally prescribed or suggested practices of the self, one comes to understand oneself as a subject with a particular way of viewing and acting in the world.'[11]

This approach has been challenged on the grounds that, in understanding the formation of gender identities, emphasis should move away from socially and contextually constructed forms of masculinity toward the kind of interior influences, often preverbal and including the individual's family background and upbringing, that psychology has classically focused on.[12] However, whilst acknowledging the importance of understanding gender identities as personalized, as well as the role of the individual in the performance of their own gender, such theories have been criticized both for being ahistorical (Lynne Segal has herself noted that Anglo-American applications of Lacanian thought concerning the ways in which gendered power is socialized into infants do little to show how such a cycle originates[13]) and for seeming to ignore or sidestep the strong collective tendencies in gender identity. Importantly, it is also hard to reconcile an approach to masculinity which places such significance on individual agency in the formation of gender identities with the consistency amongst masculine identities which we see over decades and centuries, even if we acknowledge the relative instability of any individual's masculinity over a lifetime.[14] Particularly given the historical context of this book, therefore, and the less individual nature of gender identities during the period in question, normative identities can only helpfully be understood as socially constructed but not imposed, in line with Whitehead and Barrett's approach that 'any sense of self can only come about through working to achieve a sense of "belonging" in the social world'.[15]

The interplay between these socially constructed 'normative' gender identities and the interior, 'psychological' experience of the individual, however, is also historically specific; at different times in history, masculinities have been formed in different ways. Therefore, before we can discuss the exact form of masculinity in any given period, we must historicize its construction, the most important element of which, in the interwar period, was the overt attempt by various governments and ruling elites to influence the form which masculinities took. The interwar period was one in which a range of competing normative masculinities, embodying different ideals and identities, were encouraged, formed and practised, and equally one in which personal notions of masculinity played a role in the way in which individuals performed their masculinities. This relative diversity, however, was underpinned by the attempts made, at various times, in most countries, to influence, but not necessarily prescribe, the practice of gender identities through the dissemination and promotion of key themes and tropes, central to which was the importance of a healthy body, to be achieved through exercise and diet.[16] During the 1930s, these attempts to influence the masculinities of European populations were consciously developed in order to mitigate the damage, caused by the First World War, to ideas that had tended to make an association between violence and heroism, and to prepare populations for the expected conflict which would become the Second World War. At its most overt, this shift can be seen played out in Germany through changing representations of the body. Where the earlier interwar period saw an exaltation of a simple, healthy body with a masculine ideal epitomized by the joyful physicality of naked skiing in Hans Surén's *Der Mensch und die Sonne*,[17] the 1930s saw the assertion of a harder, more perfect form, epitomized in the work of Arno Brecker who was to become Germany's 'official state sculptor' under Hitler. The impact of these shifts on the masculinities of those who had fought in the First World War is perhaps open to question; nevertheless, this is only one example of an effective Europe-wide anticipation of war which involved subtle manipulations of ideas around masculinity in preparation for the inevitable bloodshed to follow.[18]

Bearing in mind these influences, which arguably led to more concrete notions of masculinity that might be recognized in other periods, I will rely on an approach to gender identity formation which sees gender formed cumulatively, with the individual situating himself in relation to a number of normative identities, whilst incorporating the relevant elements of his own background and personality in order to form his individually practised masculinity: a process in which one cannot read individual agency but rather the impact of a broader complex of identities and circumstances. The normative masculinities toward which each individual was oriented would have varied depending on those available to them but based on the premise, discussed above, that society is largely formed around a hierarchical structure of dominant, subordinate and alternative, non-dependent, masculine identities.

* * *

To date, historical analysis of Jewish masculinity in the face of the Holocaust has overwhelmingly presented Jewish men as feminized – a description that suggests an alteration in gender practice where male and female roles and identities are confused and exchanged. It is therefore to questions of change, continuity and crisis in gender identities that one should turn to create a complete understanding of how masculinities are formed and practised. Relevant for the period in question, received wisdom tells us that gender identities are significantly redefined in wartime, both on an individual level and on a collective level. Specifically, in many periods and for many men, the effect of war has been to curtail conventional masculine practice, as, amongst other things, conscription distanced them from their work and families and thus any immediate capacity to provide or protect – although certainly the defence of the nation was an alternative form of protection on which many men could hang their masculinities. Whilst such limitations impacted heavily on gender identities, the increased opportunities that war offered to both men and women in many cases also had an overtly liberating effect. For some young men, war provided the means to escape relatively predictable futures, offering opportunities which would have been impossible during peacetime, whilst for many women the absence of men, particularly in the workforce, created the possibility of assuming new responsibilities and even the capacity to alter the ways in which society understood the role of women.

Normative identities have also historically been significantly altered by war as governments have asserted particular gendered requirements[19] or old identities have become unsustainable: the unavoidably large numbers of disabled men in the aftermath of the First World War arguably had this impact.[20] And yet despite all of these changes being largely undisputed, historians have conversely argued for the durability of gender identities in the face of war. Elizabeth Foyster stresses the importance of not assuming that changes to masculinity occur simply because they ought to, suggesting instead that periods of great social change are often times when gender proves most durable.[21] Equally, Tosh sees the changes to masculinity that do occur, as being the limited impact of major social change on an otherwise solid base of masculinity. 'Might it make more sense', he asks, in relation to the extreme social upheaval of the period 1750–1850 which saw the transition to modernity, 'to conceive of gender as a structure of practices and attitudes which was particularly *resistant* to change?'[22]

These contrasting realities direct us to what seems to be the most credible way of understanding gender in wartime: as both extremely stable and eminently flexible, a dichotomy which, when broadened to include masculinity and gender identity even outside of war, seems to remain largely valid. Despite monumental changes in society, and what might be considered a gender revolution in the last century, the structure and practice of normative gender identities have changed little and those limited changes that can be charted, for example the shift away from the honour-based masculinities of the early modern period in Western Europe,[23] tend to take place over centuries rather than decades. In contrast to this stability, the masculinities of individuals, and even the particular manifestation of any given normative identity, can fluctuate and alter hugely, just in the course of a lifetime; as Shawn McGuffey and Lindsay Rich argue, 'gender is a social construction that is constantly being modified as individuals mature'.[24]

One way of understanding this dichotomy is to see the base of masculinity as largely impervious to change, whilst the superstructure of individual performances of gender identity are flexible and adaptable. Arthur Brittan refers to this base as 'masculinism',[25] which he defines as 'the ideology that justifies and naturalizes male domination', arguing that there exist essential, inalienable, gender traits common to all masculine identities. Whilst the universality of this theory renders it deeply flawed,[26] a variation which posits the idea of a culturally specific set of core masculine traits, such as violence or competition, sustained through social conformity rather than genetics, might bear more fruit in understanding masculinity in a given time and place, posing one question with which this book grapples: are there some elements of masculine identity common to all masculinities, whether individual practice or normative identities, in the interwar period in Europe, and, if so, do they respond to the specific circumstances of the Holocaust in a different way to more peripheral elements of masculine identity and practice?

Finally, in looking at questions of change and continuity, 'crises of masculinity' – a term which is commonly used in relation to this period but rarely defined or examined – should also be considered.[27] A crisis in masculinity is usually taken to mean a time when men are significantly hindered in practising a previously stable and successful gender identity. The impact of mass unemployment in communities where masculinity is closely tied to work and financial provision for families is a good example of such a crisis, but they can also occur on an individual basis, for example when an adult man becomes ill or physically disabled and ceases to be able to perform actions previously central to his gender identity.[28] The ability to recover from a crisis, in such circumstances, usually involves either the return of the capacity to successfully practise one's masculinity (finding new work being an obvious example) or adapting one's masculine practice to conform to new circumstances. On this question, Thomas Gerschick and Adam Miller have shown that men who become disabled, after an initial depressive period, often create for themselves an alternative gender identity, based on the same themes as their original masculinity but adapted to fit their new status and capabilities.[29] In this scenario, whilst dominant masculinity might continue to see these disabled men as emasculated, the disabled men see themselves as having reclaimed their masculinity.[30] On this basis, then, and given the prevailing use of language around gender crises in attempts to understand wartime, this book will not only consider whether the notion of a crisis of masculinity is applicable in the case of Jewish men in the Holocaust, but more importantly, whether, after an initial crisis, the circumstances of the Holocaust made it possible for Jewish men to employ either of these approaches to restore or reform their gendered practice in order to again consider themselves masculine.

* * *

Beyond considering how masculinity changes and adapts, it is equally important when writing about male gender identities to understand where and with whom gender identities are formed, practised and renegotiated. Whether some relationships are more significant to the formation of masculinity than others, to what extent gender identities are practised both in the home and outside of it, and whether any division of the spheres in which gender is practised can helpfully be made. Not only are these questions key to understanding masculinity itself, but they are all central to creating the workable definition of masculinity needed to underpin any credible historical analysis of gender.

On the first question, sociologists and historians have stressed the importance of seeing masculinity as integrally tied to patriarchy and therefore highlight interactions between men and women as central to understanding gender identity. Lynne Segal illustrates well this approach in her observation that 'the meanings of "masculinity" inhere not within individual men and their behaviour, but within institutional, cultural and discursive formations conceived hierarchically with men on top',[31] as does Foyster in arguing that 'gender history, as it has been defined, is above all relational history. It seeks to examine the sexes not in isolation, but rather the relationships between the sexes'.[32] Certainly the importance of heterosocial relationship in gender formation and, to a more limited extent, practice is clear, and where men are writing about relations with women, it represents one significant way of understanding gendered practice and, potentially, the changing nature of gender identities. The approach of this book, however, will be to stress the equal importance of homosocial relationships in the practice of male gender identities in order to both problematize the relationship between hegemony and gender formation and understand patriarchy and the changing debate concerning gendered spheres of influence. On this question, Tosh has convincingly argued that, whilst in our society hegemonic masculinity is principally used to uphold a patriarchal system, this is not an essential facet of masculinity but simply the current contextualization thereof. In making this assertion, Tosh uses the example of colonialism to show how hegemonic masculinity has also been used to reinforce structures of racial, rather than gender, domination.[33] If such a paradigm shift is possible, then the notion of the necessary elevation of heterosocial over homosocial relationships in analysing masculinity is baseless, and the two must at least be considered on an equal footing in attempting to understand what power dynamic, if any, was reinforced by masculinity during the Holocaust.

In order to underpin this rejection of traditional heterosocial methods of understanding masculinity, this book will, by design, avoid taking a gender comparative approach – avoiding looking for differences between men and women and instead focusing entirely on the male experience and the implications of the Holocaust on men alone. I take this approach in spite of the arguments specifically made by historians of the Holocaust who have advocated for the importance of a comparative approach to gender analysis,[34] on which subject Tec writes, 'I realized that to concentrate on women alone would yield skewed results. In effect, knowing how intricately intertwined are the lives of women and men, I recognized that to exclude the male experiences would offer only limited insights, whereas comparisons of the experiences of both sexes would result in a broader understanding.' My concern with such an approach to the writing of gender history, however, is perhaps best illustrated by the most common example of such comparison:

> Here, at Birkenau, only a day after their arrival, the differences between the sexes was already striking. The men, in hats with cut-off brims and in trousers and coats thrown to them at random – too short, too long, too wide, too small – looked like sad black storks. The women, also wearing garments that had been distributed to them at random, had somehow succeeded in only twenty-four hours in adjusting them to their bodies and sewing up the holes, using needles made out of wooden splinters and threads pulled out of the one blanket allocated to them.[35]

Whilst this example and the comparisons it makes teach us that women in the early- to mid-twentieth century were more likely to be skilled at altering clothes than men,[36] it does not necessarily tell us anything about comparative gendered behaviour, let alone about gender identities. More interesting for a gender historian would be to look only at the women and attempt to understand the impact of such acts on their identities – did performing such a task remind them of home, did they do it to look, and therefore feel, better or as a distraction and what was the relevance/impact of this, both for themselves and for the Germans who ran the camps? Ultimately, a more nuanced and detailed understanding of Jewish lives and gender identities can be gained by studying one gender in detail than by making comparisons between the two.

The second reason to focus on homosocial as well as heterosocial relationships is found in the shift away from separate spheres theory[37] which began with Foyster and others looking at both the central role played by women in public in reinforcing the gender identities of their husbands and the use made of the home in the assertion of masculinity, in contemporary society, particularly by men unable to assert themselves in the workplace.[38] This approach has been advanced by those who argue that separate spheres theory relies too heavily upon didactic

texts which, whilst showing that society believed that women *should* inhabit
the sphere of the home, provide little evidence that they actually did so and
potentially even represent a 'defensive and impotent reaction to public freedoms
already won'.[39] Finally, criticism has focused on the realities of the overlapping
spheres of home and work for many communities and classes. Whilst spheres
theory may apply to the emerging middle classes of the nineteenth century, who
are the centre of Leonore Davidoff and Catherine Hall's original study, for other
groups, notably those whose workplace was within the home, such a division
of spheres was impossible. This last question is particularly significant here if
we consider the number of Jewish men, both independent artisans and those
who ran small businesses, who worked in the home with the help of their wives
and family and for whom the home and workplace were parts of one indistinct
body. Responding to these debates, this book relies on the approach that, even
in heterosocial environments, in order to understand male gender identity it is
important not to focus too heavily on traditional male–female dichotomies but
to look also at competing or conflicting masculinities;[40] to do so by considering
all spheres in which masculinity is formed, conditioned and practised; and to
understand those spheres as necessarily interdependent and overlapping.

Exactly because gender identity is formed and practised throughout all of
the various spheres of daily life and through engagement with other men and
with women, the final problem to consider is how one might helpfully subdivide
masculinity in order for it to be studied. A clear structure like that offered by
Tosh in his early work, which looks through the prism of spheres, dividing the
world into 'home, work and social networks', risks losing access to the spaces
between the spheres.[41] More than this, however, if we agree that, beyond
engaging with normative gender ideals, the practice of masculinity draws on
personal gendered positions, then we must consider that masculinity should
not be viewed uniquely through one's relationships with others. Amongst these
non-relational elements of masculinity, historians and sociologists stress the
role of the body and the way in which men talk about and engage with their
body in understanding gender identity. Hadley sees the body as serving as a
'crucial medium in which to discuss the social order',[42] whilst Petersen deputizes
Foucault to make the argument that 'bodies are discursively constructed within
modern systems of power'.[43] Petersen goes on to relate the body directly to
other systems of identity such as race and class, embedding it firmly in the
contrasting identities that influence gender construction, when he comments
that '[p]articular male bodies, namely the bodies of white, European, middle-
class, heterosexual men, have been constructed as the standard for measuring

and evaluating other bodies'.[44] A spheres approach to masculinity, however, lacks any obvious space for these considerations of personal influences, the body or otherwise, on gender identities – a significant enough failing to render the division of spheres unworkable as a structure for analysis. As Tosh himself has more recently commented, 'no longer can masculinity confidently be located in specifically "masculine" contexts… Its discursive traces are to be found in every area of culture and society, and are certainly not confined to explicit ideologies of manliness'.[45]

My own approach has been to look for the outward manifestations of masculine identity (e.g. pride, valuing hierarchy and paternalism) wherever they arise, and then find the elements that seem, in this period, to influence them – whether they are traditional questions of employment and affluence or more personal factors, for example the body. This process can be self-perpetuating however, since one tends to find the elements of masculinity that one is looking for, leading one to conclude that ideas of masculinity are relatively stable throughout the period. To counteract this effect, it is important, therefore, to be open to new and alternative outward manifestations of masculinity wherever they might appear, as well as to the different elements influencing them. If, as has been suggested, men did struggle once the war had begun to continue performing the same masculine roles as previously, it does not necessarily follow that their masculinities collapsed. Instead they may have adapted their masculine identities to suit their changing lives, something which is allowed for in this approach.

* * *

Finally, in seeking to understand masculinity, the historian needs to be alert to the interactions which occur between the various identities within each individual and, given the disadvantaged position of many of the subjects in question principally for reasons of race, to the contribution than can be made by the theory of intersectionality. Whilst the focus of this book is gender, each individual equally can be considered to have, amongst many more, a religious identity, a national identity and even a socio-economic identity which intersect and interact with the performance of their gender. To break down gender analysis to take account of these interactions for each individual, however, would make it impossible to draw conclusions broader than on an individual level. Moreover, whilst sensitive to the importance of these interactions, as discussed already, the consistency and continuity of masculinities over time indicate that broader collected experiences of gender may indeed take primacy over the specific identity interactions of the individual. To attempt to combine both of these elements of identity and gender, therefore, I shall follow Whitehead and Barrett in defining *masculinity* as a 'fluid arrangement of multiple subject positions which together provide the means by which the individual achieves a sense of identity',[46] and through following the principle that subject positions in the period in question were formed both through positioning one's self vis-à-vis a range of normative, socially defined, gender identities and through engaging with elements of one's own personality, physicality and background; coming together, however, not as Whitehead and Barrett would suggest to 'achieve a sense of identity' but more actively to form the practice of one's own gender identity.[47] Whilst many of these positions are enduring gendered ideals, personal or collective, many are also flexible and transient elements of one's masculinity. The notion, therefore, of a 'fluid arrangement' skilfully represents the way in which the relationship between the subject positions and identities can alter, promoting different aspects of one's gender identity at different moments in one's life and in some cases altering the subject positions themselves. Exactly what the subject positions are depends on each individual, but for every man, I will go on to argue, there are one or two key normative masculine identities toward which he orients himself at any given time.

Jewish masculinities in practice on the eve of the Holocaust

One key question remains, however, concerning the nature of the normative identities toward which Jewish men in this period oriented themselves and the basis on which we can understand how individuals negotiated different identities in the performance of their masculinity. In the aftermath of the First World War, and facing previously unknown levels of mortality and injury amongst young men, European states set about (re)forming twentieth-century masculinities. Whilst the fascist states of Germany and Italy imposed gender identities upon their citizens in order to further embed their political projects, the more democratic nations also attempted to influence gender identities to support their social and political needs.[48] Unlike these nations, however, the Jews lacked a state that might have imposed forms or imperatives of masculinity upon its people, making the definition of Jewish gender identities in the period a more complex task for the historian. Jewish men were, of course, influenced by the governments and gender positions of the countries in which they lived; however, for most, this influence vied with Jewish religious and cultural impositions to form a range of alternative masculinities. No single 'Jewish masculinity' can be understood to have existed amongst the Jews of Europe in the years immediately preceding the Holocaust. And yet, in spite of this, in seeking to understand the impact of the Holocaust on Jewish masculinities, it is imperative to form an understanding of what those multiple Jewish masculinities comprised. Specifically, I argue in the following substantive chapters that three key masculine norms – dominant (which I shall term 'assimilated'), subordinate (henceforth 'internalized') and 'independent' – when considered in the light of cultural, scientific and political developments, formed the basis of the masculinities practised by Jewish men across Europe before the Holocaust.

* * *

The population of twentieth-century Europe included a large number of acculturated families who had not been practising Jews, in terms of either religion or culture, for several generations. They spoke the local language and identified themselves first and foremost as natives of the country in which they lived rather than as Jews. Whilst many of these acculturated Jews lived in Germany, they were also present amongst the urban elites of most European countries including Poland, France and Holland.[49] However, even for these acculturated Jews, life was not often completely separate from religious practice. Both Holland's *Hoofdcommissie tot de zaken der Israelieten* (Supreme Commission for Israelite Affairs), which dealt with such questions as religious responses to military service and responded to the persecution of less acculturated Jewish minorities in parts of its empire,[50] and the Central Consistory in Paris, which trained rabbis, selected the chief rabbi and oversaw worship and religious education, were staffed almost entirely by secular Jews who oversaw the complex problems of interweaving religious and national identity on a daily basis.[51]

In contrast to these acculturated populations, each of the four countries in question also had a more 'traditional' Jewish population, some of whom practised the Jewish faith – a variety of reform, orthodox and ultra-orthodox – whilst others had effectively given up their religious adherence but retained a strong attachment to 'Jewish culture' including rituals of dress and diet or even simply by speaking Yiddish – although this latter declined greatly in the early part of the twentieth century. In Poland, these culturally Jewish populations were largely native-born Jews living both in urban and in rural environments, many in the area formerly belonging to the Russian Empire, whilst in Western

Europe, they were more often immigrant populations who had fled pogroms and later persecution in Eastern and Central Europe during the late nineteenth and early twentieth centuries. In each country, a different history of Jewish presence with its own answers to questions of affiliation, loyalty, religion and nationalism existed and was under constant development in the interwar period.

The Jewish communities of France and Belgium at this time both included large numbers of these immigrant Jews, who were not nationals of the countries in which they lived and who, whilst statistics vary, are thought to have comprised around 90 per cent of the 70,000-strong Belgian Jewish community[52] and over half of the French Jewish community of just over 300,000.[53] In stark contrast, 85 per cent of Holland's Jews at the same time were Dutch nationals with a long history in the country, who spoke little Yiddish and who might not even have been identifiable as Jewish.[54] However, even these numbers only tell a small part of the story. In the fifty years before the Holocaust, France admitted more than 100,000 Eastern European Jews from Russia, Poland and the Baltic states amongst others, many of whom retained strong religious and cultural affiliations to Judaism, and yet by 1939, only 2 per cent of school-age Jewish children in France attended a religious institution or Yiddish language school – something in the order of 2,000 out of a population of more than 300,000. The rest all attended the secular public schools of the French Republic,[55] a statistic which suggests a less-than-obvious relationship between Jewish migration and degrees of assimilation.

Political affiliations also varied greatly amongst the Jews of Europe, and whilst some Western Jews avoided expressing strong political opinions that might somehow identify them as Jewish, instead supporting more mainstream parties,[56] other Western Jews and those in Poland supported a number of different parties, from the Communists and the Bund to Zionists and Orthodox parties (although this last rarely in the West). In Poland, the political affiliations of Jewish men were further complicated by their regional loyalties and the political systems within which they had resided before the creation of independent Poland in 1918: broadly speaking whilst Galicia and the territories of the former Austro-Hungarian Empire had strong support for the Zionist cause, the former Russian territories were more traditional, voting Orthodox in far greater numbers than elsewhere.[57] Voting statistics in the period even varied greatly within one city depending on whether they were local or general elections, on which subject Antony Polonsky records the words of Abraham Meir in Krongrad that, concerning the *Sejm* elections, the *Agudah* 'fights to avoid being ignored', whilst in the *kehilah*, 'it fights for hegemony'.[58]

Finally on this topic, the question of employment and its impact on degrees of cultural integration and cross-fertilization is significant to understanding Jewish-European identities in the interwar period, particularly in the East. The shtetls of Eastern Poland are most commonly seen as the core of unintegrated Jewish communities, and yet for most who resided in them, contact with the gentile community was a daily occurrence. Traditionally in such shtetls Jews and gentiles lived quite separately, with Jews residing in the centre of town and gentiles surrounding them. To complicate this, however, gentiles also comprised many of the customers and suppliers of Jewish craftsmen and businessmen, particularly since in many cases restrictions on Jewish land ownership meant that Jews were largely unable to work as farmers to provide the raw resources that Jewish craftsmen and salesmen needed. Equally, for those Jews employed by large landowners, which was not an uncommon occurrence, work often involved acting as a go-between for a gentile landlord and his gentile peasants.

In contrast, many of the most unassimilated Jews were in fact those living in poverty in the cities of Poland, where they were often, effectively, ghettoized; urbanization only really brought assimilation where it also brought wealth and not always even then. Statistically the majority of Jews in the towns were employed in 'trade and industry'; however, such a description is misleading in so much as it sounds more lucrative, and therefore potentially assimilated, than its reality. Those who were considered 'tradesmen' also included the high numbers of street peddlers who would not necessarily have left the Jewish quarters on a regular basis; moreover, 'industry' amongst the urban Jewish populations was largely cottage industry, which employed only a small number of, mainly Jewish, workers.[59] And yet, also to be considered in this period was the rise of state-funded education and the use of the Polish language that accompanied it, which contributed to a slow secularization and integration regardless of socio-economic circumstances.[60]

It is across these nations that individuals from different religions, with varied experiences of migration, employment, assimilation and language, lived. Yet I believe it is possible to identify three key normative identities, toward which they very largely oriented themselves in different, complex ways. The purpose of defining separate normative masculine identities, however, is not to specifically attribute them to individuals; these norms are effectively ideal types,[61] and no individual directly conforms to one single normative identity. Rather, each man uniquely orients himself toward one or more of these identities, all of which are themselves fluid concepts. To attempt to define exactly who does what would be to attempt to find concrete identities where, even on an individual basis, they do not exist. It is for this reason, however, that the above, brief consideration of the cultural, political and religious diversity that existed amongst European Jews in the interwar period is significant. Such an overview informs our understanding of the normative gender identities by illustrating some of the many complex factors involved in the practice of masculinity.

* * *

The interwar period saw Jewish men orient themselves toward three masculine norms, the first of which – 'bourgeois masculinity' – was the dominant Western masculinity of the time and was created by, and reserved primarily for, gentiles. Although gentile society had clearly framed Jews, and others including homosexuals, as the 'other' on which their dominant masculinity rested, it was possible for some Jewish men, nonetheless, to access this identity, either by ignoring their Jewishness or by rejecting the antisemitic elements of the discourse. This dominant masculinity was not a static concept and continued developing, particularly in response to war, embodiment and economics, throughout the century, and yet as George Mosse concludes, its key elements remained unchanged from the mid-eighteenth century: power, honour and courage seen through a unity of 'external appearance and internal virtue'.[62] Moreover, Mosse has persuasively argued that, although variations on this masculinity did exist, in the period in question bourgeois masculinity clearly triumphed over its competitors and, as the dominant masculine norm in European gentile society, was also that most relevant to acculturated Jewish men, particularly those in Western Europe.

The First World War had sustained the previous dominance of a gender identity built upon strength and military masculinity,[63] but this identity could not survive the realities of the aftermath of the conflict, as both the impact of the war on individuals and the presence in society of the very visual effects of the war, seen in the mass of disabled and mutilated veterans, fatally undermined the image of the masculine soldier. Mosse alone has attempted to suggest that when applied to Germany, and perhaps other smaller nations, the physical realities of warfare had a lesser impact than some have suggested.[64] Whilst this may be true (and certainly a more militarized masculinity was maintained in Germany than in the rest of Europe in the interwar period and particularly as war again approached), the case for the 'traumatizing experiences and consequences of the war' on the 'militant male image' is strong.[65] The space left by the perceived failure of this military gender identity allowed several alternative masculinities to present themselves, central amongst which was a 'socialist masculinity' stressing education rather than physicality as the dominant trope of masculinity. And yet, this socialist image also failed to gain dominance for a number of reasons including its inability to manage the question of the embodied male, an image which had been sustained in spite of the damage caused by the war. Ultimately, Mosse persuasively argues, 'bourgeois masculinity' offered the only embodied gender identity which nonetheless was not overly reliant on violent or military physicality and, as such, became dominant in most interwar European societies.[66]

Whilst it sacrificed the more hardened or violent images of military masculinity, this bourgeois norm succeeded in retaining both its dominance over women and its image of the body. Exercise and physical fitness remained key to gender identity in this period and membership of sports clubs increased, yet the purpose of this physicality had changed. Instead of symbolizing power through aggression and might, the body became a way to show power through self-control, discipline and proportion, all of which were well represented by the fit and healthy, contained, strong man. These traits, combined with ideas of duty, honour and respectability, informed the dominant masculinity of the interwar period. Key to this bourgeois masculine identity was a man's ability to provide for, and manage, his own family such that they were a credit to him when in society. It also hinged, however, on his status and performance outside the home. In homosocial environments, like clubs, for both working men and gentlemen, and in their employment, men strove to prove their 'individual industry, energy and uprightness',[67] all of which contributed to their gender identity.[68]

For all the attention I have given this dominant interwar masculinity, it was not, however, an identity toward which a large number of Jewish men would have oriented themselves, perhaps due to its inherent antisemitism, which almost necessarily rejected them as subordinate. In a limited number of cases, Jewish men, most likely in Holland and France rather than Poland and Belgium, could sidestep the antisemitic imagery that rejected them and perform the dominant norm described above – a possibility most clearly available to those who did not conform to the gentile image of the Jew and were instead assimilated into mainstream bourgeois society and already, therefore, conforming to its ideas of masculinity. (For this reason I call it 'assimilated Jewish masculinity'.) Yet, beyond its direct application to those few Jewish men able to access it, this masculinity played a more significant role. Not only did many men simultaneously orient themselves toward both this norm and another – effectively sidestepping the elements of both that were most problematic to their individual performance of masculinity – but also, equally importantly, the structure of this dominant masculinity is key to understanding the contingent, subordinate form central to the gender identities of a significant number of Jewish men in the interwar period.

* * *

The second normative Jewish gender identity that I have identified in this period is the subordinate Jewish masculinity, formed when the dominant group creates the subordinate as an undesirable 'other' in order to reinforce its own hegemony. In line with this theory, the subordinate 'other' became internalized as Jewish men strove and often failed to conform to the virulently antisemitic dominant normative masculinity. The coadunation of self and 'other' that this caused in many cases resulted in a complete internalization of the subordinate type, described by Sander Gilman as 'outsiders' acceptance of the mirage of themselves generated by their reference group … as a reality'.[69] This internalization of the subordinate form, in particular the antisemitic images it painted, rested upon a stereotype which needed in no sense to be a reflection of any reality; indeed it could be so far from being a reality that it could alter, or even reverse, itself and yet retain its power.[70]

One central target of this subordinate identity was language, both spoken and written. Accused of lacking their own language (since Yiddish did not count as a language of its own and Hebrew was a language only of study and prayer for most Jewish men), it was suggested that Jews spoke *Mauschel*, a perversion of other languages through the manner of their use. In some cases, this was represented by accented speech on the part of Jews, but also extended to choice of words or subject, which might instead suffice to define the Jewish 'other', as Gilman explains, '[w]hether evolutionary or conservative, journalistic or philosophic, it could always be seen as a specific language of the Jews'.[71] Gilman goes on to argue that written language can be seen as a key element of self-hatred, significant to the internalization of the subordinate, since as a post-enlightenment signifier of culture, it was a common tool of assimilation. It follows that this attempt to assimilate the written language 'confirmed to the reference group the superiority of their language' and thereby the distance of the Jewish 'other'. Thus Jewish men reinforced their alienation from language and the dominant type through attempts, in the form of writing, to assimilate.

Whilst I do not question Gilman's theory, I would, however, suggest that it had limited impact. Requiring a high degree of linguistic self-analysis, it would have affected a relatively small number of Jewish men who chose to intellectualize their language transmission in this way. Instead, it was overwhelmingly, but not uniquely, the assault upon the Jewish body which provoked the assimilation of the subordinate identity, since it was both more easily understood and more commonly applicable, and its dissemination, in the form of scientific and political discourse, provided a top-down imposition of gender, not unlike that found in other nation states, which acted to reinforce and secure the internalization of the subordinate masculinity.

The antisemitism of the dominant masculinity included numerous, often conflicting, attacks on the Jewish body,[72] but it was predominantly the image of the Jewish male as inherently feminized, weak and feeble, damaged both by his own Jewishness and by life in the ghettos, that was internalized and contributed most obviously to the subordinate masculine identity. Portrayal of the Jewish male body as physically frail and feminine was by no means new in the twentieth century, nor was it necessarily negative, having been used by Jews as a positive element of survival in the Diaspora.[73] As Jewish masculinity became more closely linked to combat and war, however, it further excluded Jewish men who could not bear arms, and drew on this feminized body to frame their status as an other.[74]

One way of understanding the dissemination of the internalization of the subordinate type is through a consideration of writing in this period, particularly the widespread tendency amongst Jewish authors, particularly but not uniquely in Germany, at the turn of the century, to write about themes of self-hatred. Walter Rathenau, himself a Jew, wrote in 1897 of the Jewish condition including its 'unathletic build … narrow shoulders … [and] clumsy feet', and only ever referred to Jews as 'you' and his work is described by Daniel Boyarin as, the 'undertheorized total internalization of the dominant faction by Jewish men'.[75] A few years later, Otto Weininger published his *Geschlecht und Charakter*, another key example of the internalization of the subordinate masculinity, which saw twenty-five editions in twenty-five years and contained one particularly significant chapter repeatedly detailing the inherent femininity of the Jewish male.[76] *Geschlecht und Charakter* was popularized by Weininger's suicide soon after publication – an act which was presented as one of self-hatred (Weininger was a converted Jew) to suit popular discourse and might have been understood by other Jews as such, regardless of the realities of his act. Significant in its time, Weininger's work has since been cited by numerous historians for its accurate representation of the way in which the Jewish condition and Jewish gender identity were portrayed. As John Hoberman writes, 'Weininger's ostensibly ungendered defamation of the Jews as a type is in fact an unerringly precise defamation of the Jewish male as he was commonly portrayed at this time.'[77]

Just as important as these writings, Zionism, which began in the late nineteenth century but found increasing support through the early twentieth century with the rise of the nation state and antisemitic persecution, can be seen both to play on and to disseminate pre-existing ideas of Jewish subordination. With the aim of obtaining a national homeland for the Jewish people, Zionists emphasized the physical representation of feminized Jewish men, to suggest that the Diaspora, the ghetto and the loss of the land had damaged the Jews. With the ultimate aim of reviving the Jewish body, and through it the Jewish nation, the Zionists effectively reinforced and internalized the subordinate stereotype.

The primacy given in Zionist thought to the weakened Jewish body, the associated internalization of the subordinate and its public dissemination are best understood through a consideration of a number of well-publicized books and speeches by Zionists in the period, amongst the earliest of which was Theodor Herzl's 'A Solution of the Jewish Question' published in *The Jewish Chronicle* in 1896. In it Herzl wrote of life in the ghetto where 'we had become somewhat unaccustomed to bodily labour'. The strength of this sentiment and its mode of expression developed through the early twentieth century, leading to Theodor Lessing's *Der juedische Selbsthass* in which he famously wrote,

[f]or centuries, his [the Jew's] national identity has been like a small and calm pond, constantly endangered by an underlying swamp. He has had only the company of his dead, and he has forgotten their language. No soil has supported him, no history relieved him of his sins, no cultural heritage [*Bildung*] has been *his own*; his hero is the sufferer.[78]

The peak of the Zionist project as it related to the Jewish body, however, can be seen in Max Nordau's idea of the *Muskeljuden*. In 'Jewry of Muscle', published in 1903 in the *Juedische Turnzeitung* and again in 1909 in *Zionistische Schriften*, Nordau argued that Jews had been involved in the 'mortification of our own flesh'. It was time, he wrote, for their bodies to 'live again', entreating, 'let us once more become deep-chested, sturdy, sharp-eyed men'.[79]

More specifically, the themes of Zionism and the weakened Jewish body were popularized through the link made between the Jewish body and *Aliyah*, with Zionist discourses of physicality establishing an effective dichotomy between the weakened (subordinate) Jew in exile and the Zionist (dominant) Jew in Palestine, as David Biale argues, '[p]hysical strength, youth, nature, and secularism were the constellation of Zionist symbols set against the degeneracy, old age, urban and religious signs of the Exile'.[80] The strengthening of the Jewish body was not, however, entirely ideological. *Aliyah* was necessary in order to convince Britain and the world of Jewish claims in the Middle East, which was in turn necessary since the ability to provide the Jews with a homeland in Israel still, at this time, lay with the British government. The Zionist discourse of the weak Jewish body could be seen, therefore, as pragmatic politics – by persuading young people that their bodies were being damaged in the Diaspora, they could convince them to perform *Aliyah*, thereby both furthering the Zionist cause and improving their own bodies. Yet, whilst this pragmatism may indeed have been significant in understanding the reason for the Zionist representation of the Jewish body, this is, in fact, far less important than understanding the impact it was hoped this representation would have – and the intention behind this was certainly to convince European Jews that their bodies had become inherently weakened and feminized – an intention which can only have further contributed to the internalization of the subordinate other. That this approach could equally have impacted upon those with no affiliation to Zionism should also be considered, since the discourses surrounding Zionist targeted all Jews and were well disseminated through European societies at this time.

This confirmation by Zionists of the inherent weakness of European Jewry, combined with the striving for a 'new' physicality so clearly and closely based upon the dominant gentile ideal and the success of Zionism, particularly in interwar Poland, provided the perfect conditions for the dissemination of the subordinate type and its internalization, something which was further influenced, were such inducement needed, by the advancement of race science, the resultant reinforcement of antisemitic stereotypes and ultimately the establishment of 'Jewish race science' which did little to redress the antisemitism of race science and may even have aggravated it. The development of race science in this period saw the representation of Jewishness change from a religion to a race, reinforcing the stereotype as a genetic reality, providing scientific confirmation of the 'other' in existing discourses of subordination and reinforcing the division between dominant and subordinate. Moreover, the widespread interest in the development of science and race science brought these ideas to a wider audience and lent them credibility, if indeed such was needed. Ultimately, even the Jewish race scientists, who set themselves up to confront the damaging racial representation of Jewish men, conceded damagingly that Jews were, for whatever reasons and perhaps not permanently, physically weak or inferior, as John Efron notes, '[a] poor physique or neurasthenic temperament was said to have been brought on by the debilitating effects of ghetto existence or antisemitism'.[81]

Moreover, compounded by their own, sometimes chequered, intellectual pasts, the arguments of Jewish race scientists may even have damaged the

Jewish case. Ignaz Zollschan, one of the leaders of the Jewish race science movement, had himself begun his scientific life decidedly more nationalist and with more conviction concerning inherited racial characteristics, than he ended it, provoking the accusation that his scientific conversion was as much about undermining antisemitism as it was about offering an authentic scientific opinion. As persecution of Jews increased into the middle of the 1930s, Zollschan set about forming an international committee to renounce antisemitic race science and its conclusions. Whilst the committee was eventually established in 1938, the field was extremely small and compromised by the notion that it was more concerned with the political implications of science than the science itself[82] – a charge faced by many anti-fascist scientific movements in the same period, Jewish or otherwise. Ultimately, as Efron notes, 'Jewish race science [was] unable to dispel the malicious opinions of the antisemites', instead describing it as 'like all apologia written by Jews, able to offer Jewish readers comfort, dignity, and hope'.[83]

Whether through the reading of texts, such as those of Rathenau and Weininger, or by engaging with international discourses of Zionism or race science, Jewish men engaged with the gentile community and could not avoid confronting antisemitic images of the Jew. For many, but by no means all, this led to the internalization of such images and ultimately an identification with the subordinate Jewish masculinity. Depending very much on engagement with the various discourses discussed, as well as levels of assimilation and independence, some Jewish men would have been well placed to avoid this rejection as an 'other'. However, for many, if not most, who lived their lives somewhere between the extremes of assimilation and isolation, in a period of increasing acculturation when Yiddish was being quickly lost to the vernacular and Jewish religious conviction, practice and education were all on the wane, some orientation toward a normative masculinity which internalized the subordinate would have been almost unavoidable.

* * *

The third, and final, normative masculinity I would identify as key to the practice of Jewish masculinities in the interwar period – and here I depart from Connell's approach to masculinities – was an independent identity, not the product of a power relationship with the dominant norm but instead established independently thereof and developed in parallel with the dominant and subordinate identities rather than in a hierarchy.

The exact form that this independent Jewish masculinity took, however, is debated. Boyarin makes a case for a form of Jewish masculinity which, related to the notion of Diaspora as inherently female, frames masculinity around an alternative approach to power where feminization is not construed as a 'lack', as in the subordinate masculine norm, but as an active choice.[84] In Lacanian terms, key to Boyarin's theory, '[i]t was the condition of not being imperial, of being Diasporic, that presents this possibility to the Rabbis, a possibility not of a temporary disruption but of demystifying "the phallus" for what it is, a violent and destructive ideological construct',[85] and thereby creating a feminized, but still sexualized, masculinity which some might explain using the term *Edelkayt*. This approach details a masculinity, exemplified by rabbis, which eschews the elision of power and violence with masculinity found in Western gender identity, and instead orientates itself toward the body and its sexuality in a way which more closely relates to early modern masculinity than its modern successor with its racialized approach to Judaism. And yet despite an impressive understanding of ancient religious texts,[86] Boyarin does little to show the practical existence of this gender identity amongst Jewish men in general or in interwar Europe specifically.

If, for want of evidence, we leave Boyarin's religious, feminized masculinity aside, however, a lack of discussion in modern gender history continues to make the framing of any independent Jewish masculinity problematic. Studies of modern masculinity have tended to overlook the subject altogether, whilst Jewish histories often engage more actively with the assimilated end of Jewry than the traditional one, focusing heavily on the engagement between Jewish and Western cultures rather than on the points where the two bisect. One good example of this is Robin Judd's article 'Moral, Clean Men of the Jewish Faith: Jewish Rituals and Their Male Practitioners, 1843–1914', which discusses the move of *Mohelim* and *Shochetim* toward embodying a more Western masculinity based around hygiene, cleanliness and 'bourgeois respectability'[87] – themes which tie-in well with the dominant masculinity discussed above. However, whilst the article provides us with the Western stereotype of the 'Jewish' background these men are attempting to eschew – single men in unhygienic conditions (bachelorhood being a sign of limited respectability in this case) – we are told little of how those involved would have viewed themselves. It seems unlikely that Jewish culture saw its own *Mohelim* and *Shochetim* as filthy, backwards and immoral, but this reality does not form a part of the article, and the lack of any discussion of the image and self-image of the *Mohelim* and *Shochetim* perfectly frames the problems inherent in discussing this underconsidered normative identity.

On the question of this alternative masculinity, however, historians have not been entirely silent and Mitchell Hart writes,

> there did exist a significant body of literature that represented Jews and Judaism as healthy and vital, that did not feminize the male Jew, or associate him with the sorts of social and political pathologies so common in the antisemitic imagination. There might very well have been real Jewish men out there who did not internalize antisemitic imagery, who did not come to understand their own minds and bodies through the prism of the negative stereotypes of Jews.[88]

So, who are these men and what comprises their masculinity? Potentially it is to this masculinity that Stefanie Schüler-Springorum alludes when she refers to Aron Liebeck – a Jewish, East Prussian businessman born in 1856 who wrote his autobiography between the wars and the focus of her study – as a 'A Soft Hero',[89] although the argument is perhaps undermined by Liebeck's wish that his tombstone read 'here was a man, and this means, here was a fighter'.[90] Nonetheless, in so much as Liebeck's autobiography presents a man able and willing to admit to 'crying bitterly' on several occasions and to repeatedly commenting on the beauty of other men, beauty being a manly attribute connected to charisma in this case, Schüler-Springorum shows us elements of an alternative, Jewish, normative masculinity. This masculinity can also be found in broader Jewish culture and writings, for example in the relationship with the circumcised penis – whilst many elements of antisemitic discourse concerning the Jewish body have been internalized, and despite strong and constant antisemitic assaults on the circumcised penis as a site of feminization, castration and emasculation, dominant discourse seems to have retained a positive relationship with the penis.[91] This positive approach to circumcision, not as a lack but as a choice, although not a feminizing choice as Boyarin would have it, reflects this independent Jewish masculinity.

In the relationship of the Jewish male to his family, and its presentation in both Jewish and gentile discourses, we see again elements of this alternative masculinity. The image of the Jewish male as the head of a warm and stable home, and its positive reflection of both the man and the father,[92] seems to be a key element of the independent Jewish normative masculinity. Beyond the immediate family, however, this association also exists between the Jewish man and his male ancestry and is an element of Jewish masculinity that we see very clearly in practice in the Holocaust. Key examples of this association are to be found particularly in literature, and notably in stories like 'The Little Shoemakers' written by Isaac Bashevis Singer, which begins by naming nine generations of the shoemaking family of Frampol, a list which, alone, shows a clear pride in descent and heritage. The story goes on to tell the life of Reb Abba and his seven sons who, one by one, all trained as shoemakers, emigrated to America and set up new lives working as shoemakers but using a highly mechanized process. One day, several decades later when they are all grandfathers, Reb Abba goes to visit; however on arrival he is taken very ill. After several weeks it is only the finding of his shoemaking tools that brings Reb Abba back to health and thereafter he begins to make shoes again. The story ends with Reb Abba in his workshop surrounded by his seven sons all making shoes by hand and singing as they had when their father had trained them in Poland.[93] Although this was written long after the Holocaust, still it is only one example of very many where the significance of descent and paternal ancestry can be seen and is clearly linked to the gendered identity of Jewish men. This fictional representation of heritage and ancestry is equally reflected in historical writing. One example of such writing is a Leo Baeck quotation that Josef Katz notes in his diary after seeing him speak in Berlin in 1940:

> Baeck says that in these times, when the house we live in threatens to collapse, we should sit down to observe the ancient Jewish tradition of study in order to understand the spiritual heritage of our ancestors. 'We don't put our people into uniforms!' he cries. 'Never forget that you are looking with eyes and hearing with ears that are centuries older than those of your fellow men.'[94]

This independent Jewish masculinity, perhaps softer than the Western equivalent but not necessarily feminized, rooted in an embodied state, confident in its Jewishness, religious or cultural, and tied to the Jewish family and ancestry, might be understood as a descendant of Boyarin's *Edelkayt*, but seems first and foremost, to be a Jewish confrontation with itself in a modern context. Such a man might have been orthodox and lived a life steeped in Jewish tradition and isolated from gentile culture, but this was not a prerequisite. As in the Singer story, such an identity is equally possible for a Jewish man with knowledge and experience of the cultures and traditions of Judaism, even when held in balance with a Westernized existence, who manages to avoid being too closely drawn into a gendered identity linked to relationships of power with the Western dominant form.

Despite the importance of the dominant role in the formation of multiple identities, and the positive potential of the independent masculinity, still for many Jewish men, it was the internalized, subordinate masculinity which played the most significant role in underpinning individual gender identities. I do not suggest that a majority of men consciously hated themselves for their physical degeneration and wished they could look more like Erwin Huber,[95] but that the interplay between the dominant Western norm and the independent Jewish norm, when combined with the unavoidable impact of omnipresent antisemitism, drove many Jewish men into orienting themselves toward a subordinate, specifically Jewish, masculinity.

Exactly what these normative identities each comprised will be considered throughout the remainder of the book but, importantly, common to all three normative masculine identities – much as they also vary in their particular manifestations, from assimilation and the importance of culture and language to questions of descent and heritage for culturally Jewish gender identities – was a core set of masculine traits. Both providing and protecting must be understood as central to most practices of masculinity in this period and overtly present in all of the normative identities. To these should be added status, which varied more in the form it took, but is equally omnipresent in the normative identities toward which Jewish masculinities oriented themselves in the interwar period. So universal are these three signifiers of gender, within the context of European Jewry as it faced Nazi persecution in 1939, that they are perhaps best understood as the 'essential, inalienable, gender traits' which make up Brittan's 'masculinism' and as such will form the core of my own analysis.

* * *

Attempting to understand the multiple natures of Jewish masculinity in the period in question, Sharon Gillerman writes of Siegmund Breitbart, a Jewish strongman of interwar Europe, thus –

> Yet even while Breitbart was exemplifying German masculine ideals, this analysis will also suggest that a dichotomized view of a gentle ('traditional') Jewish masculinity, on the one hand, and a ('modern') capitulation to gentile culture, on the other, does not do justice to the range of conceptions of Jewish masculinity available to Jews at the time. Based on the Breitbart example, I will propose that in place of conceiving only two forms of masculinity that were mutually opposed to one another, we instead consider the Jewish masculinities that Breitbart performed, and that were perceived by different audiences, as a loose and flexible assemblage of images, a mosaic, or even a cacophony of divergent discourses.[96]

And yet, with one addition – that of the third normative identity – this is exactly what I am suggesting. Whilst I do not contest the multiple personalities and characters of Breitbart, nor the divergent masculinities they seemed to present, I do not concede that normative masculine identities were either myriad or cacophonous. Rather, as I have laid out here, normative masculinities in this period can be understood as finite and influenced by top-down social trends. Beyond these normative identities, the gender that one practised was a product of the interplay between normative masculinities and the individual elements of gender identity that each man sustained.

It is this interplay of norms and personal element of gender which make up the way each individual practised his masculinity and collectively allow us to begin to understand the impact of the Holocaust on Jewish masculinities. Using this approach it is the work of the remainder of this book to consider the ways in which men's orientation toward these normative identities changed, the impact of persecution and enclosure on both norms and individual elements of masculinities and, where change or collapse of the practise of masculinity occurred, for whatever reason, whether Jewish men were able to find mechanisms for its reassertion.

Masculinity in Crisis: Persecution and Collapse

Described in the diaries of Chaim Kaplan as a period in which Jews 'hover[ed] between destruction and construction',[1] the beginnings of occupation and war across Europe are key to understanding the impact of the Holocaust on masculine identities, and indeed Jewish identities in general. Throughout Europe, German invasion and domination brought with them an end to a period of 'construction' which, in spite of the ongoing presence of antisemitism, has been generally understood as a period of growth, success and stability for numerous Jewish communities. Yet, as Kaplan notes, whilst this stability was ending, Jewish communities had yet to be plunged into the comprehensive 'destruction' which accompanied the creation of the ghettos and camps. It is this interim period which I have termed the 'deconstruction', and which is the focus of this chapter.[2]

The 'deconstruction' was not a period which saw any unity of experience for those who lived it: depending on, amongst many other things, nationality, material wealth, social status and, for the most part, luck, individuals and families experienced this persecution in extremely diverse ways. The period of the deconstruction is, however, framed by a unity of process: during the deconstruction, the lives of almost all Jewish individuals who came under the influence of the Nazi state were marked by a more or less swift, but essentially inexorable, process of disestablishment, attrition and diminishment. At different speeds and in different ways, the lives of Europe's Jews were dismantled by the occupying forces and by their fellow nationals through a process of legal discrimination and physical diminishment, ranging from the loss of employment, the 'Aryanization'[3] of businesses and the daily struggle to support one's family, to the slow alienation of public space, seen in the eviction of Jews from schools and universities and the closing of Jewish organizations and, finally, daily humiliation and abuse, both mental and physical.[4] It is this process, the dismemberment of people's lives, which typifies and unites the experiences of the deconstruction. Despite this dissolution of their lives, however, it was also a period in which, for the most part, Jews managed to remain with their families and communities, were not physically enclosed and were not separated by age, gender or physical capacity to work and survive, as would later become the case. Encapsulating the atmosphere in Europe for Jews in late 1939 and 1940, this gradual deconstruction of lives, seemingly endless but not necessarily catastrophic or terminal, became key to the inability of many Jewish men to practise strong masculine identities.

The form that the deconstruction took varied from one city to another and from one country to another, and yet it affected Jewish communities across Europe in a startlingly similar way. Creating an atmosphere of confusion and collapse that is clearly expressed in the sources, it is notable that many works, both by contemporary diarists and by survivors writing decades after the Holocaust had ended, cannot find language to describe the period. Failing to offer either the clear trajectory or the ethical clarity of later periods, some accounts go so far as to ignore these years altogether, often beginning instead with the moment when they entered the ghettos or camps and, when questioned on what came before, returning to their childhood and to life before occupation, bypassing the deconstruction completely.[5] Whilst there are exceptions to this rule, and some diaries and accounts cover the period comprehensively, for a number of writers the deconstruction remains unrecorded and perhaps unrecordable – considered neither 'normal' life nor a part of the systematic destruction that followed.

Perhaps unsurprisingly, the nature of the deconstruction had a significant and destructive impact on the gender identities of the Jewish men who lived through it. It is this period which most closely demonstrates the emasculation that historians have sometimes presumed, and yet even if we acknowledge a general tendency toward depression and collapse in male gender identities, there remains a flaw in this simplified representation of masculinity. Whilst the emasculation of Jewish men in the early stages of Nazi persecution was closely related both to environmental questions of passivity and loss of agency and to an inability to perform established gendered norms, the extent to which this can be easily described in terms of depression, confinement and role exchange has been significantly overplayed. Moreover, such an approach ignores those elements of individual gender identities that, for many men, remained relatively strong during this period. It is with these complexities in the performance and collapse of masculinities, then, that this chapter attempts to grapple.

Before considering in detail the impact of the deconstruction on masculine identities, however, it is worth considering its exact form in the countries under consideration. The very distinct nature of occupation in each country perhaps does most to highlight the relative insignificance of particular circumstances. Instead, the parallel collapse in masculine identities found in the different countries is explained through the idea that it was the process of one's life being deconstructed, rather than the actual conditions of that life, that had the greatest impact on gender identities.

German troops entered western Poland on 1 September 1939 and very quickly pushed east, crossing the Bug River in a matter of days, forcing a formal Polish capitulation on 27 September. This was swiftly followed by the imposition of the terms of the Molotov-Ribbentrop agreement which saw the Germans withdraw to the western side of the Bug and the Russians move in to occupy its eastern bank. From September 1939 until June 1941, when Operation Barbarossa began, those Jews east of the Bug lived very different lives from those to its west. Life under the Communists was not easy for Jews: persecution on the grounds of religion and class was not uncommon, and the situation was further complicated by the large numbers of Jewish refugees from the west stranded in eastern Poland, placing a strain on already limited resources, and later by Russian deportations of Jewish and gentile Poles to Central Asia.[6] Nevertheless, Jews throughout the area managed to live relatively stable and secure lives and write off the period as painful but not damaging in the way that German occupation had briefly been and would become again after 1941. When the Germans did invade eastern Poland, ghettoization and labour camps were already well established in the west and were therefore quickly imposed on the larger cities and towns in the east, whilst smaller Jewish populations were almost immediately destroyed. For many of those Jews who lived east of the Bug, this interim period of deconstruction was therefore extremely brief, their lives changing suddenly from straitened stability under the Russians to complete destruction after the German (re)invasion.

In contrast, for Jews who remained west of the Bug or returned there after the division of Poland, the period of deconstruction was protracted, beginning with the German invasion and lasting until the establishment of the ghettos, something which did not reach all cities until late 1940 and beyond. The intervening year or more comprised some of the most random and yet extremely violent and disruptive experiences for European Jewry under occupation and is therefore key to understanding the perhaps disproportionate impact it had upon Jewish gender identities and masculinities. Following a similar pattern to western Poland, Belgium and its Jewish population experienced a rapid occupation followed by a long period of deconstruction and a late shift toward internment and deportations to camps. During some two weeks in May 1940, Germany occupied Belgium. Whilst some Jews fled Belgium, predominantly to France, most remained and, within limits, retained their freedom. The deconstruction that followed the invasion, however, whilst similar to western Poland in its pattern, contrasted starkly with the Polish experience in its detail, notably lacking, for the most part, the extremes of violence and humiliation that became commonplace in the East. Through 1940 and 1941, Belgian Jewry experienced increasing ostracization, unemployment, humiliation and confinement, and by 1942, deportations to camps in the East via holding camps in Belgium had begun, with the first transport from Malines to Auschwitz in August of 1942 representing the beginning of destruction in Belgium.

In contrast to the occupation experienced by the Jewish population of Belgium before 1942, Jews living in Holland endured an occupation more closely resembling the severity and barbarity of the later occupation of eastern Poland with their swift invasion followed closely by immediate and severe restrictions on the lives of Jews culminating in the establishment of an internment and deportation camp at Westerbork. Finally, the experiences of French Jewry were quite different again from those of Jews in the other countries in question. The German invasion began in June 1940 when over half of French Jews fled to the unoccupied zone in the south, leaving around 120,000 in Paris and the occupied north. In the south, although some limitations on work and movement were imposed, relative stability endured for some time. And despite the ultimate fate of many Jews who lived in the south, including the head of the UGIF (*L'Union générale des israélites de France*) himself,[7] and the strong antisemitism of the Vichy regime, the south was able for some time to use its position to defend Jews in both the occupied and free zones. In the north, economic exclusion and restriction began from 1940 onwards; however, by mid-1941, the mass internment and ultimate deportations of Jews had begun, culminating, when such moves were only just beginning elsewhere in Western Europe, in July 1942 with the Vel d'Hiv round-ups.[8]

Each of these countries had its own distinct experience of occupation. In each case, German intentions and different levels of compliance and power combined to ensure very different lives for Jewish inhabitants. In almost every case, Jewish companies were Aryanized, curfews were imposed, Jewish associations were closed and Jews were randomly humiliated and assaulted. The speed and severity with which this was done certainly varied greatly between countries and even cities, and yet these differences appear largely irrelevant when compared with the fact that each country experienced a period of deconstruction and confusion during which the totality of Nazi intentions remained unclear. In every case, this process gradually but steadily diminished and eroded the lives of those Jews who experienced it – a significant factor in the collapse of masculine identities ultimately linked to an inability to perform the normative identities toward which they oriented themselves.

Environments

As important as the normative and individual elements of masculinity, which are the focus of this book, is the impact that a broader gendering of society can have upon masculinities. By this I mean to suggest that a given society might actively encourage or discourage behaviours which were commonly understood to be characteristically gendered, either male or female. Where a society encourages behaviours in men which are understood to be feminine, I would argue it produces an internal contradiction for gender identities: either men continue to behave in ways they see as masculine, and risk being condemned for doing so, or they must behave as society expects, in a way they consider feminine, and risk undermining their own masculinity. It is just such a feminization of society that I argue took place during the deconstruction with universally deleterious effects upon the ability of men to perform their masculinities.

In much of pre-war European society, an association can be found between male gender identity and 'action' on one hand and femininity and 'passivity' on the other. Moreover, this division applied to all spheres of life from the workplace, the social arena and politics to household management and relationships.[9] During the deconstruction, however, this association was turned on its head as the German occupation, and the antisemitism and persecution that it imposed and encouraged appeared specifically to target men. Initial physical assaults were directed principally at men, whilst the early round-ups also involved only men, either seized as political enemies or to be co-opted as forced labour. Examples of this gendered persecution are myriad but many reflect Helen Kotlar's clear statement when Germans arrived at her door in Kurów, Poland, that 'the bandits were more interested in men than in women'[10] and her reflection that '[i]t crossed the minds of many of our women how much easier it would have been if only our men had been women'.[11] This opinion is mirrored by Jacob Frank, also living in the Lublin area of Poland, who comments, '[w]e figure this way: the women and the children, what interest would they have to harm them? But with the men, the Nazis will do what they want to do',[12] and Alexander Donat, a young man living in Warsaw, who wrote of his wife, 'Lena was sure the Germans would be vicious, but what could happen to women and children?'[13] This belief in the relative safety of women compared to men in Poland is reflected in cases in the West including Fania Freich who, living in Paris, hid her husband when the Germans came, an act which ultimately led to her own internment and that of her children[14] and in the shock expressed by Albert Hipszman when he writes, '[o]n avait aussi entendu dire qu'à Metz des allemands avaient arrêté des femmes et des enfants, mais cela apparaissait impossible à croire pour tout le monde'.[15]

Perhaps even more important than its practical implications, this gendered persecution neatly conformed to the perception held by Jews throughout Europe, that men were under greater threat both in times of war in general and, specifically, to antisemitic assaults than women. This elision of perception and reality confirmed for Jewish communities the importance of focusing their protective efforts on men and resulted in two main responses, also both centred around men: faced with economic and social hardship, notably the expropriation of businesses and limitations on movement, many Jewish communities and individuals opted for compliance rather than direct resistance; and faced with physical hardship, specifically assault, humiliation and round-ups for labour, communities encouraged men to hide or flee. Moreover, as this compliance and inactivity were considered to offer the best possible chance of survival, attempts to fight back or protest, particularly unorganized attempts, were condemned by Jews themselves as deleterious both for the individual and for the community. Such was the strength of belief in the compliant approach in Holland that the General Strike called in 1941 in support of Dutch Jewry (the only gentile uprising of its kind during the Holocaust) was suppressed by the Jewish community in fear of reprisals.

This approach to persecution, adopted almost universally across Europe by Jewish societies which had endured centuries of antisemitic persecution and understood it to be their best hope for survival, effectively forced men into positions of extreme passivity: obeying, hiding and running. Whilst many men resisted this strongly, with sources overwhelmingly showing women and children forcing men to accept their protection rather than men requesting it,[16] ultimately, the combined impact of understanding assault as predominantly targeting men, both a reality and a misconception of Nazi intent, and the imposition of passive behaviours understood to be feminine and adopted by many, if not most, men at some point established the damaging, gendered environment in which the Holocaust took place. Becoming the targets of violent antisemitic persecution, Jewish men were at once emasculated as victims, and again as passive and feminized.

In understanding the impact of targeted persecution upon Jewish men, it is also worth considering the argument that some women were empowered by the gendered nature of persecution. Whilst their spouses, sons or fathers became more and more constrained in their actions, many women, it is argued, not feeling threatened in the same way as men, used their altered circumstances to assert their own position, both within the family and within the community and in dealings with the German authorities. In exactly this vein, Dalia Ofer argues that '[m]any [women] testified that the new situation, in which the men were more often endangered and abused than the women, filled them with courage and a sense of mission. It was now their responsibility to take care of the family.'[17] One example of this empowerment can be seen in Marcel Liebman's biography, *Born Jewish*. Liebman, a teenager living in Belgium at the time of the occupation, describes his father's initial reaction to becoming unemployed, stressing his achievement in finding alternative work and ways of making money where possible and highlighting his mother's contrasting weakness, describing her as 'obliterated' and 'negated'. Once her husband began to decline, becoming depressed by his inability to act, however, Liebman's mother began to reassert herself and is clearly described as becoming stronger and taking control.[18] Based on the argument that weakened men lead to empowered women, one might equally speculate as to whether the inverse could also be true – that empowered women further increased the likelihood of men becoming disempowered and depressed. Limited source material makes drawing any conclusion on this question virtually impossible; nonetheless this argument makes an interesting contribution to understanding the outcomes of gender-specific persecution and environmental changes on male and female gender identities.

The impact of this gendering of society on Jewish men can be best understood by considering the ways in which men write about action, a theme which is notable for the frequency with which it is referenced in accounts and diaries. Primo Levi closely links a failure to act with 'shame', something he writes about at length in his work *The Drowned and the Saved*, concluding that the shame which arose for many Jews after the Holocaust came directly from having failed to act. In contrast, such shame very rarely came from action, even action which did not ultimately have a positive outcome.[19] In explaining this theory Levi comments,

> [i]t was the same shame which we knew so well, which submerged us after the selections, and every time we had to witness or undergo an outrage: the shame that the Germans never knew, the shame which the just man experiences when confronted by a crime committed by another, and he feels remorse because of its existence, because of its having been irrevocably introduced into the world of existing things, *and because his will has proven nonexistent or feeble and was incapable of putting up a good defense.*[20]

This idea of inactivity as shaming is born out in numerous other testimonies including that of Abe Mohnblum who, in an interview soon after the Holocaust, when discussing watching a man being beaten by a *Kapo*, commented, 'I couldn't do a thing. I couldn't open my mouth. It does something to a person. It does something to a bystander more than to the one who is actually beaten.'[21]

Whilst both of these examples refer directly to the camps, they eloquently describe an approach to action which seems, perhaps less overtly, to be mirrored in the deconstruction. Writing of this period, Saul Friedländer records his father's deep depression and the reality that '[d]oubtless the worse thing of all in those days was to go on waiting, reduced to complete passivity. What could my father have done? ... Nothing depended on him now. A safer hiding place depended on the good will of others, as did fleeing the country'.[22] This shame at inactivity is also clearly reflected in the responses men were forced to make in public when confronting their German occupiers, from the wearing of stars to the doffing of hats, both of which were seen as passive responses – passive in the sense that it would have taken more action to resist them than to concede. Both had a significantly damaging effect on male gender identities. Moreover, the great pride that a few men took in ignoring or actively defying these instructions casts light on the way in which even limited, and often self-destructive, action could alleviate the shame of passivity.[23]

As well as being the chosen response of the Jewish community, gendered inactivity was also imposed by the Nazi regime as it occupied cities and took over their administration. For the Jewish community at large, restrictions were introduced daily to close down organizations, limit movement and diminish association and, with the exception of the American Jewish Joint Distribution Committee which continued to function during the deconstruction, the institutions and establishments of the Jewish community were largely destroyed. Schools and libraries were closed, political organizations abolished, Jewish industry appropriated and social networks scattered. Not only did these changes impose inactivity, but also they impacted predominantly on men, who played a greater role than women in these organizations and institutions. Through the closing down of political and social groups, men were again forced into passive behaviours they would have understood to be feminine. Yitzhak Katznelson's experiences are one example of the impact of inactivity through loss of association. A Polish poet actively involved in Jewish cultural life, Katznelson found that the German invasion and the resulting inactivity led to crippling depression – something he was able to escape only after the establishment of the Warsaw ghetto and his involvement with Dror, a Jewish underground organization, which inspired his return to writing.[24]

One final element of the shame of passivity can be found in the capacity for self-reflection that it offered. Levi writes that his shame was worst on Sundays, since that was the day when work was reduced and the camp inmates had more time to reflect upon their actions, '[c]oming out of the darkness', he wrote, 'one suffered because of the reacquired consciousness of having been diminished'.[25] Again if applied to the deconstruction, one might argue that continuing to live within one's old society, community and home, whilst the bulwarks of that society are demolished, could lead to a similar reflectivity. Jewish men in this period were more likely to be at home and unemployed than in earlier or later years, allowing ample time for reflection on their own inactivity and the changes in their lives.

The importance of the capacity to act in this context is further highlighted if we consider that those Jews who were able to remain active often cite that activity as being of importance in sustaining their strength and reference it specifically when discussing behaviours which might be directly associated with male gender identity. Moshe Flinker, a Dutch Jew and still a teenager writing during the Holocaust, observed that activity was necessary to 'better my soul or to elevate my spirit'.[26] Flinker's privileged situation living in Belgium during the deconstruction enabled him to continue to be active, remaining in education, regularly discussing employment and developing ideas for life after the war. Later, having decided that once the war had ended he would become a politician, Flinker commented, 'I now understand that ideas and thoughts are worthless if one cannot convert them into action.'[27] In contrast, periods in which Flinker recorded bouts of depression seem linked to imposed inactivity. Raymond-Raoul Lambert, living in the free zone of France, was rare in his success at using the occupation to increase his capacity to act, becoming a key player in the French Jewish community as president of the UGIF until his deportation and death in October 1943. Whilst working for the Jewish community, Lambert retained his freedom of movement and his power and ability to affect events. The impact of this ability to act is clear throughout his diary but particularly in the winter of 1941 when he commented, 'I am acting and that is what matters.'[28] A few weeks later he wrote '[t]aking action is intoxicating and satisfying.'[29] Importantly, Lambert often associated the ability to act with his role as a father and protector, reinforcing the connection between action and a strong male gender identity.

The significance of action, perhaps even despite its potential threat, is made particularly clear by Liebman and his brother who describe being called up for labour duty, showing delight as men in their ability to act and commenting,

> [t]here was an element of dread and a kind of pride in the excitement we felt. Yes, pride! And I'm sure my memory does not deceive me on this point. When my brother and I paid a visit to some friends that afternoon to say goodbye to them,

we quite openly and without inhibition displayed an air of resolve, a martial demeanour, as if we were obeying a call-up order that turned us into soldiers fighting for a noble cause. I can picture myself walking along the street next to Henri, at a marching pace, admiring my brother's calmness and determined to emulate him by remaining steadfast in the face of the test to come.[30]

Even in dire circumstances the elision of action, physicality and martial behaviour was enough to encourage strong male gender identities. Of course, examples such as these are limited and those men who managed to retain or increase their power or ability to act in this period are few; nonetheless, those who did, even for a brief time, clearly saw it as an important element in sustaining their identity and strength, reinforcing the idea that an inability to act would have had the opposite effect. For the most part, the initial targeted persecution of men, leading to the imposition of passivity by Jewish families and communities, combined with the destruction of Jewish institutions which accompanied occupation forced men into positions of passivity and inaction which conflicted with their traditional ideas of male gender identity as active and created the debilitating and emasculating gendered environment in which the deconstruction took place.

Normative masculinities

Whilst the gendered environment is important in understanding the impact of the Holocaust on masculinities, it was the inability of Jewish men during the deconstruction to perform the normative identities toward which they had previously oriented themselves that had perhaps the most damaging impact upon masculinities during the Holocaust. Whilst each Jewish man's ability to orient himself toward normative masculine identities was particular, affected by myriad influences including his work and continued potential to earn money, his status within the community and his ability to protect his family, it is hard to escape the conclusion that ostracism, economic exclusion and assault made it virtually impossible for most men to attempt to perform any normative identity during the deconstruction. Although some men succeeded in mitigating this damage, very few managed to avoid it altogether – a failure which underpinned the loss of masculinity which typified the Jewish male experience of the deconstruction.

Amongst the core elements of gender identity which made up masculinism, and key to the central normative identities of the period, the capacity to provide (which I will, hereafter, call 'provision') seems to have presented many of the most immediate and obvious problems for Jewish masculinity during the deconstruction. Performed primarily through employment and financial support of families, provision reinforced masculinity through the feeding, clothing and housing of one's family, and one's degree of comfort confirmed for the individual, to some extent, his own status and success. As Nazi Germany occupied countries across Europe, however, the combination of Aryanization of Jewish businesses and the ban placed on Jews working in the professions resulted in the immediate impoverishment of families and the impossibility of adequate provision. The damage caused by this situation was exacerbated by the realities of Jewish trade: whilst large numbers of Polish Jews owned factories, less than half employed more than five men, compared with 93 per cent of non-Jewish factories.[31] Instead, the Jewish economy comprised primarily small cottage industries which, rather than hiring outside assistance, often employed their own family members. In such a work climate, the expropriation of one Jewish business could damage the material wealth of several related families whilst also removing the possibility of reliance on one's close community for financial support. For those men who did not own their own businesses, the German occupation was equally damaging. As lawyers, doctors, teachers and other professionals were forced to give up practice, first being barred from working for gentiles and later altogether, they were equally left with no means to make money or to support their families.

Whilst these policies impacted upon all members of Jewish families, the immediate effect was most keenly felt by breadwinners who, as the people upon whom the onus of provision generally rested, were most exposed to the immediate ramifications of unemployment. Joanna Dobschiner writes of her father, who had previously run his own company in Germany, going out every day in Amsterdam and failing to find work. She notes his unsuccessful return on many nights, 'a beaten, tired, human being'.[32] Similarly, Abram Lancman records his father's collapse after the decline of his pharmaceutical business, a decline closely linked to the appropriation of property and goods essential to its successful functioning. Lancman's sister was forced to take over running the family business and, when she did so, Abram records that she 'understood immediately the extent of our father's embarrassment, the depth of his grief and the reason for his collapse',[33] highlighting not only the impact of unemployment and disenfranchisement upon men but also, more significantly, the extent to which even their families were sheltered from the full impact of the deconstruction of their lives.

It is important, however, not to overemphasize the impact of economic exclusion on the capacity of Jewish men to continue to provide. In a minority of cases, Jewish owners were able to use the expropriation of their business to establish a sustainable way of providing for their families: hiding tools and materials in order to sell them or continuing to work clandestinely, donating goods, or even entire businesses, to particular gentile families in exchange for later support or hiding goods or people, for financial benefit.[34] Similarly, some men in the professions, barred from working at their chosen careers, were resourceful in finding ways to earn money by working privately, often on the black market, or by selling possessions. Liebman's father, despite losing his job, continued to make money through small-time trading, and his success clearly represented a key element of his strength and morale.[35] Nevertheless, whilst it is important to note the sustained efforts men made to perform this element of their masculine identity and the success of a few, for most the continuation of work and provision was limited and temporary, and the overall impact of this comprehensive economic exclusion was disastrous for Jewish men attempting to provide for their families and thereby extremely damaging to their masculine identities.

The second key element of masculinism, the capacity to protect, was, much like provision, rendered almost impossible by the German occupation. During the deconstruction, particularly in the West, instances of murder or deportation of Jews were less frequent than they would become. For many, therefore, the focus of protection was from public assault and round-ups for forced labour, both of which occurred in every country under study and were common in some places. In a few cases, men were able to protect themselves and others from this threat – occasionally using bribes to free sons from custody or to distract marauding soldiers or policemen from assaulting people in the home – however a lack of work made money limited in such cases and attempted bribes risked increasing the anger of the assailant. When assaults did occur, therefore, both on men and on women, there was little that other men could do to stop them – and the impact of such impotence upon male gender identities was significant.[36]

Assaults on women when they came, moreover, often occurred when men were out of the home and more than one example exists of German occupying forces knocking on a door, only for the men to flee and the women to become victims of assault.[37] Such occurrences are predominantly recorded by women; nevertheless we can speculate as to the catastrophic impact they would have had on the masculinity of any man forced to flee, both by his own fear of persecution or by his wife's pressure to protect himself for her sake and for the sake of their children.[38] Frank describes exactly this attitude and expectation concerning the gendering of assault when he recounts German soldiers arriving prepared to appropriate the materials from his tailor's workshop.[39] Frank records his wife saying, 'Officer, you can do with me anything what you want – but my husband, he is the father of my two children ... if you'll do that to him something [*sic*] he would not be able to feed my kids.'[40] Whilst a quotation such as this suggests that there continued to be a belief in the ability of men to protect their families, it also highlights the incredible pressure placed upon Jewish men in this period to continue performing this role which, for many, was simply impossible. Ultimately, to the extent to which it relied upon an ability to protect one's dependents, much as in the case of provision, the capacity of men to perform their normative masculine identities was largely voided, with an incalculable impact on their overall identities.

Significantly, however, in very few cases did this inability to protect their families lead men to stop attempting to do so. Rather, the importance attached to the efforts made to protect, even where they were unlikely to have any real impact, is clearly shown by the numbers of men who returned from relative safety, predominantly in the east, in order to defend their families. As the Germans invaded Poland, large groups of Jewish men fled east across the Dnieper and Bug rivers into areas of Poland they believed would be safe from German invasion. Initially a response to calls by the Polish government for men to regroup in the east for a counteroffensive, this exodus became a way for men to protect themselves and attempt to establish new lives which might later allow their families to join them.[41] However, for many men the act of, what felt like, abandoning their families became unbearable and they returned, often from situations of relative security, in order to fulfil what they saw as their duty to protect. In exactly this way Alexander Bronowski left Lublin and reached relative safety in Bialystok before applying for his wife to join him. Her application was rejected, as was his subsequent application to return, so Bronowski chose instead to return illegally to Poland.[42] Similarly, Jacob Frank reached safety in Russia before choosing to return to Poland on the basis that security for himself alone had little value,[43] and Alexander Donat, who also fled to Russia, returned for his wife who refused to leave, fled again, and finally returned for a second time, commented, in language clearly denoting its relevance to his masculinity, 'I was there to stand and fall with them [his wife and son], to shield and protect.'[44]

This process of flight and return as a method of protection cannot be easily seen mirrored in the West. For many men in the West, rejoining one's family in an attempt to provide such protection was less relevant since, in many cases,

Holland, Belgium and France had been the countries to which the family had fled together initially, and onward escape was often impossible due to a lack of documents and passports. Nevertheless, ongoing attempts to protect family members in whatever way possible are found in every country in question. Where all else failed, for some men, attempts to die or be deported with their families were a final attempt at protection. Following the occupation of Lvov, Leon Wells was arrested along with many of the town's men, including his own father, and taken to a sports field where the men were separated into groups, his group being taken to a cellar and viciously beaten. When Wells regained consciousness the first thing he claims to have seen was his father's face; having heard screams from the cellar and assuming the boys were being killed, his father had volunteered to join the group in order to die with his son.[45] Similarly, when Liebman's brother was arrested in Antwerp and taken to a holding camp for deportation, his father ordered the whole family to pack their belongings so that they might all report for deportation together. Although his father ultimately decided against such a course of action, the instinct to die together, or at least to enter the unknown together, seems clearly to have been a protective one.

Individual attempts to protect families were also made by innumerable Jewish men in whatever way was offered by their circumstances. Lucien Duckstein describes surviving the Vél d'hiv round-up in Paris because his father, a French prisoner of war in the First World War, was able to secure special treatment in the form of food and protection.[46] Also exercising his position within the gentile community, Liebman's father, early in the occupation, decided to act in an attempt to protect not only his own family but also all of Belgian Jewry. To this end he organized an audience with the queen, which he was granted, and although his efforts were ultimately unsuccessful, they were nonetheless clearly significant both to himself and to his son.[47] Such examples as these as much reflect the futility of continued attempts to protect one's family as they show the importance for individuals of making those attempts. Liebman records his father being lifted from depression when he was 'restored to his duties as head of the family – to which he attached such extraordinary importance'[48] and his final collapse came, both in the eyes of himself and his son, only when he sent his children away to stay in hiding and 'ceased to be [their] protector'.[49] Whilst these attempts to protect, against the odds, illustrate the importance of such actions for gender identities, they should not distract from the harsh reality that, for most Jewish men, the ability to protect was barely an option to be attempted, let alone something at which they might succeed. Furthermore, the fact that both of these examples come from Western Europe clearly illustrates the greater capacity that many men in the West had to act during the initial phases of persecution when compared to Jewish men in Poland.

The final element of masculinism significant to understanding the inability of many Jewish men to perform the normative gender identities toward which they oriented themselves was status – not that status was marked in the same way for all men, but that for all men status had significant gender implications. Status questions are also, however, the most complicated element of masculinism to identify since, more than protection or provision, status not only impacted upon gender identities but also intersected with other strands of identity including racial, religious and class. More importantly, just as identities overlap, so too do signifiers of identity, an intersection epitomized by Sam Pivnik when he writes of his uncle, '[he] had been a handsome man – I remember the photographs – but now he was an elder of the town, with a beard to match. He had status; we boys knew that'.[50] In this period, the beard would have been understood as both a signifier of religious identity and of social status, and so the public cutting of beards during the Holocaust can be seen not only as a humiliation of the individual's religious status and identity but also as an assault on the masculine identity and social status of the men who wore them.

The point during the deconstruction at which these broader questions of status became particularly significant to issues of masculinity can most clearly be seen with the loss of access to public space: where public space had previously offered an area of male domination in which men, Jewish or otherwise, had conducted male homosocial interaction and formed and asserted their status and position, the deconstruction saw the loss of ownership of that space, with rules of conduct being imposed from above and the alienation of Jews from within that space. The severity of this shift is summarized by Samuel Shryver who, living in Amsterdam, commented, '[t]hey [Jews] were not allowed to participate or to do anything that had to do with the public',[51] whilst its impact can be seen in Kaplan's reference to the 'excommunication' of men from their 'legitimate social or moral community'.[52] This impact was then exacerbated by the numerous humiliations which took place within the space that Jewish men had formerly felt to be their own, and the subsequent collapse in status shows clear links to gender identity.

The initial alienation from the public space came for Jewish men soon after occupation as bans were placed upon walking on the pavement or using certain types of public transport, and in many countries, curfews were placed on the movements of Jewish men and women altogether. Dominance in the street shifted from being gendered to being racial and with it the position of those Jewish men who had previously asserted their status in the public space was diminished. This is something which Kaplan notes repeatedly in his diary and is reflected in the comments of Josef Katz that 'walking by myself I feel excluded from human society. The streets are poorly paved, and the puddles and garbage make it hard to walk on the cobblestones. I wonder how it feels to be walking up there on the sidewalk?'[53] Emmanuel Ringelblum also makes repeated references to Jewish men being forced to walk in the street rather than on the pavements, a repetition which attests to the importance this appropriation of space had for those who experienced it.[54] The damage caused by this loss of domination and space was, however, exacerbated by the loss of interaction which occurred in the streets as men ceased to find the space secure enough to conduct such relationships. As a means of establishing, advancing and proving one's status and manly credentials, this homosocial interaction was a key element of gender performance, and its loss had a significant impact upon masculinities, particularly when combined with the closing of Jewish institutions – traditionally the other site of male homosocial relations.

Although managed at different speeds in the countries in question, in all cases German occupation regimes chose to close down Jewish organizations and institutions. The involvement of Jewish men in political parties, whether specifically Jewish or not, was an early casualty of occupation, followed by involvement in cultural organizations such as orchestras, Jewish theatres and male clubs designed for leisure and sports. For younger men, the exclusion from higher education, a space clearly used for developing masculine identities whether through intellectual achievement, sporting prowess or simply socialization, was critical. Equally, the closing of Jewish schools impacted indirectly on Jewish men as they lost a means through which to assert their position in the Jewish community – as Yitzhak Zuckerman, a Jew originally from Vilnius who fought at the head of the Jewish Combat Organisation (Żydowska Organizacja Bojowa – ŻOB) in the Warsaw Ghetto Uprising, explains in his *Chronicle of the Warsaw Ghetto*, sending one's children to religious school was, for many, not a testament to religious commitment but instead a means of proving and sustaining one's place within society.[55] Ultimately, the numerous limitations placed on Jewish involvement in public space in all its many guises, particularly when combined with the loss of work spaces which also represented sites of male status and interaction, left men either using public space, but risking assault, humiliation, alienation and the loss of status that necessarily accompanied those experiences, or confined to the home, away from their traditional space of domination and at risk of depression.[56]

The stress placed in accounts by Polish-Jewish men on efforts to move east in order to rejoin the army, or to involve themselves in public defence, provides another way of understanding the status value of being associated with society, in this case through public action. On this subject Mary Berg referenced her uncle walking from city to city looking for his army regiment[57] whilst Calel Perechodnik, who later became a member of the Jewish Ghetto Police in the Otwock ghetto, was keen to note that he, his brother and his father all tried to enlist when Germany invaded Poland.[58] The preponderance of accounts in Yizkor books[59] written by young men is also not unrelated to the fact that many of them fled east to join the army and avoided ghettoization. Amongst them Dr Asher Heller recorded his flight east along with a group of town men in the Wald Yizkor book,[60] Sholom-Abner Bernstein fled from Łódź to Dereczin with his father and brother[61] and Motl Eisenberg fled Szydłowiec in a group of men and, although they did not attempt to join the army, Eisenberg is keen to note his respect for and support of their efforts, recording, '[o]nce in a while a truck drives by filled with armed Polish soldiers. Whenever that happens, the Jews jump up from their seats, remove their hats and greet the soldiers sincerely'.[62] Later during the Holocaust, Ringelblum recalls the heroism of Jewish troops fighting with the Polish army in this early period in attempts to stop the German invasion, recording that, even when all the other soldiers in a battalion had fled, the Jews would stay.[63]

A similar emphasis on commitment to military and social involvement can be found in the numerous references made by those who did not flee, to efforts to join in civil defence, in particular ditch digging in Warsaw. Chaim Kaplan records joining efforts to build defences against the German invasion, noting that it was the first time he has ever done physical labour – interestingly an action which freed him briefly from earlier depression and suggests the potential impact that such social involvement could have upon masculinity.[64] Finally Lancman records attempting to defend his building during the bombardment of Warsaw, noting that he was aided by another Jewish man but that no one else was willing to risk their life in this way.[65] Such comments might simply be understood as attempts to prove the involvement of Jews in order to rebut frequent suggestions that they were separate from society or weak;[66] but it also seems important to these Jewish men and their families to assert the homosocial bonds built up in this period as proof of masculine involvement and cohesion. This emphasis on the place of Jews in the public domain before the German victory contrasts sharply with their immediate eviction from that space once the Germans took power and should be understood as a key example of how masculinity is formed and its importance: the loss of such a sense of masculine camaraderie and space clearly being seen as significant.

Despite their loss of dominance within the public space, Jewish men, nonetheless, continued to spend a good deal of time occupying that space, and it was in this limited occupation that the most damage to their status was done, through acts of humiliation. Many historians have suggested that during this period Jewish men were driven into their homes, both as a response to their own depression and to avoid public humiliation, something made possible by unemployment and existing gender roles. Commonly cited is the example of women doing the shopping, and yet whilst women may in many cases have done the shopping, there are enough examples of men going out to do the shopping, and references to this being a male task, for us to question assumptions in this respect. It is worth noting, on this point, Victor Klemperer's comments that he did the grocery shopping because women could not get served in many of the shops (this is particularly significant in Klemperer's case since his wife was gentile). Julian Castle Stanford, originally from Düsseldorf but residing in Holland, commented that men were visible in the streets as they were commonly doing the family shopping,[67] and it is Mary Berg's father in Poland who queued in line for bread during an air raid despite the fact that his wife, an American citizen, might have been afforded more protection in the event of an assault.[68] Equally, Kaplan, who was based in Warsaw, comments that men who had never before bought anything got up in the night to queue for food saying, '[e]very important man now carries a bag full of potatoes on his back, and a live chicken or a duck in his hand,'[69] and Sara Zyskind records her father coming home from the breadlines where men with beards were being pulled out and sent home.[70] Therefore, whilst acknowledging that many men in this period did lose work and stay at home, which was in itself damaging to their status and gender, the sustained nature of public humiliation to which Jewish men were subjected was possible only because of their continued and unavoidable presence in the streets.

Throughout the period of occupation, particularly in Poland and the other eastern territories, ritual humiliations were visited upon Jewish men during the time they spent unavoidably in public space, by both Germans and gentile locals. On a daily basis, diaries and accounts from the Holocaust record examples of humiliation ranging from the wearing of the star and doffing of hats to forced dancing and singing in public and even the desecration of holy articles. In many of these cases, the act of humiliation itself was not targeted toward gender identities, particularly true in the case of attacks which focused on religious symbols (including phylacteries, locks or scriptures) or sites; nonetheless, the collective impact of these humiliations was to diminish the status of the Jew as a man, not only because they were endured or observed by almost all men regardless of their religious affiliation but also because religious identity was inextricably linked to gender identity, and an assault on one's religion was not just an assault on the Jew but on the Jewish man.

Some of the most frequently referenced, and clearly extremely damaging, humiliations visited upon Jewish men in this period were enforced acts of obeisance to the Germans, chief amongst which was the forced doffing of hats. Kaplan recorded that '[s]ome psychopathic Nazi is demanding that every passer-by take his hat off in his honour. Many fled, many hid, many were caught for their transgression and beaten'[71] whilst Ringelblum made repeated references to such events including the relatively innocuous note that '[i]n Lublin the Jews have to take their hats off to the German guards'.[72] These are just two examples of comments found in many of the written and recorded accounts of the Holocaust. For numerous men, the humiliation of tipping one's hat was so great that they would try to avoid it, often at great risk to their personal safety. Many also avoided the problem by not wearing a hat at all, an omission which, at this time and in the east in winter, would provoke anything from surprise to overt ridicule and shame,[73] and the fact that men continued to do this is testament to their need to avoid the more extreme humiliation of the act of doffing their hat. Not dissimilarly, Michael Zylberberg noted that on returning to his village (Plock) he found that many men were refusing to leave their homes because they did not wish to salute the Germans[74] – a rejection of obeisance which, in the circumstances, might seem disproportionate, unless we consider its indirect impact upon status and masculinities.

Of course not all Jewish men found that forced obeisance diminished their status and, living in Warsaw when the Germans invaded, Władysław Szpilman recorded how his father went out of his way to find Germans and to greet them with exaggerated bows.[75] Whilst this seems to have provided Szpilman's father with a degree of hard-earned, childlike pleasure, he is perhaps the exception that proves the rule. Both Szpilman and his brother had decided they could not bow to Germans, a decision which effectively placed them under house arrest avoiding the possibility of meeting a German, refusing to bow and the beating that would necessarily follow. Ultimately many men were beaten either for failing to doff their hat or indeed *for* doffing them, and we should not downplay the arbitrary violence that seemed to be linked to various acts of humiliation. Nonetheless, most commonly referenced by men, and most humiliating for them, seems to be the doffing of the hat rather than the potential or actual violence attached to the act.[76]

Also of particular note, and mentioned briefly already, was the undermining of status through the humiliating public cutting of beards and locks – more commonly referenced as having been seen happening to other men than written about as a personal experience. The distancing of such attacks from those who recount them may be linked to the fact that a large number of the available diaries and accounts were written by younger men who were often relatively assimilated, or at least beardless; nevertheless, those accounts written by Jewish men who wore beards, even if not locks, still rarely reference personal experiences and perhaps indicate the extreme shame that such an act seems to have induced in the individual.[77] Similarly, Ringelblum's account of the abuse of several men held for days in a labour camp and assaulted, which places particular focus on the cutting of their hair, indicates the particularly visceral response that such treatment provoked, even when compared with acts of near torture.[78]

The beard and, equally, sidelocks were first and foremost symbols of religion and for many men their cutting was a severe assault on their religious identity. They were also, however, a symbol of masculinity, both specifically for practising Jews, for whom masculinity was linked to religious commitment, adulthood and even status within the religious community, but also for gentile and assimilated masculine identities in this period, and an assault on the beard necessarily impacted upon both religious and gender identities. Moreover, simply the wearing of a beard in the period diminished one's status since it instilled one with a fear and altered one's public behaviour, as Zyskind commented, '[w]ell-known and respected Jews, whose bearded faces had never failed to arouse veneration, now slunk like shadows along the walls of houses, desperately trying to elude detection'.[79] Much as the refusal to shave was a religious one, the loss of position, freedom and status that came with this decision and its affect upon how 'well-known and respected' one was clearly show its impact on questions of identity broader than purely religious. Not only, therefore, was the removal of the beard itself humiliating, but living with a beard and effectively in hiding, or living without a beard after its removal, would have been equally damaging and a constant reminder of one's diminished status and therefore diminished capacity to conform to any normative masculine identity.

The final humiliation regularly referenced by Jewish men as impacting upon the question of status is the wearing of the yellow star in public, referred to by Kaplan as his 'badge of shame'[80] and described by Kahane as the 'branding' of Jews, in his comment that '[t]he armband singled out its owner like an animal.'[81] Maurice White and his father, living in occupied Paris, found the shame so unbearable that they refused to wear their stars, citing this decision, and its impact upon their lives, as a key reason for their ultimately choice to leave behind the women in their family and move to the unoccupied zone where the star was not worn at that time.[82] Although women also referenced the shame that they felt in wearing the star, it was men who extended this to seeing the star as representing their being owned by someone else and who were most likely to have had particular trouble wearing it in public. Whilst in a few cases this gendered difference is tied to the perceived ease with which women could remove the star – there are more accounts of women doing this than men since they were considered less likely to 'look Jewish'[83] – in general women did wear their stars, and simply do not seem to write about humiliation in the same way as men. Moreover, this gendering of humiliations of status exists more generally, and whilst accounts written by women do occasionally reference the range of humiliations of status described above, they are overwhelmingly to be found in the accounts written by men in the Holocaust.[84]

In a very different way, unemployment, already discussed at length in relation to provision, also impacted upon status and masculine identity since one's work and one's role within the community were intricately linked. Herman Kruk, who was himself a Polish refugee having fled Warsaw for Vilnius, described other Jewish refugees arriving and listed their former professions '[a] week ago a landlord, the director of a bank, an industrialist; today hungry, naked and hunched up. Ten days ago a merchant, a factory supervisor, a cobbler, a baker; today naked and barefoot, crushed'.[85] The significance of their current circumstances, Kruk makes clear, is found in what they have lost and what they were formerly. Similarly Bernstein, writing in the *Dereczin Memorial* book, noted the link between employment and status, '[m]y status in the mean time had also changed: before I was a teacher, a person who commanded respect; but now, as a Jew, I found myself outside the framework of the law; I was worse than a dog in their eyes'.[86] Moreover, different types of labour had a specific status attached to them. Zuckerman records shovelling snow on behalf of his father, although he was too young, because, 'I did not want him to suffer the humiliation of the physical labor'.[87] For a man such as Zuckerman's father, the very act of physical labour, regardless of assault or public space, was a humiliation of status to be avoided.

The relationship with public space was not, however, universal. The extent of alienation, and therefore humiliation and loss of status, for any individual depended on a range of factors including which country and even city one lived in, the extent of native gentile complicity[88] and the German presence on the streets. For some, therefore, a relatively safe public presence remained an option for some time during the deconstruction and was significant in the sustaining of status and therefore in the performance of normative masculine identities. Even beyond this and in strong contrast to the numerous and deep humiliations visited upon most men, a few Jewish men in this period experienced a reversal of this trend, and their diaries and accounts note in some detail the rare occasions when gentiles, and sometimes even Germans, showed them the respect that they had become used to forgoing. Notably these were not acts of kindness and they rarely affected the material well-being of the individual concerned. Instead, exactly because they were not materially beneficial, these can be seen as acts which reinstated traditional notions of respect, restoring pride and a sense of status to the Jews involved, even if only for a short time. Again, given their limited impact on questions of sustenance, employment and liberty, which in this period might seem to have been more pressing, the fact that such events are as well detailed as they are shows their clear significance to those involved.

Castle Stanford relates an experience on a tram in Amsterdam when one gentile doffed his cap to him and another offered him a seat. On another occasion when he offered to give up his seat on a train, several gentiles refused to take it. When Castle Stanford explained that he would be in trouble if a German found him sitting whilst gentiles stood, a number of men left the carriage in order to enable him to sit without fear of reprisal. These were not acts of kindness that Castle Stanford notes, he does not note that he was particularly uncomfortable or needed the seat overly much, but rather acts of respect, which clearly frame the corresponding humiliations as showing a lack of respect rather than as physically damaging.[89] Similarly, Katz specifically recorded an occasion on which he observed a Catholic priest raise his hat to a group of Jews being forced to clean the streets whilst being taunted by Polish children.[90] Examples such as these are rare, however, when they do occur, they are dwelt on with some attention, and their restorative nature for those involved clearly shows the importance of status to those individuals.

Accounts are not, of course, all unified on this topic. Humiliation is a particularly personal experience, and those who recorded their stories immediately after the war, particularly those who did so with an eye to assisting prosecutions against the perpetrators of the Holocaust, tended to place particular emphasis on those crimes they believed would receive the worst punishments: thus physical abuse took precedence over mental or emotional abuse. Moreover, as Ofer notes, men writing in this period were keen to stress the collective experience, and thereby the universality, of the Holocaust, making a record of events in order to ensure that knowledge of the Holocaust could not be suppressed (as many Germans had threatened during the war) rather than writing simply for personal record, as was more common later.[91] Early accounts, therefore, leant toward detailing the most sensational or shocking events and away from the mundane humiliation which in fact seems to have had a deeper impact on its victims. That not all accounts reference such humiliation is therefore unsurprising; nonetheless, that so many men, in the process of recording their personal experiences, do mention humiliation and loss of status is a good indication of its importance to the individual, even if not to his understanding of the collective.

Almost without exception, sources show that the performance of those elements of normative masculine identities common to almost all men, here called masculinism, was almost entirely impossible. Despite significant and ongoing efforts, Jewish men were largely unable to protect and provide for their families, or to maintain a sense of their own status within society and the public space, when faced with the assault of antisemitic occupation. Nevertheless, there were also elements of masculinity particular to each of the three normative identities outlined earlier, which should be considered in attempting to understand the complexities of interactions between the deconstruction and male Jewish gender identities.

For those men who oriented themselves principally toward an assimilated normative masculine identity, perhaps the most significant outcome of occupation and persecution was rejection from the group to which they understood themselves to belong. For those who did not identify themselves as Jewish, whether in a religious or a cultural capacity, the gentile community was their own, and the rejection of Jews by that society which occurred across Europe to a greater or lesser degree was particularly damaging to the gender identities of assimilated Jewish men. This eviction from their own space and social milieu might have been mitigated, in a limited sense, at the beginning of occupation since the earliest assaults were largely targeted at those men with a stereotypically Jewish appearance. Nevertheless, as persecution increased, and particularly after the wearing of the star became mandatory, assimilated Jews were as easily targeted as any others and they experienced the same humiliation as other Jewish men. One notable absence in the testimonies of assimilated Jews when compared with those of more traditionally religious or cultural Jews, however, is seen in the discussions of antisemitic assaults which occurred, particularly in Poland, in the decades before the Holocaust. For some men these formative experiences seem to have acted as a preparation for the humiliation and early persecution of the deconstruction,[92] whilst for others, often from cities which provided a degree of anonymity, such acts were more alien. This is not to suggest that the antisemitism of the interwar period prepared Jewish men for genocide or the Holocaust; rather it should be noted simply that the physical assaults and antisemitic persecutions of the pre-war period, particularly childhood experiences, are often cited by men as a forerunner to the early humiliations and ostracism of the persecution.

Also key to understanding the ways in the which the deconstruction impacted on assimilated Jewish men is the way in which they were able to exploit friendships and associations with gentiles during the early period of social and economic exclusion, and thereby mitigate its impact. Yet, despite these limited benefits, it is clear that once persecution became established, assaults and humiliations increased against all Jews and assimilated Jews were, if anything, increasingly vulnerable as they were ostracized by the gentile communities they would have considered their own. In contrast, Jews who remained within the Jewish community were less isolated by the occupation and persecution, retaining, as they did, their contacts, associations and communities for a longer period.

For those men who oriented themselves toward an independent Jewish masculinity, deconstruction had a very different impact, central to which was the question of descent and heritage. In contrast to assimilated masculinities, independent male gender identity was associated closely with familial descent, inherited business and continuity of the male line, all of which were severely threatened by the deconstruction. Evidence does also suggest, however, that during the early persecution of the deconstruction, this sense of heritage (associated particularly with living in a Jewish community) also brought with it, for some, a heightened sense of unity and belonging – a point alluded to by Ringelblum who notes the importance of the historical past for Jews in understanding themselves both as individuals and within their community. After speaking with a Jewish scholar, Ringelblum records, '[t]here's been the growth of a strong sense of historical consciousness recently. We tie in fact after fact from our daily experience with the events of history', going on to note, '[t]he Jews created another world for themselves in the past, living in it to forget the world around them.'[93] Similarly Yosef Kermish, writing after the Holocaust about the reasons for which Jews recorded their experiences, cited the opinion of Simon Dubnow, a celebrated Jewish historian and writer, that 'Jewish history is the chain uniting the generations, and someone who does not know the past is not a Jew.'[94]

Finally, understanding the impact of the deconstruction on those whose normative identity was based around the internalization of the subordinate type is perhaps most complex in this period. Relatively easy to pinpoint in the pre-war period, the subordinate masculinity seems effectively to have been consumed by the Holocaust, and references to it are very few both during the years of the deconstruction and later in the ghettoization and hiding of the destruction. One noticeable reaction, however, is a limited intensification, or perhaps reinforcement, of discourses of 'self-hatred' in the earliest part of the deconstruction. For many Jews in the period before the war, 'self-hatred' had manifested itself in a distancing from their Judaism combined with an overt criticism of the 'Jewish character'. The effect of the deconstruction was to force these Jews into unavoidable contact with those they had previously disdained and it is in the attempt to negotiate the shift toward closer contact with traditional Judaism that we see some of the few references of the period to the Jewish body. Joseph Schupack writes of his brother being arrested, for reasons the family cannot decipher, '[h]e was tall, broad-shouldered, strong and abounded in good health ... My brother's physical appearance contradicted the Nazis' racial theory'. Significantly, this physical distinction was noteworthy to Schupack, and played a role in his understanding of his brother's arrest and detention.[95] More common, however, was the continuation of self-hatred which manifested itself in the internalization of antisemitic stereotypes of Jewish masculinity. Particularly notable in this way is the surprise described by numerous survivors in the Dereczin Memorial book upon meeting Dr Yekhezkiel Atlas. Those who wrote in the book were universally astonished to find that Atlas, a famous Jewish partisan leader known as a brave fighter, was, in fact, 'a short, scrawny young man, wearing a short officer's jacket, whose appearance was very much like that of a Jew: dark hair and dark eyes'.[96] Of course, these examples are too limited to allow a detailed discussion of their implications; nonetheless, it seems to be in representations of the body that the subordinate masculinity made itself clear during the deconstruction.

Individual elements of masculinities

Besides the attempts men make to orient themselves toward normative ideals of masculinity, there exist numerous more personal and individual elements of male gender identity, formed and shaped within the family and dependent on, amongst other things, relationships, physique and one's own interests and strengths. As a boy matures, his personal physical and intellectual attributes are added to existing preverbal experiences and the influences of parenting: a physically strong man will likely develop different ideas of masculinity from a weaker man. During the deconstruction, the ability of men to sustain these elements of their gender identities, whatever they might be, varied greatly depending on what exactly was significant to their personal masculinity. Broadly speaking, however, this was a period in which men were, predominantly, able to continue to perform the individual elements of their masculinity with comparatively few hindrances. I do not suggest that the deconstruction did not challenge these individual elements on a daily basis, forcing men to reconsider questions related to, amongst other things, their bodies, clothing, emotions and knowledge; yet in comparison to the almost impossible task of performing normative masculine identities, such individual elements, perhaps due to their flexibility, were well adapted and sustained during the deconstruction.

Of the body and its relationship to masculinity, Gerschick and Miller uncompromisingly write '[t]he body is a central foundation of how men define themselves and how they are defined by others'.[97] More particularly, it is generally agreed that, as Gilman writes, 'the Jew at the *fin de siècle* is the male Jew', an elision of gender and race which ensured that even seemingly ungendered antisemitism directed at the body was inherently an assault on the male Jew. For these reasons, but also because of its significance in enduring discussions of Jews and the Jewish man, the body ought to play a key role in our understanding of masculinity during the deconstruction. And yet, in order to write about the body during the deconstruction, the historian must necessarily write from an absence of sources. Perhaps surprisingly, very little is said about the male body during this period, either in diaries written during the Holocaust or by those who recorded their experiences later. Whilst we cannot say why the body seems to go largely unnoticed, its absence in this period does contrast sharply with the period of destruction that followed, in which Jewish men wrote more openly about their bodies. Two main contrasts are helpful in better understanding this shift in the approach to the body that Jewish men seem to have experienced between the deconstruction and later enclosure: representations of starvation and personal space. The deconstruction, for many men but with very definite exceptions, was not a period of extreme starvation, and although sources of food were scarce, many men were able to acquire enough to avoid going hungry.[98] Equally, the deconstruction was a period in which many people remained in their homes and in their own spaces, and did not see a significant encroachment on their personal space:[99] both manageable realities which seem to have limited the extent to which men felt the need to discuss their bodies. In stark contrast, the period of enclosure, which I shall go on to discuss in more detail, was both marked by a degree of starvation for virtually all families and the almost total loss of space which accompanied the move from private homes into the ghettos or hiding. In both cases it seems that it was these extremes of enclosure which forced men into closer contact with the realities of their male bodies and which provokes a discussion thereof, the loss of privacy particularly eliciting a number of comments, on the edges concerning sexuality, about bodies and their realities.

Clothing, and the individual's relationship with it, seems to have had a similar trajectory to that of the body in Holocaust writing. The period of deconstruction impacted upon most resources, and very definitely upon clothing, evidence for which can be found in the records of the Winterhilfe in Germany[100] as well as throughout Poland and the West, particularly for those Jews who were displaced or fled and lost many of their personal belongings. Nonetheless, the impact of this shortage seems rarely to have been severe enough to make it into people's memories or even indeed their diaries when writing about the deconstruction. Szpilman does note a particular decline in standards of appearance once war begins;[101] however, although he is not entirely alone, he is something of an exception in writing thus. Again, in contrast, once people had entered the ghettos or hiding, clothing and the problems it presented became a common subject of discussion. Although there is no certainty around why men during the deconstruction chose rarely to mention their bodies or attire, the contrast presented between this and the later period of enclosure, when both subjects were regularly referenced and clearly traumatic for the men involved, suggests that the absence of early references may simply reflect the relative unimportance of the subject. Men in the deconstruction were perhaps sufficiently content with, or at least unconcerned by, their bodies and their presentation to ensure that the subject remained a relatively insignificant and unrecorded element of daily life.

One might counter this argument concerning the relative stability of the body and attire as elements of masculine identity in the deconstruction, by arguing, following Mary Langerwey, that women tend to be more embodied than men,[102] and that men are, therefore, less likely to consider or reference their bodies regardless of their circumstances, an argument which Langerwey particularly uses to explain the different impact of sexual and physical assault upon men and women during the Holocaust. If this were indeed the case, then one might argue that the limited references men make to their bodies say little about their ability to sustain this particular element of masculine identity in the circumstances of deconstruction, and instead can help us only to understand more generally their limited relationships with their bodies. However, not only does a broader study of masculinity in the interwar period show a clear and overt connection between men and the body,[103] but, as discussed already, the stark contrast between the silence of the deconstruction and the multiple references and discussion found in the later period of destruction and ghettoization suggests instead that where it became a significant or problematic element of their lives men were very much aware of their bodies. We can conclude, therefore, that silence should be understood as evidence of, at least, a neutral relationship with the body and, thereby, argue that masculinity seen in terms of physicality was not severely challenged during the deconstruction.

When considering the emotional capacity of men to manage the experiences of the Holocaust, however, quite the opposite was true. During the deconstruction, numerous Jewish men seem to have been unable to manage their depression, succumbing to sustained periods of intense emotional collapse. Numerous sources speak of men falling into a depression, usually following loss of work and confinement to the home. Amongst many others, Fania Freich, a Pole living in France wrote, 'I am now here with my husband, and my husband is sick, ninety-nine percent sick, and this is the end of life. We have no courage. We have no morale.'[104] Similarly Kaplan repeatedly referenced not only his own depression, his broken heart when his radio was taken away and his inability to continue writing his diary due to sadness and depression,[105] but also that of his friends including A.W., who appeared, '[s]o broken and crushed. He had turned grey, his voice was hoarse and low, he was sloppily dressed – the inner beauty that had always illumined the face of this scholar was gone. He was a broken man'.[106] Likewise Yitzhak Katznelson was noted as being 'in the throes of utter depressions. His creative powers were numbered and had ceased to function'.[107] Roman Halter speaks about his father falling into a 'deep depression from which little could rouse him',[108] Friedländer describes his father as appearing to 'founder in a sort of wordless sadness'[109] and Pivnik writes, '[l]ooking into my father's face I could see that all the fight – all the life – had gone out of him'.[110]

Yet, whilst I do not dispute the veracity of these references to depression, nor their relevance to discussions of masculinity, it is important to note that in some cases these accounts are written by the wives and relatives of men experiencing this depression. Whilst this does not invalidate them – indeed it is perhaps unlikely that men would chose to document their own depression and collapse whatever its reality – it is interesting to consider conversely how men wrote about women and their emotional response to persecution.[111] In such cases we find that men very often recorded their wives as experiencing similar, although usually more transitory, emotional collapse. On 9 December 1939, soon after the Polish surrender to Germany, Adam Czerniaków, later to become head of the Warsaw *Judenrat*, noted in his diary, '[m]y wife does not cease crying',[112] whilst around the same time Chaim Kaplan commented that '[h]ysterical women gasp and wail and beat their breasts'.[113] In a similar vein Michael Diment comments that the 'quiet crying and sobbing of women was heard long into the night'[114] but makes no references to a similar, or any, collapse amongst men.

In the light of this parallel framing of the emotional state of the other sex, the historian must consider whether, in accounts of the Holocaust, the concept of depression is in itself a tool of gender negotiation. Seen in this light, each gender may be largely incapable of recording its own depression (although given the range of admissions recorded in the diaries and accounts of the Holocaust this seems perhaps too simple an answer) and, in describing the diminished coping capacity of the other, seeks to draw attention to its own gendered strength. Moreover, in many cases those who record their partner's collapse simultaneously assert their own strength and resilience, often either in caring for that partner or in assuming the burdens of their duties and caring for the family. Barbara Stimler is an exception to this when she records her mother's collapse as her husband (Barbara's father) is taken away. In a similar pattern, however, Barbara uses her mother's collapse to assert her own emotional strength writing, '[s]o I could see I am going to be breadwinner here. I went over to them and I begged them to give me a job there'.[115]

Nonetheless, even taking into account this process of mutual diminishment, there are certainly fewer references to depression and collapse amongst women, particularly as a sustained emotional response rather than a fleeting outcry,[116] than amongst men in this period, which suggests, whilst acknowledging the problematic nature of sources on this question, that we can begin to understand sustained depression in this period as gendered. If, then, men did indeed experience depression during the period of deconstruction, something which clearly has implications for male gender identities, a second question arises as to the impact this depression might have had upon the performance of masculine roles, most significantly the exercise of power and control within the home.

This discussion is where historians have had most to say on the question of Jewish masculinity in the Holocaust and where, perhaps, they have most seriously erred. Arguments have tended to suggest that many of those men who were depressed experienced collapse and emasculation, consequently opting out of making decisions in the home, supporting their families and, notably, seeking ways to escape the Holocaust. Significantly these arguments are used to reinforce the idea that as men abandoned their 'duties', their wives assumed them, supporting the conclusion that women rose to the challenges presented by the Holocaust. That this connection is made, notably using sources written by women, is perhaps unsurprising since, although men were not universally decision makers in the home before the Holocaust, the home was the place where a loss of power by men could most clearly be translated into increased or assumed power for women.[117] However, for a number of reasons, the universality with which this conclusion has been applied should be questioned. Whilst, of course, examples exist of men absolving themselves of all decision-making duties or responsibilities within the home and family, this was a relatively rare occurrence. Instead, sources suggest that far more common were men who, although extremely depressed, continued to function, attempting to provide and protect as discussed above, but also acting as head of the household, making significant decisions for their families and thereby sustaining a key element of their own gender identities.

One particularly illustrative example is the conclusion that women played a key role in exploring ways to emigrate and escape German occupation, whilst men tended not to be closely involved. Where families who had found a means to escape did not leave, this is also often blamed on the refusal of men to leave their communities and businesses and is linked to the inactivity of depression that accompanied disenfranchisement and exclusion. For the most part, both the realities of women more than men seeking opportunities to emigrate and the suggestion that decisions to stay were often taken by the men in the family have strong historical grounding – although this latter is certainly a vast generalization and as Donat writes of his flight east, his decision to return for his wife and child, and his wife's subsequent refusal to leave, '[s]he took me on a tour of our beautiful seven-room apartment and talked about how miserable life was in Russia',[118] so Elisabeth Harrison describes her father's early decision to leave Germany for the United Kingdom and her mother's refusal to go any further than Holland where they had friends, commenting, '[i]t was the only time he listened to my mother, and the worst mistake he ever made'.[119] However, the way in which these realities have been extrapolated to draw conclusions about masculine identity must be challenged. Numerous sources show that the decision not to emigrate was rarely a passive failure to act, which might reflect an emasculated identity, but instead was a clear and conscious decision that survival was more likely in the home, surrounded by one's resources, contacts and community, than as an anonymous refugee. That for many families this was a disastrous decision is not under question, but the nature of the decision that men made should be.[120]

Yitzhak Zuckerman's father, in making his decision that the family would stay in Krakow rather than attempt to flee Poland, is a perfect example of this active decision-making. Whilst it may ultimately have been the wrong decision, Zuckerman's account never described it as a default decision, even less a failure to decide. His father had seen numerous families attempt to flee and return materially diminished, often having lost their homes, goods or money in the process and with family members either dead or injured.[121] For him, therefore, survival seemed better served by deciding to remain. Such decisions were particularly reached by men who remembered the First World War and the damaging displacement of people which accompanied it.[122] Jafa Wallach describes her father's attempts, in exactly this way, to use his experiences in the First World War to predict events in the Second World War. This led him to put all his money into the family farm which, he believed, would not depreciate like money. The area in which they lived, however, was occupied by the Russians who collectivized their land and animals, leaving them destitute and her father heartbroken. Equally, Sem Hartz's family discussed leaving Holland but decided to stay, based on their positive experiences in the country during the First World War.[123] In neither case could these decisions be understood as a lack of action, but rather only as incorrect action, catastrophic as they later proved to be.

It is important, therefore, to understand these choices concerning emigration as an exercise of the individual's masculinity through decision-making and familial control, rather than as an example of its absence and therefore of the feminization and collapse of which they are accused. Of course, men rarely made these decisions entirely alone and often such choices were made in larger family units – with more junior members deferring to elders and parents – or within couples, with numerous sources speaking of marital fights concerning the decisions around whether or not to emigrate.[124] Ultimately, whilst each family managed this decision in its own way, in very few cases are men documented as making decisions to stay which might be seen as representing a failure to act or could be understood as a product of the emasculation of the individual.

Even leaving aside the particular decision as to whether or not to flee, decision-making within the home, and the reinforcement of masculine identities it implies, can be found in numerous other instances amongst men who would otherwise be considered as depressed. Roman Halter's father is described on several occasions during the deconstruction as being in a deep depression, and yet it is not a contradiction for his son also to detail his father's attempts to draw resources from the Aryanization of the family business, to hide possessions for later use or sale and to remain a strong and commanding patriarch.[125] Similarly, Pivnik notes, 'Father, a broken man though he was becoming, still had the energy to smuggle scraps of cloth out of Rossner's uniform factory and he'd sit at home at Number 77, cross-legged on the floor with his needle and thread, making clothes for gentiles in exchange for flour or sausage',[126] whilst Katznelson, who became severely depressed and stopped writing or associating in any way during the deconstruction, retained an entirely different position with regard to his family, his biographer noting, '[h]e was a devoted husband and father, and in the bosom of his family he radiated warmth and glow … He loved them all dearly and in their midst he was intensely happy, in spite of the cold and hunger'.[127] Whilst this latter is not an assertion of power, it is a clear example of the ability to distinguish between one's role within the family and one's response to more global problems and to sustain a strong patriarchal position despite compromising depression.

One final way in which Jewish men were able to sustain personal elements of their male gender identities during the Holocaust was through exercising their intellect. For those men who practised their masculinity as much through their intelligence as their bodies, the deconstruction offered relative stability. Of course these men still had to endure the abolition of the numerous clubs and associations within which they were used to asserting their intellects and, perhaps more damagingly, were also extremely vulnerable to loss of work, with all its contingent implications for gender identity: as Edmund Kessler notes, Jewish white-collar work decreased much faster than blue-collar work and those who 'worked with their minds using pen and paper' were now required to 'wield shovels and picks'.[128] However, in spite of these limitations, ongoing gendered performance through the intellect can be seen first and foremost in the number of men who record others asking for their advice as their circumstances changed during the deconstruction. Understanding events as they progressed through the war and counselling family or community accordingly, as Elie Wiesel so proudly reports his father doing, were central elements of masculine identity for many Jewish men in this period.[129]

Moreover, as relevant to religious or culturally Jewish men as to assimilated men, sources suggest that the deconstruction was a period in which intellectuals were defended and supported by their communities, further allowing them to sustain this element of their gender identities. As long as these men remained in their homes, the capacity to wield pen and paper was not completely removed from them and access to work and books was an important element of sustaining morale. And although outside of the scope of this book, the diaries of both Mihail Sebastian in Bucharest and Victor Klemperer in Dresden are particularly clear on this subject, detailing the available options, particularly in the early period of persecution, for intellectuals in continuing to function as such.[130]

Any discussion of gender identity should, however, include a consideration of the impact of age upon masculinity. Both due to a lack of sources for certain age groups and a close correlation between age and circumstance, however, conclusions on the subject remain problematic. For a raft of reasons, as already discussed, including family loyalties and physical strength, survivors of the Holocaust and therefore also the available sources come predominantly from men who were in their late teens or early twenties during the Holocaust. Where older men survived it was often because they had fled early on in the Holocaust, and in many cases did not, therefore, actively experience much of the Holocaust or even the deconstruction. Moreover, where sources from older men *do* exist, their circumstances are often so different from those of younger men that it is difficult to compare their experiences. Whilst young men had family ties, they very often had limited responsibilities. Older men, in contrast, were often struggling to provide for and support children and wives, a level of responsibility which significantly altered the way in which they acted. And yet, perhaps surprisingly, where they can be charted, behaviours impacting on masculine identity vary less between the age groups than one might imagine.

In the initial phases of persecution, younger men were more able to flee than older men, since leaving behind parents was a very different decision to abandoning children. Yet, within a relatively short period many of the younger men had chosen to return to their families, effectively placing themselves in similar a position to the older men. Added to this, sources show this period to be predominantly one of inaction, and for obvious reasons age divides inactivity less than it does action. In contrast, as the next chapter discusses, when activity and reconstruction became possible, through employment, social involvement and even resistance activities, men of different ages did respond differently. In particular, where homosocial interaction and hierarchy reasserted itself, we see significant references to age and masculinity. During the deconstruction, however, where homosocial activity was suppressed and passivity was the dominant position, the deconstruction of masculine gender identity and the internalizing of activity within the family and the self seem to have similarly affected and been performed by men of all ages, even if their initial reactions to invasion varied.

* * *

Philip Friedman, the historian and survivor, distinguishes between responses to the Holocaust in Western and Central Europe, where slow change allowed for the gentle adaptation of society and sustained social codes, and in Eastern Europe, where faster change, due to Soviet control in 1939, and 'radical equalization' occurred, writing, '[i]n the east the German abuses and atrocities followed one upon another so rapidly that no new social order could be established. It was not only a radical but a continual revolution, which maintained a constant state of flux in the society'.[131] Yet, whilst this is an interesting comparison with an acute use of language, in fact, conversely, although the speed of change in Western and Central Europe may have allowed for social adaptation, the evidence regarding gender identity suggests something quite different. Masculinities in Western and Central Europe exactly experienced a state of continual revolution in the months and years following German invasion. Moreover, it was this state of constant flux regarding those elements of life which impacted on gender identities and made it impossible for masculinities to stabilize and reform themselves after the initial damage of occupation, economic exclusion and loss of status.

Another way to understand this is through Gerschick and Miller's argument that men who become physically disabled, for whatever reason, respond, after an initial period of depression linked to an inability to perform their gender identities, with a reassertion of their masculinity. This process, according to Gerschick and Miller, occurs in one of three different ways: reformulation, reliance or rejection.[132] The first response involves the 'redefinition of hegemonic characteristics on their own [the disabled person's] terms' – a response which often relies heavily upon having the financial means to alter one's lifestyle to suit one's new situation. 'Reliance' requires less adjustment and is instead based on stressing, even more firmly, certain elements of the hegemonic masculinity of one's society and through asserting one's own ability to conform to those ideals in spite of physical limitations. Finally, 'rejection', which often comes after some time and once other options have been exhausted, involves the renunciation of hegemonic standards and 'either the creation of one's own principles and practices or the denial of masculinity's importance in one's life'.[133] Above all, however, what all three of these reformulations require is the space and stability to assess one's own abilities and capacities and to develop a theory of masculinity which plays to those strengths whilst minimizing one's limitations. In much the same way, Jewish men in the deconstruction very often experienced a loss of the capacity to perform the normative masculine identities toward which they had previously oriented themselves. Significantly, however, the process of the deconstruction, as a constant and incremental erosion, removed exactly the space and stability which Gerschick and Millar show to be so important for the reconstruction or reassertion of normative gender identities, and neatly explains one reason why the deconstruction was a particularly damaging period and process for the masculine identities of Jewish men.

Whilst men encountered unassailable problems in attempting to conform to the normative identities with which they associated, many individual elements of masculinity were, in contrast, relatively resilient. Ranging from one's relationship with the body to questions of decision-making in the home and the community, men seem, during the deconstruction, to have been able to continue engaging with these individual elements of their gender identities. Nevertheless, in Gerschick and Miller's argument that to ignore normative notions of gender is to 'court gender annihilation',[134] we can see clearly why the ability of Jews to access many of the individual elements of gender identities was not enough to defend them from the incredibly damaging impact of the 'constant revolution', experienced during the deconstruction, on their ability to perform their normative identities and ultimately led to their inability to successfully practise their masculinities. This is particularly the case when we add to this deconstruction of normative roles the enormous impact of the broader gendering of society which saw Jewish men being pushed toward behaviour patterns they themselves understood to be inherently passive, and therefore feminine.

Masculinity Reasserted: Enclosure and Stability

The period of enclosure which followed the deconstruction offered a complete contrast to that which had preceded, both as a process and in its impact on masculine identities.[1] The period is identifiable as one in which many European Jews either went into hiding in fear of deportation or murder or were forced into ghettos as part of a broader strategy enacted by the German occupation. Whilst for most people this enclosure presented a daily struggle simply to survive, it also represented the point at which 'normal' lives in one's home and community ceased and, with that, the inexorable decline and deconstruction of those lives also ceased, and instead entered a new phase which whilst unbearable was, as will be shown, often more stable than that which had come before.

Historical discussions of Jewish male gender identities are even less common in works concerning the period of enclosure than in those concerning the preceding deconstruction. And yet, often without any chronological distinction, historians of the Holocaust have applied their understanding of the impact of the deconstruction on gender identities to the enclosure that followed: thus representing Jewish men throughout the Holocaust as weak and emasculated. Much of the existing scholarship highlights sources which describe men as being confined to the home, restricted in their movement and depressed, and yet, whilst these conditions and responses were indeed daily occurrences during the deconstruction, they were far from common in the period of enclosure which followed.[2] The impact of this conflation of the two periods has been to promote the collapse of masculinity into a universal Holocaust experience, instead of seeing it as an experience which remained largely confined to the deconstruction. One of the clearest examples of this tendency is found in *Hitler's Ghettos*, where Gustav Corni effectively argues that the weak character of many men resulted in their too speedy consumption of rations and, ultimately, their deaths, writing, 'sources demonstrate that women were generally more disciplined than men in this terrible task of self-control and this very probably accounts for their lower mortality rate.'[3] Corni's reference for this conclusion is Michal Unger's article

'The Status and Plight of Women in the Lodz Ghetto' which itself comments, in relation to men's higher mortality rates in the ghettos, '[b]y inference, women were better able than men to tolerate the ghetto conditions'.[4] Leaving aside the fact that Unger's comment is unreferenced, making the basis for both comments unclear, such conclusions should still be rejected since, whilst men in the ghettos certainly did have a higher mortality rate than women, Unger seemingly ignores a range of relevant facts, including that women can survive on fewer calories than men, that the chief cause of death in the ghettos, heart disease, commonly kills more men than women,[5] and that men in the ghettos often undertook more physically demanding work than women.

An approach which sees men as being weakened and demoralized by ghettoization should, however, also be challenged on a substantive level, since many Jewish men were, in fact, able to use the experience of enclosure, particularly ghettoization, to revitalize their gender identities. As this chapter will go on to detail, in a reversal of the impact of the deconstruction on masculinities, the combination of a masculine environment in the ghettos, which encouraged and enabled action, and the conditions of enclosure, which allowed many Jewish men to once again perform, within clear limits, the key elements of their normative gender identities seems to have allowed many men to begin to reassert strong masculine identities. And whilst my analysis of this period particularly focused on the ghettos in German-occupied Poland, due to the sheer number of Jewish men who experienced them and because of the clarity they offer in comparison with the more complex, less common, Western alternatives of hiding or resistance work, it can also be applied more broadly. Ultimately, I shall suggest that the ghettos, and to a lesser extent alternative situations of enclosure like hiding, offered Jewish men the possibility of reasserting strong masculine identities where stability, principally of living conditions and expectations, existed – a stability which contrasts starkly with the persistent change that had marked the deconstruction.[6]

Any approach which represents the ghettos as even relatively stable, empowering and masculine, however, requires an explanation of how these extreme conditions could ever provoke such a description. Indeed Isaiah Trunk refers to the Łódź ghetto as 'something like a camp with a milder administration';[7] Leni Yahil observes that '[t]he ghetto's function was essentially no different from that of the labour camp: both were designed to exploit the Jews and to destroy them "naturally"'[8] and numerous survivors stress the impossibility of conducting a 'normal' life inside the ghetto when one's entire being was focused simply on survival.[9] Yet, whilst acknowledging absolutely the backbreaking hardship and horrors that the Jewish people experienced in the ghettos, an approach which seeks to ignore or overlook life beyond mere survival provokes two challenges: not only does extensive academic work stress both the existence and importance of ongoing cultural and social lives maintained in the ghettos, but sources also indicate an active reassertion of masculinities in the period, underpinned by a perception of limited autonomy and a sense of living within a Jewish micro-society.[10] Arguably, for many Jews the ghetto provided a false, but nonetheless powerful and beguiling, sense of political autonomy, social freedom and Jewish independence which gave its inhabitants the illusion of a security they had not found before its walls were erected.[11] The calm with which Donat anticipated the establishment of the ghetto, commenting that 'people actually began to hope that the rumors about establishing a ghetto which would seal off the Jews from the rest of Warsaw were true,'[12] or Kruk's note in his diary that, for many, entering the ghetto created a sense of 'relief that people will finally be with their own and not exposed to all sorts of provocations'[13] can only be understood in the context of this reading of the ghettos – a fatal misreading but nevertheless one which created the possibility of the reassertion of masculinities.

A sense of increased security within a Jewish society can be found in numerous voices from the ghettos, amongst them Vladka Meed, a Polish Jew, born and raised in Warsaw who worked on both sides of the ghetto wall to support the uprising, wrote,

> [t]he stilled ghetto streets were dear to me; they were closer to me than the liveliness and cheerfulness of the streets on the Aryan side. Within the ghetto was my own bitter reality, my own world where I no longer had to maintain my forced smile before my Polish neighbors. Here my ears were no longer assailed by their acrimonious remarks about the Jews deserving all that was coming to them and about Hitler's purging Poland of the Jewish plague; here there was not the constant fear of being unmasked as a Jewess – here I was among my own.[14]

Similarly Stanislaw Adler, who worked for the Jewish police inside the Warsaw ghetto, writes, significantly in a chapter entitled 'The Period of Normalization in the Quarter',

> [t]herefore, when the Jews found themselves behind the walls of the ghetto, though under unbearably harsh conditions of existence, they felt relieved of fear for their lives. Until then, they could be slain with impunity by any indiscriminate soldier or even by a civilian, since in practice, and sometimes also in theory, they were deprived of the benefits and protections of the law. Therefore, the walls of the shut-in Jewish Quarter provided the only protection possible in those days. Besides, the lone soldier desiring to go on a rampage

through the ghetto for plunder or any other purpose undoubtedly would fear the reaction of a mob brought to desperation, and would therefore have to temper his ardour somehow. Jews felt more peace of mind and hope of survival.[15]

Beyond the sense of comfort of unity in a Jewish society which the ghettos seemed to offer, it is even possible to understand the ghettos, more controversially, as having created a sense of limited autonomy which was of particular significance for the reassertion of masculinities. It is beyond question that the Jews in the ghettos were completely powerless; moreover, it is clear that where the *Judenräte* did exercise some limited powers, it was power entirely conferred, and which might be immediately revoked, by the German authorities. Nonetheless, either the ghetto population was not privy to this truth about their situation or they chose to ignore it. For, as Daniel Feierstein argues, many saw the ghettos as a way of achieving Jewish autonomy,[16] which is perhaps not that surprising if we consider that many ghettos included a system of government with its own police, court, rabbinical authority, post offices and currencies amongst other things. As Marek Web notes, 'Indeed, on the surface it looked as if the ghetto had total autonomy over its own affairs.'[17]

This analysis of ghetto life, whilst controversial, is supported by myriad contemporary sources, from Zuckerman who noted that 'the autonomy of the ghetto wasn't only a delusion. It was, of course, "an autonomy of corpses", but there was some development in our enterprise,'[18] to Kaplan who commented that 'Polish Jewry has become a self-contained organism'[19] and Perechodnik, who repeatedly wrote of the Jews governing themselves, the limited influence of Germans and the protection that the ghetto provided from marauding Poles.[20] Ultimately the power that the ghetto authorities exerted over their populations and the attempts they made to appear to have influence with the Germans all contributed to a false, but widely held, belief that the ghetto was, at least in part, governed by Jews.

But what of the argument made by some survivors that the unbearably hard life that most lived in the ghettos precluded them from also living a 'normal' existence with everyday concerns such as gender identity? Importantly in this regard it is worth noting that masculinities, and gender identities more generally, do not necessarily require a conscious thought process – when Roman Halter says he was too hungry to think about gender, it is not a contradiction to say he might still have been practising a strong masculine identity. Also relevant, however, are contemporary sources which, whilst stressing the horrors of existence in the ghettos, also clearly note the ongoing nature of daily life – *Oneg Shabbat* recorded that 'street emotions' in the ghettos included '[o]ptimism and pessimism. Joy and sadness. Hopes and resignation. Illusion and apathy ... Cowardice and courage.' In line with this argument Eric Sterling describes the ghetto as 'a transitional life ... where many Jews maintained their hope, their faith, and their culture while enduring harsh and atrocious conditions' and when Janine David records the struggles of her parents' marriage, her father staying out late gambling and drinking, and her mother's seduction by a more attentive male friend, she need not necessarily be writing from the ghetto at all. Almost irrespective of the circumstances, gender identities form a part of the lives men live, even if not consciously, and the ghettos of the Holocaust, their horrendous conditions notwithstanding, are no exception to this and should not be easily dismissed.

Amongst Jews in the West, any suggestion of a sense of community or autonomy is more complex, however. A sense of unity, both as a community and a unity and purpose, can be seen amongst the members of the Eclaireurs israélite de France (EIF), the French Jewish scouting movement formed in 1923 which became a focus for Zionism and clandestine activities for young Jewish men and women during the Holocaust.[21] Equally, other examples of Jewish communities in the West seem to provoke a similar sense of unity, for example, Hermann Bodner speaks very warmly of being involved in a Belgian underground organization with a number of other Jews and the impact of being trained by a Jew from Germany.[22] These are, for the most part, however, no more than exceptions. Most Jewish men in the West involved with underground groups joined organizations whose membership was overwhelmingly gentile. In some cases, the group knew that the individual was Jewish but in many others this knowledge was entirely hidden. Whilst this made it virtually impossible for these men to have a sense of Jewish community like that found in many of the Polish ghettos and the EIF, they nevertheless often found a unity of purpose within these organizations. The fact that many men emphasize membership of such an organization with great pride, even when, if pressed, they admit that they played a rather silent role, shows the importance simply of belonging to a community and the empowerment it offered.[23]

For some Jewish men in hiding in the West, enclosure offered this same sense of unity and empowerment, again not directly linked to their identity as Jews, through living in the community of their family. This is particularly the case for Otto Frank who, following a period of extreme emotional and personal turmoil during the deconstruction,[24] described his period in hiding thus:

> I have to say that in a certain way it was a happy time. I think of all the good that we experienced, whilst all discomfort, longing, conflicts and fears disappear.

How fine it was to live in such close contact with the ones I loved, to speak to my wife about the children and about future plans, to help the girls with their studies, to read classics with them and to speak about all kinds of problems and all views about life.[25]

Finally, Dan Kampelmacher, an Austrian by birth but living in Holland during the war, who belonged to a Zionist group which placed young Jewish men on remote farms during the war, noted, '[s]ometimes I had the feeling of being on an island that provided some security, and which I shouldn't leave for the time being'.[26]

Again, for the most part, however, it is impossible to suggest that hiding spaces provided the level of stability required to even begin to reassert one's masculinity for, as Meed noted, '[o]ften a *melina* turned the hiding Jew into a bundle of nerves and fears, less a person than a hunted animal'.[27] For those in the West who could find neither the stability of a relatively secure hiding place nor a resistance group, the deconstruction effectively extended either until their capture or until the end of the war. One clear example of this was the father of Marcel Liebman who spent the war in Belgium. Whilst he was able to find a hiding place for Marcel and his brother, thereby allowing them some stability, he himself remained for the duration of the war in a limbo between legal existence and hiding, a constantly shifting position which at no time allowed for any stability or reassertion of masculinity.[28] Nevertheless where some stability was possible, the sense of unity and the contingent boost to gender identities are clear – making the case again for the importance of such unity when it could be found.

Based upon a sense of autonomy and a life within a Jewish society, the collected testimonies of Jews in the ghettos, in hiding or involved in organized resistance in the West show a greater sense of control over one's own life than during the deconstruction. That this sense of autonomy was a perception rather than a reality is indisputable; nonetheless it impacted heavily on the way in which lives were lived, ultimately providing a strong basis for the reassertion of masculinities for which this chapter argues.

Environment

The previous chapter argued that the deconstruction encouraged a series of behaviours that would have been understood as feminine, behaviours which forced Jewish men into passivity and, in doing so, made the practice of traditional active masculinity almost impossible. Relying on the same understanding of gendered environments, the period of enclosure, in contrast, can in many cases be seen as foregrounding behaviours which would have been understood as overtly masculine in nature; the societies and authorities within the ghettos of occupied Poland encouraged men to act wherever possible, and in doing so enabled them to perform in ways that they would have considered masculine, thus providing the potential to practise strong gender identities. This environment of action is very clearly alluded to by Adler who, in writing of the 'Homeric battles' that men fought to gain a place in the Order Service (the Jewish Police, henceforth OS), notes, 'for most men in the prime of life, there was a need for some kind of occupation, some kind of discipline, after more than a year of compulsory and oppressive idleness'.[29] Not all men were ultimately able to access the elements of masculinism which this environment made possible, and yet the gendered environment itself was universal within many, if not most, of the ghettos – action was encouraged even if not every man had the capacity to act.

This positive approach to action with its connotations of masculinity can be found throughout the sources from the ghettos, particularly amongst those who fought the Germans. Simcha Rotem writes of a fellow resister and friend killed in a bunker during the Warsaw ghetto uprising, '[a]s he lay wounded, he insulted and cursed the Germans and challenged them to approach him. They didn't dare and came close only after pumping a full magazine of ammunition into his body, which they then mutilated'[30] whilst another resistance fighter writing after the Warsaw ghetto uprising says,

> [t]his rising didn't result from any political reckoning, any calculation of purpose and powers, whether right or wrong; it wasn't based on any estimation whatever, no matter how preposterous, even if seemingly logical. It wasn't self-defence, either; nor was it – according to some opinions – a simple impulse of despair. The rising was an heroic gesture of those who have squared their accounts with the degenerated world and didn't count on anybody nor anything. The nation on which an unprecedented slaughter had been performed, bade the ages a fiery dying farewell – through this nation's best sons.[31]

This representation of action for its own sake as inherently masculine is carried through the sources and seen equally in Draegerova who comments, 'our end is not a decline, but rather it is a death knowingly chosen by strong men'[32] and *Oneg Shabbat* which records the response of S.Z. Stupnicki to a questionnaire distributed in the ghetto, 'Jews don't feel like passive victims but rather as active fighters. The dead fallen in this gigantic battle for freedom are war heroes, active combatants. The Jewish folk-masses are saturated with this consciousness which strengthens their persistence, their readiness to give battle and to endure until the final victory.[33]

Of course action, where it risked the lives of others in the ghetto, was not uncontentious. Both armed resisters and smugglers received their share of opprobrium from the community, and yet both were also clearly lauded for their efforts. Diment records the murder of a man caught smuggling grain into the Lukacze ghetto, but rather than condemning him concludes that his actions did not put people off smuggling; on the contrary they became more daring, more keen not to die of hunger but to die fighting to survive.[34] Similarly Ringelblum writes about the Resistance in the ghetto fighting the German army. He knows their struggle is futile and yet he sees their actions as heroic nonetheless. In a passage entitled '"Little Stalingrad" Defends Itself' he lauds the actions of the resisters describing, 'desperate young men, armed with poor quality revolvers, who knew that extermination awaited them'.[35] Exactly what was understood as action in these circumstances was broad and ranged from perhaps heroic acts of self-sacrifice to more quotidian acts of finding work, both for themselves and for their family, or using connections to find accommodation within the ghettos. Moreover all of these elements of 'action' were available to both men and women in the ghettos, of course, although perhaps not in equal measure. Nonetheless the same sense of action, and even the same act, had different implications for male and female gender identities and could therefore, for men, have the effect of creating an environment gendered masculine, in which action was rewarded and respected.[36]

Beyond this, the existence of an environment which was gendered male within the ghettos can also be seen in the gendered discourses which pepper the writings of ghetto inhabitants and which were conspicuous for their absence during the deconstruction. Diaries and accounts from the ghettos are filled with descriptions that belittle, undermine and make comparisons between the masculinity of the writer and other men, all of which are key elements of active masculine identities and part of the traditional language of gender. [37] One of the clearest examples of these comparisons of masculinity is found in the description Ionas Turkov provides of the two leaders of the OS in the Warsaw ghetto: of Shmerling he notes, 'la carrure athlétique, grand, fort, un cou de taureau' whilst of Tshaplinski he comments, '[i]l passait pour l'officier le plus beau et le plus elegant de la police juive'.[38] The positivity of Turkov's comments, however, is relatively uncommon, and writings from the ghettos more usually describe the masculinity of others unfavourably – perhaps an act which helped in many cases to bolster one's own gender identity – examples of which range from attacks on the individual, 'that small ridiculous roly-poly manikin with his round belly, his cut-off caftan, his tiny yarmulke and fattened cheeks'[39] or Adler's description of Lejkin, an applicant for the OS, as a 'caricature-like figure … in his *rejtuzy* (jodhpurs), and his canary-yellow cardigan, the future "Napoleon of the Order Service"',[40] to entire groups – either those with power like the Jewish police 'these little young men, dressed up in high shiny boots and uniform caps'[41] or those explicitly without power, notably German-Jewish refugees.[42]

Not overtly derogatory, but clearly a commentary of sorts on masculinity, is the story of David Feinberg, who attempted to break out of the Łachwa ghetto in 1942 – at the last minute he was set upon by the town rabbi (someone who might be considered the most feminized of men) and a group of women who forced him to turn back for fear of reprisals. Ultimately the Jews of the Łachwa ghetto were killed and Feinberg was powerless to stop it.[43] The association of Feinberg's final decision to stay with a rabbi and women is a subtle denigration of his masculinity and again makes it clear that gendered analysis of events continued to hold significance in the ghettos. In representing Feinberg's actions as unmasculine, his detractors show that there was still, at this time, scope for being seen as masculine.[44] Similarly, in September 1942 writing in the Warsaw ghetto, Abraham Lewin noted, 'I saw with my own eyes how a young, strong man and a young, attractive woman were shot.'[45] Even at that advanced stage of the Holocaust, Lewin's description of the young man as 'strong' and the young woman as 'attractive' show a sustained gender discourse within the ghetto using the same language of gender as found before the war. Finally, the *Chronicle of the Łódź Ghetto* refers to the 'last and final privilege' – to take a 'bag and a stick' with you when deported.[46] Although some women did also use sticks, they were, nevertheless, a significant piece of a man's gendered paraphernalia and, as such, both the fact that this right was retained until relatively late and that its removal is referenced in the *Chronicle* show its ongoing importance in ghetto life and, therefore, the ongoing insistence of questions of masculinity and gender identity.

Finally, the male-gendered environment in the ghettos was reinforced by the strong patriarchalism inherent in its organizational structure. The ghettos of Eastern Europe were managed almost exclusively by Jewish men. However, more than this, many of them were men who had played important roles in pre-war Jewish society.[47] As such they were men who respected, and belonged to, traditional patriarchal hierarchies, and it was these hierarchies that they replicated in the ghettos.[48] Furthermore, the structure of the ghettos was established by the Germans, who also functioned through a strongly patriarchal organizational system and whose influence penetrated the entire ghetto leadership, perhaps seen most clearly in Adler's reference to the *Führerprinzip* in the Warsaw ghetto. Adler's point is that the ghetto employed an extremely complex and well-developed bureaucracy which mimicked that of the Germans; his comments, however, can be extended to include the nature of the hierarchy employed.[49] The hierarchy promoted by the ghetto leadership also created new levels of status, which in turn reinforced a gendered atmosphere in the ghetto. Most notable in this regard is the infighting seen amongst the members of the *Judenrat*, and even on occasion amongst their wives.[50] With reference to these struggles for status and position Corni stresses that '[f]rom what is known about the subject, this was not a conflict based on profound ideological differences, but was purely a question of power'.[51] In this case, as in others, the struggle for power itself seems to be a struggle for, and display of, masculinity, even if in some cases women were involved, and contrasts starkly with a lack of such competition in sources from the deconstruction, since a lack of institutions and organizations of power made struggles within any such institution impossible and is proof of the very different gendered environments in the two periods.

For a few Jewish men in the West, the conditions of this period created a similarly male-gendered environment. Particularly this can be seen in the case of the EIF, sources from which time and again emphasize the action of those involved and their attempts to improve themselves, both by assisting others (for example, helping young children to cross into Switzerland and avoid deportation) and by spreading Zionism and religious Jewish practice amongst their group. Just as in the ghettos, this valuing of action over passivity created an environment which seemed to be gendered masculine. This was most obviously seen in the practice of *La Route* – a process of mentoring and self-development which allowed a young man to 'prendre sa position d'homme'.[52] Despite the limitations presented by the persecution of Jews and the clandestine activities in which they were also involved, sources suggest that this practice continued throughout the war with young men taking the time to develop their masculine identity in this overt way, something which clearly indicates a strongly male-gendered environment. Moreover, for the young men in the EIF, power struggles, like those in the ghettos, existed and attest to the ongoing discourse of masculinity that encouraged such battles.[53]

Involvement in gentile underground organizations similarly provided a male environment which encouraged, and even required, action from many young Jewish men in the West during this period, offering a stark contrast to their experiences during the deconstruction. The underground organizations of the West, as was also the case in many, if not most, similar Polish organizations, whilst involving women – performing select, dangerous and extremely important roles – largely comprised men, and were established with the primary aim of acting, whether just in a defensive manner or whether proactively attempting to sabotage German efforts. This sense of action, very different from the sense of passivity during the deconstruction, can be most clearly seen in Samuel Schryver's comments when helping his mother and sister to escape from Westerbork, '[w]hen you are in the resistance you do things differently'. Later when he protects his mother from deportation by finding her a hospital bed, an almost impossible thing to achieve, he simply but proudly comments, 'I got it done.'[54] Nonetheless, for most Jews in Western Europe, particularly those in hiding, this kind of gendered environment encouraging action was not available in the way it was for many of those in the ghettos.

Normative masculinities

Where the deconstruction had little by little rendered Jewish men virtually incapable of performing the normative identities toward which they had previously oriented themselves, life in the ghettos, in spite of its horrendous hardships, offered the possibility of, or perhaps imposed, a lifestyle where those norms could again become a reality. Building upon an environment which encouraged action, opportunities to provide and protect, as well as gain status, were all, to varying degrees, available and practised by Jewish men in the ghettos and were key to the reassertion of tentative and intermittently strong masculine identities. Whilst for a considerable number of men, who entered a ghetto starving and penniless without any influence or connections and died almost immediately, establishing any stability whatsoever in their lives was impossible, those who did achieve even limited stability were offered the possibility of reasserting their masculinity through the renewed performance of normative gender identities.

The ghettos of German-occupied Poland encouraged men to seek work, industry and opportunity in ways that had not been open to them since the German invasion and allowed them, within clear limits, to attempt to provide for and protect their families. Certainly there was no possibility of re-establishing careers, or finding work that suited an individual's skills and interests or could be compared to pre-war employment; nonetheless high levels of employment in the larger ghettos combined with a belief in a productionist agenda[55] and employment-linked rations meant that the notion of provision became an option for many men once the ghettos were established and for some time after. By July 1940, 40,000 of the 146,000 Jews in Łódź ghetto were employed in *ressorts* (workshops) and offices and by March 1942 production workers alone numbered 53,000.[56] Eliasz Tabaksblat, writing in the *Chronicle of Łódź Ghetto*, goes as far as to suggest that in 1942–43, 95 per cent of the ghetto was employed. This number is likely an exaggeration; nevertheless it denotes a trajectory of employment very different from that seen before the establishment of the ghettos. In Warsaw, employment figures were lower, perhaps 30 per cent of the ghetto population was in work; however, this is still estimated to represent the involvement in the working process of all men aged 15–60 who were fit for work.[57]

Most immediately, the work that these statistics represent provided food: lunch during the day,[58] and limited money with which to buy more food when it was available, thereby avoiding starvation. The benefits of such work for entire families were, however, far more wide ranging. From their establishment, and in line with interwar approaches to economics, the ghetto authorities considered family as dependents of the worker. Gainful employment for the individual, therefore, had ramifications for their entire family. One example of how this theory was applied can be seen in Łódź ghetto where the OS petitioned the *Judenrat* for improved conditions, with extra food and fuel. Whilst their request was denied, the OS mess was extended to provide food for the men's families,[59] a move which established the policemen themselves as de facto providers for their families. For most this provision was aimed at immediate family with whom they lodged in the ghetto, however in some cases it could also extend to men providing for family in hiding or in other ghettos, as in the case of Perechodnik who regularly sent money to provide for his mother who lived in another town.[60]

Beyond the provision of food and shelter, men's roles as workers in many ghettos, perhaps more decisively, offered protection, both for themselves and for their families. One means of protection came in the form of the 'work card' which, in various ghettos, at different times, was the basis upon which one's legal existence, and therefore the right to ration cards, limited supplies, accommodation and the 'right' not to be deported, rested.[61] Whilst it was certainly not the case that those with work cards were never deported, on several occasions where it was found that someone listed for deportation did possess a work card, their status as a worker was enough to save them, at least in the short term. This was affirmed in Łódź in June 1942 when several men with work cards were listed for deportation, but were not ultimately deported because of their status as workers. The *Ghetto Chronicle* noted that '[t]his incident ought to be regarded as extremely important and significant', [62] reinforcing the link between work and protection established by Mordechai Rumkowski, the controversial head of the Łódź ghetto *Judenrat*, and confirmed in his speech of 17 January 1942 in which he stated 'only work can secure one's existence'.[63] Beyond saving himself, there were also occasions where a man could use his work card to secure the safety of his immediate family or even extended family or family friends.

Some types of employment offered men further opportunities to protect their families, and members of the OS were in a particularly strong position not only to protect but also to use their position to provide their families with employment and preferable accommodation. Perechodnik, as a Jewish policeman, records a round-up in the Otwock ghetto in which, although initially threatened with deportation, the families of policemen were ultimately offered protection. In light of this, Perechodnik criticizes the behaviour of a police colleague who had given up his armband and had in order to be deported with his wife suggesting that he had shown 'contempt' for his uniform.[64] Not in fact a member of the OS, Michael Zylberberg pretended to be a policeman in order to save himself and later the wife and child of a friend, an act which shows the power held by the OS.[65] Zylberberg records that he did not tell his own wife about this event, or several others it later transpires, as it would seem instead that he was attempting to protect her, assuming the danger both of the act and of knowledge of the act, burdening himself alone with the responsibility in a traditionally masculine way.[66]

Clear in the administration of some ghettos, but in the discourses of individuals in many more, and perhaps of most importance in understanding the role played by work in the reassertion of masculine identities, was the productionist agenda. Whilst the administration of ghettos had quite varied approaches to the question of production, and whilst the belief that exploiting the labour potential of a ghetto would secure its ongoing existence was not universal, the hope that the safety of Jewry could be best secured by making a ghetto productive was uppermost in the minds of many Jews. Particularly early on in the life of the ghettos, when mass extermination was barely conceivable for the Jews, the most logical explanation for their existence was as de facto labour camps. It followed, therefore, that a productive ghetto would not be liquidated and, equally, that a productive Jew would not be liquidated. On an individual level this approach is manifest in the observation that '[t]here are Jews who wear ribbons on their arms that read: "Jews useful for the economy"'[67] and in Joseph Hurwitz's diary which records, '[w]e need employment to save our families from starving to death and from annihilation'.[68] The importance of productionism to the collective is summarized by Yisrael Gutman when he writes,

> [b]oth in the maintenance of industry, and in our work in individual units, we must prove that contrary to the accepted assumption that we are not fit for any kind of work, we have been very useful, and under present wartime conditions, there is no viable substitute for us. Work in general, and work for the Wehrmacht in particular, are the order of the day.[69]

Whilst Kessler also notes that 'the Jewish masses rapidly became proletarians in their efforts to keep the Jewish community alive. The slogan of making the Jewish masses productive was translated into reality so as to rebut the accusation that Jews are an antisocial unproductive element'.[70]

Ultimately the theory that there was no viable substitute for the Jews and their labour proved irrelevant to German decision makers, and yet something, perhaps the need to feel at least partially in control of their own destinies, compelled ghetto populations to believe in productionism and to act accordingly. By adhering to the productionist agenda, the individual could provide food for his family and potentially use his position to find work for family or friends whilst believing that he was not only protecting himself and his family due to his role as a necessary worker, but also the broader stability of the ghetto as an entity, and thereby, reinforcing his own safety and that of his family.[71] Arguably, however, this collective effort also caused conflict, both for the individual and for the community. Although not directly referenced in diaries, one might suggest that the sense of masculinity that came with being able to protect one's family must have been balanced by a shame or emasculation associated with aiding one's oppressor. Without sources, any such conclusion must remain speculative, yet more concrete is the impact of productionism on the collective, since the necessary corollary of one's own contribution supporting the continued existence of the ghetto labour force is that another man's limited contribution might actively undermine it. As Gutman noted during deportations in Warsaw 'skilled workers in the various workshops complained about the employment of unskilled workers, claiming that they endangered the continued existence of the shops and the skilled or professional nucleus'.[72]

Of equal importance, the sense of being able to provide for one's family seems to have extended beyond formal employment, and the belief that some had in the ghetto as a semi-autonomous entity, considered already, seems to have encouraged many ghetto inhabitants to see themselves as autonomous and therefore as having the power to act to provide for their families. This will to provide was manifested in numerous ways but included smuggling, bribery and the exploiting of connections or position to secure food and shelter. As Trunk comments, '[i]n the ghettos (for example, Warsaw, Vilnius, Bialystok et al.), the individual ... could attempt somehow to keep himself from going under with his own strength, independent of the ghetto administration.'[73] In most ghettos smuggling played a central role in sustaining ghetto life and those who took part in it, whether on an individual level or in large scale movement of food and goods, were able to perform an act seen as daring and dangerous, and therefore masculine, whilst also providing for their loved ones. And again, although smuggling was by no means carried out uniquely by men, where it was, it was accompanied by a discourse of masculinity. Diane Plotkin quotes Max Glauben, a young smuggler in the Warsaw ghetto: 'I was frightened most of the time. I don't think I ever felt like a hero. None of us did. I felt like I was being a provider, like I was defying the Nazis, like I was keeping some Jewish people alive and not allowing the Nazis to get the best of me'[74] – although Glauben denies heroism he cites two key elements of masculinism – provision and protection – in his reason for smuggling.

Men, however, were not the only workers and they were certainly not the only smugglers; the requirement that smugglers be able to move easily in and out of the ghetto favoured children, whilst the need to spend periods of time passing as a gentile made smuggling easier for women than men. On this basis historians have suggested that the importance of work and smuggling for provision had a significant impact on power brokering within families – Corni cites an example of a young child who sat at the head of the table at mealtimes as befitted his status as provider,[75] whilst Unger comments, '[w]hen a mother and children worked while the father did not – a situation which arose frequently – family tensions sometimes built up'.[76] However, with the exception of Donat, who writes of his humiliation at having to ask his wife for money to buy cigarettes, there seem not to be examples of such issues arising in the sources analysed for this study,[77] which in turn casts doubt on the frequency and gendered relevance of such situations.

Moreover, those few cases that we know of, and particularly that cited by Corni, reinforce the argument that work promoted masculine identities since they illustrate the continued reliance on a patriarchal social and familial structure which rewarded provision. Whilst the masculinity of that child's father might well be undermined, the fact that the child, as chief provider, becomes patriarch shows the importance of provision, a traditionally masculine act. It follows, therefore, that in families where the father remained the chief provider – and statistics from the ghettos suggest that men continued to be paid more than women or children and were more likely to be employed – he would be rewarded for doing so, retaining his role as patriarch and consequently reinforcing his own masculinity.

Further reinforcing this traditional patriarchal structure, at least in the Warsaw ghetto, were the ghetto's agreed priorities, seen in a letter to the Jewish communal self-help organization on 24 June 1942 concerning employment for refugees. The letter noted that any available assistance should be aimed at men, despite the fact that they constituted a minority amongst the refugees. Clearly, in spite of their statistical minority, it was understood that men's employment was more important than that of women,[78] which illustrates the argument that a masculine space and discourse existed in the ghetto: whilst women and children also worked, earned money, provided food and protected their families, for men to work was to conform to the male-gendered environment which prevailed in the ghetto, and thus reinforced their masculinity.

Finally, we hear numerous examples of random acts performed by men to protect their friends, family or comrades. Such events show men performing key elements of masculinism but, as importantly, the way in which they are recorded makes it clear that they were overtly understood as masculine. Both men themselves and their families are keen to note acts of heroism and bravery and tend to record them in a way which shows the masculine defiance of the man involved.[79] Janine David records her father leading the family away from the *Umschlagplatz*,[80] an act of masculine bravado which saves the lives of his family – as a German confronted them, shouted at her father and pointed a gun at his chest, Janine records her father keeping his cool and almost seeming to smile.[81] Similarly, writing of himself, Zylberberg records changing route through the sewers when trying to escape, going on to comment, 'Thank God I had decided to change the route, or we should all have died'[82] and Jakob Breitowicz, in one of many such descriptions, writes about his role in helping several Jews to escape a deportation train, '[a]s the train gathered speed, I began to work on the door and noticed that there was something wrong with the lock'.[83] In both cases the men do not simply record these heroic, masculine, actions but they also attribute them directly, and uniquely, to themselves.

Certainly for many of those in Western Europe these elements of normative masculine identity could not be so clearly reasserted as they were in the ghettos. Particularly for those in hiding, the diversity of circumstances and even conditions makes any universal conclusions even harder than for those in ghettos or resistance organizations and renders discourses of productionism largely irrelevant. Nevertheless, the important role played by provision and protection for those in the West who were able to access these elements highlights their ongoing significance in discourses of gender. Some Jewish individuals and families in Western Europe, whom I shall go on to discuss in more detail, were able to find a comparatively stable hiding place which offered men the chance to reassert elements of their masculine identities. For many, simply the fact of finding that hiding place, when others could not, was a masculine act, leading to their own and their family's survival, a point stressed by Hans Angress who tells the story of a friend who went into hiding on the advice of Hans's brother. After the war, the friend directly credits Hans's brother with his survival and thereby with the ultimate ability to protect.[84] Beyond the masculinity inherent in finding a hiding place for one's family, installing one's family in that space and then conducting a relatively stable existence for whatever time possible were both ways through which men were able to provide for and protect their families.

One example of this is Benno Benninga, who describes how his father found a hiding place for his entire family in Holland and was able to pay for it using diamonds in which he had invested early on in the war. Benninga's account shows his father's clear satisfaction in his ability to provide for and protect his family. Once installed, the family settled into traditional gendered patterns with the male host, Benninga and his father sitting down to play cards together regularly in the evening. Later this situation became abusive, with their hostess regularly asking them to leave, accusing the family of theft and verbally assaulting them. However, whilst these circumstances were particularly damaging to Benninga's father, who tried to protect his wife and children from the worst of the situation, significantly, the realities of hiding, enclosure or reliance were initially reaffirming for his father's masculinity and it was predominantly the uncontrollable behaviour of their hostess that limited his masculine ability to provide and protect.[85] A similar masculine reassertion can be seen with Alex Meijer's father who was very clearly proud of his success in finding a hiding place (in a farm in the Dutch countryside) and in equipping it in advance with provisions and their possessions to support their time in hiding. As with Benninga's family, the Meijer family settled into very traditional gender patterns of behaviour whilst in hiding, with Meijer Sr. behaving in an overtly patriarchal manner, taking control of educating and disciplining his children, and delegating housework to his wife and daughter whilst he and his son spent periods of time smoking together and playing cards.[86] Effectively, not only did Meijer Sr.'s masculinity benefit from providing his family with a hiding place offering relative security but the hiding place that he had sourced then allowed him to perform his role as patriarch, thereby doubly asserting his normative masculine identity.

Also very clearly a mark of male achievement, Otto Berets responded, when asked if he would like someone to take his children from the family hiding place he had organized to another, 'I have protected my family and my children up to this point, I will protect them further.'[87] A similar sense of limited stability in his situation of hiding allowed Otto Frank to continue performing his role as patriarch within his family, and Miep Gies, who supported the family throughout their period in hiding, later wrote that whilst in hiding Frank grew in confidence and decisiveness, losing much of the nervousness that she felt had characterized his behaviour during the deconstruction.[88] Finally is the example of Joseph van West who, initially in hiding alone on a chicken farm in Holland, lost both his mother and sister in a round-up.[89] On hearing the news of their internment, van West gave up his hiding and returned to Amsterdam no longer caring about his own survival. However, on reaching Amsterdam he found a letter from his wife requesting his help. In his testimony, van West is insistent that it was only the fact that someone needed him that kept him alive at that time. He was able then to organize hiding for himself and his wife, and for his mother- and father-in-law in a nearby house, allowing him to continue providing food for all three and protecting them when required. Joseph van West makes it clear in his account that he preferred this situation greatly to the period of the deconstruction which he had spent in Amsterdam since he was much safer and with his family.

Ultimately, for men in hiding with their families, enclosure more easily allowed, at least for a period, a sense of masculine assertion than for those who were in hiding alone. For men on their own, either because of their age or because families were often separated in order to find suitable hiding spaces, a lack of involvement with others made it virtually impossible to protect or provide, let alone seek any type of status and, as with the deconstruction, where these were lacking, relative success in performing individual elements of masculinity, for example physical improvement, had a minimal impact. Some few men, however, were able to combine situations of hiding with working clandestinely, often for underground organizations, and were able to assert elements of their masculinity through that route. Sem Hartz spent some time hiding alone, forging stamps for false identity documents and communicating with another man in hiding nearby through writing notes and letters. Whilst forging documents seems to have allowed Hartz to feel that he was achieving something, both acting and protecting others, his association with a neighbour supported this action by providing a limited amount of homosocial interaction and engagement, effectively provided an audience for his achievements. In much the same way, Eric Baruch who, like many men, hid in a number of different places throughout the war, often alone and always without his family, found masculine assertion by assisting in hiding others. At one point placed in a castle in Belgium, Baruch was involved in designing and building false walls and hidden rooms to assist in concealing a number of Jews and Communists, masculine actions and skills in which Baruch shows clear pride.[90]

Another option for some young Jewish men in the West was 'hiding' in plain sight, often posing as itinerant farm labourers and finding work in rural locations using false papers. Many of these men speak in very masculine terms of the period, working to provide for and protect themselves, whilst also often using the minimal money or food they earned to support other family members in hiding.[91] Jewish men working on farms in this period were also able to assert their masculinity on a more basic level through the labour they undertook, which both provided them with status, on the farms and locally, as well as making them physically fit – which of course meant that they developed a more 'masculine' body. This is something else which Kampelmacher emphasizes, showing great pride in the work he undertook when placed by the resistance on a farm in Holland which later turned out to be notorious for testing its workers with hard labour.[92] Joseph Brenig seemed equally to thrive whilst working on a farm in France, performing physical feats he had not known he was capable of and being part of the local community. Brenig explains that he became so absorbed in this new life and false identity that he virtually forgot his former existence, something which heightened his sense of masculine achievement as a farm labourer. Whilst there are few other examples of men admitting to assuming their false identities quite so overtly as Brenig, the way in which many write about the period leads one to wonder whether Brenig was not alone in this act and in finding that it reinforced his masculine identity.[93]

For those in the West involved with underground resistance organizations, the opportunities to reassert their masculinities, in many of the same ways as in the East, through the normative elements of their gender identities – particularly providing and protecting – were numerous. Relatively well equipped, one way in which many of these groups allowed men to reassert their normative masculinities was through training in, and the use of, weaponry, which not only allowed men to feel powerful but also, importantly, enabled them to at least attempt to protect both themselves and others. Whilst many testimonies are relatively circumspect when it comes to detail, when asked what they had done in the resistance, most men made immediate and repeated references to weapons training.[94] A teenaged member of a resistance group, Harry Alexander, records how, if tackled by Germans, the younger members of his group would run whilst the older members stayed to fight and draw the attention of the Germans.[95] Clearly for these men, protecting other, younger, members of one's group was as significant as protecting oneself and family. In the case of Samuel Schryver, this extended beyond protection to violent action and he speaks, with clear masculine pride, of when his boxing club (eight young men) 'knocked the daylights out of those two dozen Nazis'.[96] Equally important, raids on German convoys and relationships with local farmers and communities allowed these Jewish men to feel that they were again providers. And whilst, for the most part, the men in this situation were young men without wives or children, provision for themselves and their groups remained of key importance to the reinforcement of male gender identities.

The final element of masculinism undermined so severely during the deconstruction was status. However, whist the resurgence of providing and protecting in the ghettos closely mirrored that which was lost in the deconstruction, the reestablishment of status was more complex, effectively returning as something quite other than it had previously been. The assertion of status through the use of public space seen before the war, and so badly damaged by the deconstruction, remained largely inaccessible in the period that followed. Instead, the sense of the ghetto as a Jewish society and the return to public life in the form of ghetto organizations and events including theatres, libraries and political meetings, the importance of which is discussed in numerous diaries and accounts, contributed to a reassertion of status underpinned by the newly gained power and positions which provided status for many Jewish men in the ghettos.

Key to these positions and power were leadership roles, which many exercised for the first time in the ghettos. Regardless of the extent to which the power they seemed to exert was in fact referred, or even imagined, the *Judenräte*, OS, housing committees and most other organizations with significant influence were predominantly peopled by men, and the power they seemed to wield translated into masculine status. Moreover, these roles and positions of power re-established a hierarchy where men wielded power over other men, providing the homosocial masculine exchanges central to masculine identities.

The *Judenräte*, the highest echelons of Jewish ghetto leadership, however, far from providing the best example of the impact of this male ability to wield power, in fact raise most questions for the historian concerning the limits of this power, and perhaps consequently concerning the limits of the masculinities of those involved. Direct contact with the German occupying authorities meant that many members of the *Judenräte* had a greater understanding of their own powerlessness than those below them. Often forced into positions of leadership, these men faced both the disappointment and anger of the Jews who looked to them for impossible solutions and the humiliating derision of the Germans with whom they dealt.[97] Immediately aware of their limited bargaining power, members of the *Judenräte* were later amongst the first to understand the true nature of the Germans' intentions toward the Jews, and throughout the period placed themselves in physical danger from contact with the Germans. That several entire *Judenräte*, as well as many individual members, were killed by the Germans as a display of power only confirms the very real danger of their position despite the power they also wielded within the Jewish community.

To further undermine the impact of their roles on their own gender identities, the *Judenräte* also faced challenges to their power from the ghetto community. In Warsaw, Trunk argues, for example, that '[t]he Jewish Society for Social Aid (Z.T.O.S.) … had such social prestige that the *Judenrat*, whether it wanted to or not, had to reckon with their position.'[98] Similarly, Sterling quotes Zuckerman of the Jewish Combat Organisation (ŻOB) in Warsaw saying,

[a]nd so we defeated the *Judenrat*. The situation reached a stage where Mark Lichtenbaum[99] didn't know whom to fear more: the Germans or the Jewish Combat Organisation. When the Germans came to him and insisted that he appear before the Jewish activists and organise the pacific evacuation of the ghetto, he answered them: I am not the government in the ghetto. There is another government: the Jewish Combat Organisation.[100]

Whilst this should certainly be read as containing a degree of bravado on the part of the ŻOB, nonetheless it raises clear questions concerning the dominance of the *Judenrat* in the Warsaw ghetto.[101]

Regardless of who prevailed, however, Feierstein argues that the struggle for power itself was masculine.[102] These realities of life for many members of the *Judenräte* lead one to conclude that the idea of masculinity exercised through power and leadership is an extremely questionable assumption in their case,[103] and yet one might also argue that it was exactly their exposure to danger which placed these men in a position to reinforce their masculinities. The vulnerability of the *Judenräte* before the Germans was based directly upon their position within the ghettos; chosen in many cases specifically for their influence within the pre-war Jewish community,[104] it was only as men of influence and fame that they were useful to the Germans for their sacrificial value. Thus their arrest, detention or humiliation by the German authorities, whilst having an undeniably negative impact, also served to affirm their position and status. Some have argued, moreover, that the poor reputation of the *Judenräte* amongst the Jews has anyway been exaggerated. Specifically, Corni has suggested that negative appraisals of the *Judenräte* and their members, with which the historian is well acquainted, are a product of post-war Israeli sociopolitical influences rather than contemporary opinion – an argument which is reinforced by numerous diaries from the ghettos which seem to hold the *Judenräte* in high esteem.[105] If this was indeed the case, then the respect in which they were held within the ghetto would also have acted to reinforce masculine identities amongst the members of the *Judenräte*. Finally, on a more practical level, as overall managers of the ghetto, the *Judenräte* controlled housing, food distribution, work, security and taxation and were therefore well placed to exercise power, even if this power brought with it extra responsibilities or burdens. In some cases, although heavily dependent upon their particular circumstances, these men would have been able to exploit this power to reinforce their masculine identities.

For those Jewish men one or two levels down the ghetto administration, the impact of power and responsibility seems to have had clearer results for gender identities. Still with enough power to influence events to their own advantage, but without the notoriety and heightened risk of those at the very top, men with less visible roles in the ghetto administration were able to perform numerous acts to gain status and to reinforce their masculinity. One of the clearest examples of this is given by Stanislaw Adler, a lawyer before the war, who worked in the Warsaw ghetto administration for many years and recorded the numerous acts of personal benefit that this work afforded.[106] Adler, or so his account would suggest, did not avail himself of such opportunities, but he notes many others who did, and his style of living suggests that somehow he was able to use his position to survive the war with only limited hardship. Perks for those working in the ghetto organization, depending on their position, included not only the usual ability to protect and provide for their families that were synonymous with being a worker, but also access to better housing and food, the ability to find work for members of their families, protection from deportation and forced labour, advanced information concerning German plans and, perhaps most importantly, the self-esteem and power that came with leadership itself. Of course the perks of involvement in the ghetto administrations were not available to most Jewish men and varied depending on one's position; nevertheless, particularly in the bigger ghettos, large unwieldy organizational structures, involving a little over 12,000 people (mainly men) in Łódź and at least 6,000 in the Warsaw Jewish Council which employed only 500 workers before the war, provided access to power for significant numbers of Jewish men. The fact that the ghetto administration, in contrast to the *Judenräte* or the OS, would also have employed a small number of women reinforces rather than undermines the impact of these positions of power on masculinities since the nature of these women's roles largely underscored the strongly patriarchal structure of the ghetto administration and therefore the masculinity of those men it employed.

The OS were another group of men who used their leadership and power within the ghettos to assert their status and thereby their male gender identities. A Jewish police force, entirely staffed by men,[107] the OS, as well as furnishing them with the daily ability to protect and provide, enabled its workers to reinforce their masculinity through traditional masculine tropes – physicality, in many cases violence, uniform and order. In contrast to the *Judenräte* which tended to comprise men of experience and standing, each OS was made up of younger men with no previous experience of power, who were often outsiders from other cities with few family ties.[108] For these men the OS offered the novel experience of leadership and power. As Turkov notes, Scherinski, who was central to the Warsaw OS, had few troubles recruiting men since, 'ces gens avaient vu dans cette 'institution' nouvelle créée un moyen de faire carrière, une source de revenues et une occasion d'assouvir leur soif de pouvoir'.[109] Drawing strongly on masculinities prevalent in much of Europe since the First World War, but also upon that of the dominant Germans, the OS seem to have thrived through an esprit de corps, seen in Kaplan's writings but also made clear by Adler, despite his own professed detachment.[110]

Beyond the image that the OS had of themselves as masculine, the broader ghetto community, despite many misgivings about their behaviour, clearly also saw the OS as masculine, with their position and power conferring upon them a status within the ghetto community, something which would also have acted to reinforce the masculinities of those involved. In this vein Kaplan comments, '[t]he residents of the ghetto are beginning to think they are in Tel Aviv. Strong, bona fide policemen from among our brothers, to whom you can speak in Yiddish'.[111] Very few had anything positive to say about the OS, but many accounts still include a grudging acknowledgement of their masculinity.

Beyond these, numerous other positions of power existed in many of the ghettos of German-occupied Poland, roles which might be best described using Dan Michman's term 'leadership' in contrast to the 'headship' of the *Judenräte* and OS. Whilst those in 'headship' roles are given power through an organized system and often appointed from outside the group, Michman suggests that 'leadership' is associated with those who are 'spontaneously' recognized from within the group – many of these alternative leadership roles existed in the ghetto structures, from underground organizations to military veterans and social elders, and were, as much as positions of 'headship', used to reinforce the masculinity of the men who held them.[112] Of particular note in this regard are the men who were involved in the resistance organizations of the ghettos, many of whom used their roles to assert themselves as leaders and to exercise a degree of power and influence, in some cases over their own troops, and more universally, as they became seen by the *Judenrat* as 'an alternative to the conventional form of leadership, to be activated when mediation failed'.[113]

This was particularly the case for those men involved in resistance organizations run along military lines, such as Pinkus Kartin, a former captain in the international brigades during the Spanish Civil War and founder of the People's Guard established in the Warsaw ghetto.[114] Led by a triumvirate of men along traditionally military lines, the patriarchal leadership structure of the ŻOB also clearly acted to reinforce the masculinities of its members. In his post-war account, Rotem writes about his work with the ŻOB in Warsaw noting that Zuckerman, their leader, referred to him as 'the major link of the ZOB, my aide-de-camp and assistant',[115] a position of power with strong masculine associations. As in many other cases, however, status through position remained a more elusive element of normative masculinities for Jewish men in Western resistance organizations than for some in the east. Whilst the resistance organizations of the ghettos were run by Jews, evidence suggests that Jewish members of western resistance organizations were often slightly disadvantaged, either due to the need to remain circumspect concerning their Jewish identities or because of foreign nationalities and accents – many were German or Austrian Jews with clear accents which could only partially be explained with reference to Alsace-Lorraine. Consequently, Jewish men in Western resistance organizations were rarely able to rise in the ranks and thereby assert their status, either through power over others or through use of the public space.[116]

The assertion of status, even if not through leadership roles, was also available to more junior members of resistance organizations both in the East and the West, however, and pride in their activities can clearly be seen in the very masculine language used by many rank-and-file members of resistance groups in accounts of their work. One example of this is Mary Berg's description of a group of volunteer farmers as 'ranks of boys and girls who march along the ghetto streets, returning from work outside. All of them are tanned by the sun and refreshed by the free air they have breathed in the fields beyond the city'.[117] References to marching in ranks as well as to tans and fresh air associate this Zionist group closely to pre-war movements in Europe and Palestine which espoused new ideals of strong Jewish masculinity. Likewise the Pioneering Youth movements, Brith Hehalutzim and Toporol,[118] which in Sosnowiec became powerful enough to challenge Merin, the head of the Jewish Council,[119] all involved themselves to some degree in agricultural work and spoke in terms clearly affirming their masculinity. Involved in Toporol in the ghetto, Janina Bauman commented, '[w]hat a day! Eight long hours of hard physical work under the blue sky. Can't imagine anything better'.[120]

Resistance organizations in the West also had direct connections with male scouting organizations and reinforced a predominantly male membership with similar themes of physicality and strength to those seen in the ghettos. Most obviously this link can be seen in the testimony of Joseph Brenig who, received support from the Oeuvre de Secours aux Enfants (OSE – a French organization which hid Jewish children during the war), even though they were unable to care for him directly due to his age. The OSE provided him not only with material support but, perhaps more importantly, with a community, a group of young Jewish men with whom he could live and struggle. On many occasions he was fed and protected by the OSE and on one particular occasion he and his group seem to have enacted strong masculinities, if only temporarily, when they were provided with uniforms and 'marched' to a field where they pretended to be a scout troop for several weeks before 'marching' back to the local railway station and returning the outfits.[121] Similarly, asserting masculine pride and action through his involvement in the resistance, Wacław Poterański wrote, '[i]n those days especially, nothing was as important as the Movement. We had to amass force and turn it into acts that would be transformed by the meaning of those days'.[122]

There were, of course, women involved throughout the resistance in all countries, and yet accounts suggest that men and women were treated differently and, in many cases, in ways that were affirming of strong male gender identities. A member of a Dutch, gentile, resistance group during the war, Jonkje Grandia-Smits clearly commented, 'it was a man's world',[123] Freddie Knoller called his French resistance group 'the boys'[124] and David Lederman, from an orthodox Belgian family, recounts his time in the underground like a Boys' Own adventure story including tales of seducing women, stealing life-saving rubber stamps from under the noses of Nazi generals and narrow escapes, finally commenting of his own actions, '[y]ou've got to have a little dose of courage to do that'.[125] This was equally true of ghetto resistance groups. Michael Checinski writes about his resistance 'cell' in the Łódź ghetto, which included six other men and one woman, Genia Szlak, whose role he described as, to 'service us, in other words, she delivers to us instructions and assignments from the leadership'.[126]

Poterański underscores the division of labour this suggests in noting that the majority of leaders in resistance groups in Łódź were men, at least until near the end of life in the ghetto when a few women were admitted. In the main, however, he suggests, women were more important in forming resistance links outside the ghetto than in resistance organization within the ghetto.[127] Perhaps this division of labour was not quite so clear-cut in reality as in these accounts; nonetheless, it is significant that writers have chosen to represent it as such: a significance which hints at its importance for their own masculinities. Were it required, Vladka Meed's description of five fellow resisters shot and killed outside the Warsaw ghetto says everything one would need to know about ongoing strong gender roles and identities even in mixed organizations. Of the five, three were men and were described thus: Zygmunt, '[h]e had risked his life to save his comrades, and had perished in the attempt'; Yurek, '[h]e had always volunteered for the most arduous tasks and had carried out the most dangerous missions eagerly and skillfully'; and Luszek who distinguished himself in battle and was rewarded with a revolver. In stark contrast, the two women killed with them in identical circumstances are described as 'an exquisite but modest girl, like a mother to her brothers ... zeal, devotion ... carried out her duties faithfully' and 'eighteen, vivacious, stunning, sprightly, always witty'.[128]

Almost identical gendered language can be seen in descriptions of those in the resistance organizations in hiding in the Polish forests as in the ghettos. Amongst them Harold Werner describes four brothers from a town called Zahajki, between 13 and 25: '[t]he oldest ... tall and broad-shouldered, with a dark complexion, curly thick black hair, and a fierce look in his eyes. The second ... also tall, dark and fierce looking ... wore a German hat at a rakish angle.' The youngest they called 'the Patzan', about whom Werner comments, '[h]e disliked being called Patzan ("little one"). He wanted to be treated as an equal. He smoked cigarettes and even drank a little with the older partisans. He could ride a horse and had proven himself many times as a fearless fighter against the Germans'.[129]

The same language as is used by those in the ghettos can again be seen to be used by those involved in the clandestine resistance organization, the EIF, in France. In his recorded testimony, Roger Climaud, a member of the 6éme, records, with some swagger, living under the same roof as several members of the Gestapo and regularly eating with them, and he notes with pride that, of around two thousand children he attempted to save, only one was deported.[130] Maurice Behrnson, also a member of the 6éme and part of a group which joined the maquis after their own organization was disbanded in 1943, writes of the Jewish recruits immediately, 'nous sommes devenus très puissants', noting that they were considered the most organized and disciplined in the maquis.[131] Effectively, these examples show that the status and position that the EIF afforded these men clearly allowed them to assert strong masculine identities and the existence of numerous women in the organization, as with the ghetto resistance, does not seem to have diminish the gendered impact of these actions.

Finally, we see leadership and power as being relevant to the masculinities of individuals who were not involved in any organization or group, but simply asserting themselves within the community. This is particularly the case in times of danger or stress, for example in Adler's account of his experiences whilst leading a group of Jews to safely:

> [i]n my left hand I grab some warm clothes that I have not had time to put on and rush into the kitchen. I grab the butcher's chopper (an axe), placed there some time ago for such an emergency as this, and, leading the group, consisting of Lola, Dr. Lewinson, his mother, Giterman's wife and son, and also M., who has just arrived. I escape down the staircase in total silence. I look around attentively. I am now calm, controlled, resolved to rush upon the enemy and split his head.[132]

Adler goes on to recount other similar stories of his assumed leadership whilst hiding in a bunker,[133] ending by recording the words of a respected colleague concerning their own work, '[t]he captains are the last to leave the sinking ship'. Clearly Adler sees himself as a captain and draws a good deal of self-respect and masculine pride from that role. We equally see this language of captaincy and sacrifice in the words of Czerniakow, who in 1942 speaks of his resolve to emulate the captain of a ship[134] and Raymond-Raoul Lambert who, in very different circumstances in France, writes that 'duty compels me to be the last to leave the ship'.[135]

Whilst the circumstances of enclosure seen in this period seem to have promoted the masculinist capacities of provide, protect and status, the three central masculine identities, assimilated, subordinate and independent were, in contrast, of relatively little significance in the reformation of most male gender identities. Conditions varied between ghettos and some record a strong tendency toward support for more traditional Jews whilst others, particularly Łódź, clearly favoured those men with an assimilated identity, yet still, with only one significant exception, it is hard to find a close association between these identities and masculine practice in this period.

This exception is the case of men who oriented themselves toward a specifically Jewish masculinity and whose relationships with descent and heritage seen in the deconstruction became, in the ghettos, a positive association which provided strength and reinforcement to masculine identities. The most obvious example of this phenomenon is the case of Harold Werner who, coming from a strictly orthodox family in which women wore wigs, boys wore locks and the family kept strictly kosher, seemed to compare himself to Moses when he wrote, 'I told them we should not delay our mission because of Passover. Just the opposite. Helping the Jews escape from the Włodawa ghetto was like taking the Jews out of Egypt.'[136] Werner also writes of persuading the Włodawa ghetto Jews to go with him, describing how he told them the stories from the *Haggaddah*, the Jewish text which tells the story of the liberation of the Jewish people from slavery in Egypt, and 'they understood my message'.[137] That not only this entire process is affirming of Werner's relationship to his heritage but also it directly links to his masculine identity is seen in comments he makes when meeting Jews who had just escaped from the ghettos: '[t]hey told us that the concept of Jewish partisans had only been a fantasy to them, and here they were looking at us, heroes with guns and grenades – real soldiers'.[138] This language, moreover, ties back to the significance of military behaviour as one key signifier of masculinity found during enclosure and particularly in the organizations of the ghettos.

Making a similar allusion to masculinity through reference to the Jewish religion, Zuckerman wrote,

> I must say that never, in any incident, not even in most difficult moments, in the most difficult emotional distress, not only did I not regret but I blessed the day I came to Warsaw, even in the days of Treblinka. I didn't regret being where I was because I knew I had to be there. I thought: how could I have lived if I had been in some quiet place?! That is, to this very day, I have never blamed or accused anyone. And I don't blame myself either; no, I wasn't led like Isaac to the sacrifice – absolutely not! Not even at moments when I faced death, I had no regrets or complaints.[139]

Drawing on the strength of their forebears, Zylberberg records that in the ghetto a poem was performed entitled 'Masada', the story of a Jewish enclave which resisted the Romans until, ultimately, they committed suicide. The poem included a song which became popular in the ghetto about the link between generations and the line, '[t]he chain has not been broken; the chain continues, from parents to children, from father to son. This is how our parents danced … So we, too, will keep on dancing.'[140]

This focus on descent and heritage can also specifically be found amongst the Hasidic community and is recorded in Yaffa Eliach's book *Hasidic Tales of the Holocaust*, the first chapter of which is entitled 'Ancestors and Faith.'[141] This chapter most significantly begins by referring to the suffering of the Holocaust, and the testimonies of that suffering, as 'a song, a hymn of praise, a testimony to the eternity of the Jewish people and the greatness of their spirit' and includes a story told in the Sosnowiec ghetto which began, 'My dear son Mendel, for fifteen generations in an unbroken chain from father to son, the Halberstam family have … [been] scholars, rabbis and Hasidic zaddikim.'[142] The book also tells the story of Rabbi Israel Spira of Bluzhov who was strangled by a German in the Bochnia ghetto using the silk halatl that he had been given by his grandfather and that had belonged to many generations of his family. That he does not die in this attempt on his life the rabbi later attributes entirely to the halatl and its importance to his family.[143]

Individual elements of masculinities

Whilst the ghettos and the relative stability they seem to have offered allowed for some the successful practice of normative masculine identities, many individual elements of masculinity in the same period, in particular contrast to their relative resilience during the deconstruction, became almost immediately unsustainable for all but the most affluent ghetto inhabitants. Chief amongst these elements was the relationship of the individual with his body, the clearest impact of which was, for many men, a more overt embodiment, contrasting strongly with the lack of embodiment evident in the pre-war period and during the destruction. Where men had previously been aware of their bodies – but only overtly in particular prescribed circumstances, for example in athletics clubs – the destruction and enclosure forced men into constant and open engagement with their bodies. This shift was the product of two particular changes; in the first case, life in the ghettos placed an emphasis on masculinities tied to physicality which necessarily promoted the role of the body, but, perhaps more importantly, this increased embodiment was a natural product of the shrinking of lives which took place during the Holocaust and left little beyond the relationship between the self and the body. The extent to which individuals were able to control, protect or use their bodies became not only significant to physical survival but also to mental survival and identity, gendered or otherwise. Conspicuous as an exception – which seems to highlight the more common increase in embodiment – David Kahane describes an almost total alienation from his body whilst in the Lvov ghetto; specifically, he recorded being made to wear an armband denoting his place of work, and therefore his right to remain in the ghetto, as a 'calamity' which made him 'no longer the master of his body, but a property of the Arbeitsamt.'[144]

For a select few in the West, this overt embodiment was positive and added to the reassertion of masculinity during this period. Some young Jewish men involved with underground organizations in the West were able to use their situations to assert their physicality, a key individual element of masculinities which elsewhere suffered greatly during this period of destruction. This assertion of physicality was particularly the case for those Jews who were members of organizations based in rural locations on farms and which required their members to labour on the farms. Maintaining a strong body – or even developing a strength and physique that you had not previously had – was made possible due to a sufficient supply of food which, although it remained scarce during the war and the question of ration coupons appears frequently in the sources, almost never reached the starvation rations (and less) that those in the east survived on. Freddie Knoller, working with the French Resistance as a courier, speaks of doing physical work in order to keep himself strong[145] whilst Jacques Breitberg, fresh from the harvest in French farms and placed by the Resistance with a group of antisemitic young men unaware of his Judaism, challenges the group to arm-wrestle and in his testimony comments, 'I was strong, my muscles... I was strong. Nobody was as strong as me.'[146] Similarly Joseph Brenig comments proudly of his time working on farms in France, 'Hard physical labour – I became extremely good at this.'[147]

However, whilst bodies could occasionally be a positive element of masculinity in the period of enclosure and were, during this period, used to reinforce masculinities through asserting or diminishing the masculinity of others – something I have considered already – in the ghettos, and despite a more overt sense of embodiment, it is clear that, for most men, their own body became an insurmountable obstacle to the sustaining of the individual elements of gender identity. Perhaps the clearest example of this can be found in the diary of Oskar Rosenfeld. Written during several years spent in the Łódź ghetto whilst already in his fifties, Rosenfeld describes himself thus:

> A slight uneasiness seizes the body. The abdomen gets loose and eventually sags. Hesitant, almost fearful, the hand feels the restless body, finds bones, ribs, finds limbs, and discovers the self, suddenly becoming aware that not so long ago one was fatter, meatier, and one is surprised how quickly the body decays ... The abdomen has been sagging, giving the feeling of directly encountering the bowels.[148]

Rosenfeld goes on to talk about his physical condition as a pain which starts in the back of the head and spreads over the forehead and eyes. Significantly, he notes that whilst this pain is initially comforting as it 'gave the illusion of eventual redemption', it soon changed and became 'something bad for which there was no remedy'.[149] Similar language of the body can be found in numerous testimonies including that of Janine David which records her father trying on his suit in the ghetto for one final time before selling it and commenting, '[y]et I was never a fat man, my shoulders were all muscle. Where has it gone to? Can a body melt like this?'[150] Similarly embodied, the fictional stories written by Josef Zelkowicz whilst also in the Łódź ghetto include the line,

> [t]hese hands used to be real hands! The heavy loads they lifted. And when my arms were arms and my shoulders were shoulders, I could lift two-meter loads on each, and on top a man could sit and I could dance to a Cossack's tune. And now? You call these arms? Rags, sticks, willow branches like they wave on the Feast of Tabernacles, after being pounded on the floor – but I mustn't sin with my words.[151]

In writing this, and in relating his physical collapse to his ability to work and to how other people viewed him and his role in society, Zelkowicz clearly conveys a negatively association between his body and his masculinity.

That for many the damage caused to the body was reflected in a loss of interest in one's physical appearance, hygiene and dress is unsurprising, particularly given the conditions of the ghettos and many hiding spaces, and yet it is noticeable that women in this period are particularly, and overtly, critical of this failing amongst men. Jafa Wallach, in hiding in Poland with her husband and brothers, repeatedly noted her horror at their failure to attempt to keep themselves clean or preserve their clothes, contrasting this with her own decision to use a small amount of her drinking water each day to clean herself and to save a dress so she would have something to wear when they left hiding,[152] and Janine David's mother requested that her husband try on his suit once more before it was sold so that she could see him as he used to be. We cannot know in what way these opinions were communicated to the men in question, or how it impacted on their masculinities, but we can speculate as to the impact that this judgement of the body could have had upon men who must already have known that their bodies, and their relationships with their bodies, had changed beyond recognition.

Importantly, however, the condemnation of Jewish men's appearances that we find amongst their wives and families has been repeated by historians in the judgements they have made about Jewish men, something which is most clearly seen in the often repeated use of the story from Birkenau concerning women adapting their camp uniforms. As historians relate this story, women are seen to be proud and successful for the alterations they make whilst the men who continue to wear ill-fitting clothes are clearly condemned for their failure to find clothes that afforded them any benefits, aesthetical or practical.[153] Ultimately, it is clear that, regardless of whether it is tied to increased embodiment or a negative judgement from others, Jewish men were unable to maintain a strong relationship with their bodies during the period of ghettoization.

Beyond these almost universal elements of individual masculinity which almost all men must have experienced in some form or another during the period, there were also individual elements of masculinity particular only to certain men, many of which suffered equally from distinct changes in society which saw the elimination or diminution of certain masculine identities and the assertion of new ones. Again in the ghettos, whilst some particular gender identities thrived, others could not be sustained in the conditions they faced and, as new social structures emerged, with them came new elements of masculinities.

There are numerous historical discourses around the subject of identities, foremost class, religious and racial, in the ghettos of the Holocaust. Amongst them Philip Friedman, in *Roads to Extinction: Essays on the Holocaust*, writes,

> [c]lass distinctions in the ghetto were based less on the prewar criteria of monetary wealth and professional or intellectual achievement than on factors related directly to survival under the new conditions: shrewdness, audacity, indifference to the plight of others, physical strength, manual dexterity, and the external factors such as access to the German authorities.[154]

Whilst Friedman is writing about class and not gender, his conclusions might equally usefully be applied to masculinities: in the ghettos, masculinities were reasserted; those best suited to the conditions and opportunities offered by ghetto life came to the fore, whilst those less able to adapt often continued to struggle.

As Jewish society in Poland entered the ghettos, at very different times and in hugely varied circumstances, most men lost their social status and playing fields were levelled as they became disconnected from the possessions, finances, employment and connections which had previously defined them. Emerging from this struggle came a new elite, *di voyle* in Warsaw and *di shtarke* in Vilnius, who, according to Friedman, are a *lumpenbourgeoisie* interested only in amassing money and power.[155] Although Friedman does not necessarily associate this group directly with the *Judenrat* and OS, he argues that profiteering on the part of the *lumpenbourgeoisie* was often associated with, or assisted by, those groups, tying them all together in a rejection of pre-war social and ethical standards. Friedman concedes that not all historians agree with him that the structure of society and elites changed so significantly in this period, stressing instead continuities with pre-war Kehillot and their social classes and codes.[156] However, my analysis of masculinity during ghettoization tends to bear out Friedman's conclusions: moving away from masculinities reliant upon subtle distinctions of position and class and often favouring those with intellectual prowess, the ghetto seemed instead to favour those men whose masculinities relied upon physical prowess, cunning or bald financial achievement. Often, moreover, these identities relied on overtly negative character traits which were nevertheless understood to be masculine. In 'When a Horse Runs Wild …' Zelkowicz writes about queuing in the ghetto noting,

> [o]ne may literally push one's way into a queue by wielding one's fists like machetes. Those who lack the strength to do this, or who still think in pre-war terms and cannot bring themselves to beat up old people, women and children, are in a bad way indeed. Their reluctance indicates that they have not adapted to the conditions and must depart from the world.[157]

It is clear that whilst this behaviour may not be morally positive in any sense, it was both necessary and a sign of strength.

Two individual elements of masculinities that particularly suffered in this transition were intellect and religious piety. The Jewish intelligentsia, which had thrived in pre-war Polish society and been comparatively well treated by the deconstruction, struggled to assert itself once inside the ghetto. A few individuals were able to move into positions of power in the ghetto administration, but the existence of a dedicated soup kitchen for the intelligentsia hints at the struggle that most encountered in the ghetto, despite the emergence of intellectual groups, reading circles, libraries and lectures.[158] The provision of such a soup kitchen certainly indicates a sustained respect for the intelligentsia – nonetheless it seems to have been a respect based on past glory rather than on contemporary standing. This can be seen in the rather wistful respect Zuckerman affords his subjects when writing about those members of the intelligentsia whom he knew in the ghetto including Katznelson, Czudner and Danieliwicz. Whilst keen to acknowledge their intellects and his relationship with them, he seems to question their relevance in ghetto society and points out that many of them died of starvation immediately upon entering the ghettos.[159]

Formerly employed in work like journalism and academia, the intelligentsia were removed from the roles and structures which had afforded them their position in pre-war society and found themselves unable to thrive in ghetto employment, which often required practical skills they lacked, whether physical or commercial. As Corni explains it, 'ghettoization meant the collapse of the many social ties on which the Jewish elites had traditionally built their hegemonic role'.[160] Corni goes on to suggest, through a study of 'the outcomes of various confiscations carried out during the initial phase [of ghettoization]', that some members of the intelligentsia must have succeeded in entering the ghetto with a significant portion of their wealth and property intact. Yet whilst this may be correct, and goes some way to explaining their relative strength during the deconstruction, there is no evidence that such constantly dwindling fortunes, unless the means could be found to replenish them, were able to sustain the masculinities of the men who had earned them. Moreover, the early confiscations that took place in the ghetto, combined with high inflation, meant that wealth alone was rarely sufficient to sustain a family for long. Combined with these problems came some degree of humiliation, as Rosenfeld records,

> [c]ome here and look at this wonder. University professors, who held forth in the lecture hall, running around with a pot looking for soup, famous singers pushing coal carts, lawyers standing guard in a carnival uniform (armband and colourful cap), renowned chemists and actors waiting in front of decaying barracks for a call to be placed with some resort (straw, junk…).

Ultimately, as Friedman notes, 'their [the intelligensia's] outlook for the future was hopeless', an opinion sustained by the statistically higher number of suicides amongst the intelligentsia than other groups.[161] In the world of the ghetto it seems that members of the intelligentsia were unable to make themselves relevant.[162]

In the same vein, religious elites, in spite of receiving sustained respect from within the community, seem not to have managed to reassert their masculinities or indeed their identities more generally once inside the ghettos. Limited examples exist to the contrary including the account by Abram Lancman of an occasion on which his grandfather and others were praying and passing around the scrolls:[163]

> [m]y grandfather, Hanoch Hejnoch, a septuagenarian, embraced one of the heavy Scrolls and danced with it as lightly and as enthusiastically as a boy, refusing to part with it to anyone … He danced and danced, throwing off the blanket of gloom shrouding this Simhat Torah, and went on dancing with total abandon … Like me, they [the others who watched] have engraved upon their minds the image of the heroic old man, crowned with a halo of piety, radiating joy as he whirled around the room. In spite of our terror, no-one tried to stop him, out of courtesy to this revered and devout Hasid, for whom all thoughts of martyrdom were as nothing compared to his love for the Torah, the code and centrepiece of his life, to be honoured above all else.[164]

The use of the word 'heroic' in this case confirms the clear respect that the ensemble had for the old man and his religious identity, which would also have been central to his masculinity. In a very different situation Pivnik notes the resilience of religious identities and their positive impact when he records a group of men being deported from the ghetto, writing, 'I looked at the men praying, their faces grey and frightened under their hats. But their eyes were bright with optimism as they took comfort from the words they were reciting. They *knew* that God would help us. Hadn't that been His promise all along? He would find a way, give us a sign.'[165] Whilst Pivnik goes on to write '[b]ut he didn't', clearly himself lacking any faith in religious salvation, this does not diminish the importance of faith to those he is describing nor the role it seems to have played in their understanding of the ghetto and the Holocaust.

There are comments recorded by Ringelblum and others, which note a degree of respect accorded to Jews who continued to wear long beards and coats, since in openly defining themselves as religious they made themselves vulnerable to persecution.[166] Here however, we see a contrast – whilst sources show others paying respect to religious elites, they clearly show the elites themselves struggling significantly with their identities. The overwhelming experience was that survival in the ghetto necessitated the rejection of religious strictures and practice, which were often outlawed either by the Jewish authorities or the Germans, and provoked conflict damaging to one's masculine identity. In this way Pivnik describes a fight between his parents after his mother is able to obtain some pork. His father refuses to eat it and attempts to throw it away; however he is overridden by his wife who insists that it be fed to the children, thereby undermining both his religious and his paternal identities. For many religious Jewish men, whilst others may have respected them, the ghetto presented a particular struggle, often leading them to depression and shame directly linked to the attacks which Ringelblum references – a shame we see clearly in Leo Laufner's description of his father having his beard cut and his subsequent collapse:

> [h]e felt so badly because it was so undignified for him. I remember when they actually pulled his beard out. He was almost crying, as old a man as he was. And he put his handkerchief around the part of the beard that was still left across his face, tied in a knot at the top. He wore it like when you have a toothache. It was degrading, and this kept on for a long time. It was tragic; it was very, very bad.[167]

In contrast to these experiences, one element of masculine identities continued to dominate as much in the ghettos as before. Previously discussed in relation to the assertion of status in the ghettos, although not available to all, a military identity, linked to the masculinity of uniform, order and hierarchy, thrived in the ghettos, thanks both to the special conditions accorded to veterans and to an ongoing respect and reverence for military behaviour and dress. Particularly amongst Jews from the *Altreich*,[168] and despite laws forbidding it, the retention of documentation and decorations pertaining to past wars was common. Proclamation No. 380 from the occupying authorities in the Łódź ghetto, stating that Jews from the *Altreich* were to be resettled unless they were employed or decorated either with iron crosses or for sustaining wounds in battle, seemed to affirm that this masculinity was equally respected by the Germans as by the men themselves.[169] However, when faced with exemption from resettlement, and the belief that they were favoured by this exemption, many still chose to conceal their documentation.[170] There are several reasons why they might have done this, and we cannot ignore the implications of such a proclamation on families, as well as the general belief that refugees, of which these documents would have been proof, were not welcome in the ghettos; nonetheless to smuggle such documents into the ghetto at great personal risk and then chose not to benefit from their use does suggest that the documents themselves had some value to these men as signifiers of their masculine prowess.

Similarly inexplicable, except by acknowledging a reverence for veterans and their achievements, is the gift of a dead man's medals, made to Adam Czerniakow and noted in his diary. That Czerniakow chooses to note this, despite very rarely referencing specific or personal details, suggests that the medals were something Czerniakow held in high esteem.[171] This respect for the trappings of military life extended beyond veterans to a sustained high opinion of the masculinity of those involved in other militaristic groups. Adler notes a particular importance placed on discipline, marching and military protocols in the training of the OS,[172] whilst Lancman suggests that it was impossible to believe that men in uniform could commit such atrocious acts as Germans in the ghettos did[173] – despite the military men in question being their captors, Lancman is still unable to grasp that they might behave incorrectly, so strong is the pull of their uniform for him. With the same respect for the trappings of the military, and in spite of the realities of occupation, Zuckerman records Gershuni, a colleague from the Dror, a Jewish Zionist youth movement which was active in the Warsaw ghetto and organized resistance cells during the ghetto uprising, whose 'eyes bulged out of their sockets when he saw the SS marching in procession' and Pivnik comments on being 'mesmerized' by the *Wehrmacht*.[174]

Beyond the changing status of the elements of masculinity mentioned above, the ghettos also provided the potential for Jewish men to redefine themselves, incorporating new elements of identity into their masculinities, As Feierstein writes, '[i]n what terms, in what context, with what possibilities should Jews think about themselves as Jews? How could they redefine this identity after the rise of Nazism? This was the first great problem to be resolved, which is clear in every story told by survivors of the resistance organizations'.[175] This potential remodelling, linked to the questions of subordinate and Jewish normative identity discussed earlier, was not only available to the resistance, however. To Judaism in general, as seen before the war with the establishment of Jewish settlements in Palestine, the possibility of a new identity and a new masculinity was open.

Linked to my assertion of an atmosphere of action in the ghettos came an active masculinity, focused less on the traditional questions of whom one knew, where one lived and who one was and instead looking more centrally at what one did. The action in question was often work, although not necessarily, but need not have been manual labour. As *Oneg Shabbat* recorded, '[t]he only element which is not rotten is the working man; the only hope rests with him'.[176] *Oneg Shabbat* also records an obituary to a man named Diamant, describing him as 'an elderly worker, educated by the workshop and the Party'.[177] Again here the stress, and the respect, is placed on his role as a worker and his roots. In line with this respect for men of work and action, an obituary in the *Chronicle of Łódź Ghetto* for Jakob Szulman, who ran a hospital, noted, '[g]hetto society has lost an extremely useful, righteous, and noble man of great merit'. In such a respectful obituary, the word 'useful' is notable, and perhaps nods at a changing notion of action as relevant to how one is seen by society. The work of David Shavit, who wrote about reading habits in the ghettos, seems to support this argument for a changed masculinity showing that, although a wide range of books were read during ghettoization, trends show a leaning toward books which involved strong, mainly lower class, physically masculine heroes including factual studies of coal miners, like that by Cronin, or peasants, including works written by Silone. Where fiction was read, it was often war-based with soldiers for heroes in works including those by Remarque, Zola and Tolstoy.[178]

One particular example of the masculine respect accorded to men of action can be seen in various discussions concerning the porters of Warsaw. Kaplan writes of three porters condemned to die, describing them as 'virile men with strength in their loins', and details their physical fight for survival. Kaplan's respect for their masculinity, contingent on their physical and active self-defence, is clear despite their ultimately desperate situation.[179] Lancman also writes about the Warsaw porters conceding that they no longer had the strength or 'swagger' of their pre-war selves but suggesting that this had anyway been vulgar and uncouth. Once in the ghetto they succeed in retaining their 'honour', demanding the right to continue working as porters and earning their living, again therefore citing their masculinity in their roots and their work.[180] Finally, stressing the particular importance of physical labour, *Oneg Shabbat* accords a similar respect to rickshaw drivers when reporting discussions concerning taxation on the basis that they 'work hard substituting for horses' with 'toil and sweat'.[181]

Lancman goes on from writing about Warsaw porters, however, to define another new masculinity forged in the ghetto: 'a new strong man was born, the wheeler-dealer, who looked out only for himself and to blazes with the rest'.[182] This masculinity, closely linked to *di voyle* and *di shtarke* mentioned above, whilst not relying on physicality, was nonetheless a masculinity of action since it required men to do as much as possible for the benefit of themselves and their families and rewarded them for doing so. In Łódź particularly this shift was underscored by the speech that Rumkowski gave to all newcomers to the ghetto in which he commented,

> I understand the bitterness of people with higher education who are forced to push wagons through the streets. It cannot be helped. The Łódź worker long ago accepted the fact that the ghetto places all kinds of obligations on its inhabitants, without regard for their former social positions. After all, everything is not done for me but for the good of the whole community.[183]

Linked to these new identities was the key element of knowledge, not an intellectual knowledge of literature or science but knowledge concerning survival. During this period, men were extremely keen to prove their masculinity through the display of information pertaining to the functioning of the ghetto and the war effort and, through that, to how best to survive the war. In this way, Jafa Wallach, in hiding in Poland, records that, as the front approached, the gentile Pole hiding them brought them a map and 'the boys dug in and became experts in the strategy of the fighting forces'[184] and Alexander Bronowski, in hiding in a village, in 1944 wrote, '[o]n Sundays the villagers came to them [his hosts] to talk, and I joined in. They listened intently to every word I said about Poland under occupation and the rebellion in Warsaw'.[185] In a few cases this masculinity was extended to the men placing themselves in danger whilst gaining such knowledge, whether by reading illegal newspapers and pamphlets or listening to the radio[186] – particularly for many in hiding in the West, the possession of radios, and the relaying of their news, was a role played entirely by men who received some clear respect for the transmission. Johanna Dobschiner recounts how, whilst in hiding with another young woman and several men, only the men listened to the radio, which they kept in their own room.[187] Similarly, Kampelmacher writes about reading the paper and listening to the radio and proudly recounts how, on arriving at a new farm, his opinions on the war effort were sought and respected.[188]

For many men, however, the importance of knowledge was manifested in a more patriarchal role of counsellor to friends and family or leader in plans to escape or hide. *Oneg Shabbat* recorded, '[w]e would be the fathers, the teachers and educators of the future. We would be the grandfathers of the bards who tell to the grandsons, to the young the story of victories and defeats, of keeping alive and of perishing.'[189] Speaking of a wiser, patriarchal knowledge, Kaplan notes being sought out by his friends for advice concerning how to get out of the ghetto.[190] Finally, in contrast to this, usually, but not always, younger men closely relate masculinity to the danger and pressure of possessing knowledge, rather than its transmission. In her diary, Mary Berg writes of a boyfriend Romek who comments, 'Little girl, it is good that you don't understand too much. I am happy that you don't suffer as I do.'[191] Here Romek equates his knowledge with suffering, but at the same time displays his masculinity over Berg, his adult to her child, his man to her woman. Almost identical are the reported words of Rumkowski that 'If I were to tell you everything I know, you would not sleep. So I *alone* am the one who does not sleep,'[192] and Zylberberg's decision, mentioned earlier, not to tell his wife that he has risked his life to save another woman so as to protect her from the resulting fear.[193] Similarly Adler shows great pride in writing about hiding in the ghetto and is keen to note his knowledge of the shelter, in this case the locations of some vents as the shelter is running low on oxygen.[194] Even for those in hiding who had limited opportunities either to acquire or to disseminate knowledge, where such knowledge was possible it became a significant element of male gender identity.

Another element of identity particular to the individual, and with an impact on gender, was age. Yet, despite life in the ghettos and in hiding presenting quite different problems for older and younger men due to their circumstances, responsibilities and opportunities, in fact, whilst this led to a diverse range of experiences, for most men, the impact of age on gender identity does not seem to have been as significant as one might anticipate. The only exception to this seems to be for men old enough to have grown up children who, if they reached the ghettos at all (I can find scant few accounts of such men entering hiding), struggled to find work, particularly given its more physically demanding nature, and, reliant upon their children, often failed completely to reassert their masculinities. For young men without ties and middle-aged men with dependants and greater responsibilities, the ghettos offered a range of ways for masculinities to reassert themselves – for younger men this reassertion often came in the guise of status through youthful action in organizations, resistance or political groups or through work, whilst for older men more commonly employment and provision for family provided the means by which they were able to re-establish the patriarchal *status quo ante.*

Many, particularly young, men, in this period, with limited responsibilities beyond contributing to a family run by one or both parents seem to have found strength and masculinity through the social activities of the ghetto, and in many cases through resistance or resistance-style organizations. This is not to say that they were free to do as they please; many of these young men had, by necessity, to find work both to contribute financially and to ensure their legitimate existence in the ghetto, but evidence suggests that they had enough freedom to involve themselves in ghetto life as well. Dawid Sierakowiak is one good example of this and the combination of his involvement in politics and education clearly contributes to his having a strong masculine identity for some part of his time in the Łódź ghetto.[195] In a different way, the young leader of a group of escapees in the Sutzkever poem, *The House on the Vingri,* who ultimately leaves to join the Polish partisans built his masculine identity around respect for his youth, vigour and his physical strength.

In a few cases the ghettos were even entered with some anticipation by young men for whom they appeared to offer new opportunities.[196] The emigration of many of the upper echelons of Jewish society, particularly Jewish men, before, or at the beginning of, the war seemed to present new potential for a generation eager to test itself away from the antisemitic strictures it had known, and created space for the development of their burgeoning masculinities. Further, statistics concerning the social make-up of ghetto leadership in various cities suggest that whilst the *Judenräte* were peopled by men of experience and standing in the community, the OS tended to be younger men with fewer ties and no social standing of which to speak: a situation which provided an opportunity for young men to cut their teeth and assert themselves.[197] Although life was hard for young people, sources show a good degree of optimism concerning their chances of survival; *Oneg Shabbat* recorded a eulogy given in the ghetto which included the words 'Hear O Jewish Youth! Maybe among you, here in this hall, there is, there are potential Weissenbergs. Do not lose courage! Keep strong and gather power.'[198]

For those young men with premature responsibilities or older men with families to support, the manner of remasculation was often quite different to that experienced by those with fewer ties, but the outcomes were quite similar. Older men seem to have reasserted their masculinities through more traditional avenues: through work and provision, and through knowledge and advice giving. More particularly, this reassertion, upon entering the ghetto seems to have rejuvenated many Jewish men who had become depressed by the deconstruction. Roman Halter clearly described his father before the ghetto as severely depressed and making a limited contribution to the family, however, upon entering the ghetto he was significantly revived, finding work, arranging housing, and, even after being admitted to hospital where he ultimately died, remaining the keeper of the family valuables, and the man to whom they all turned when they needed support. For Leon Wells it was the very act of premature ageing and assumption of responsibility that solidified the reassertion of his masculinity. Writing after he entered the Lvov ghetto and found his two brothers, aged 13 and 15, waiting to be deported in the next *Aktion*, Wells writes, '[t]his was enough. I knew now where my duty lay, what I had to do. First I gave them a proper scolding. Then I looked round the room in dismay'.[199] He goes on from here to write about applying for jobs to provide protection for his family, exactly reflecting the reassertion we see in numerous other cases. Interestingly, it is at this point, where Wells assumes responsibility for his brothers, that he ceases to make his regular references to older men including his father and uncles and their advice. Effectively Wells becomes a man when he takes charge.

One significant difference between men of different ages in the reassertion of masculinity however, can be found in the way in which traditional conflicts of masculinity are described in the sources. Particularly those young men seeking to establish, rather than re-establish, their masculinity appear to have used altered notions of masculinity to promote themselves over their fathers – we can only assume that this meant diminishing their fathers' masculinity in the process, although most sources come from younger men, which makes this hard to prove. William Schiff in the Krakow ghetto provided for both his own family and that of his girlfriend and says of his father '[n]ow it seemed like my daddy was my child, and I was the father. He just cried all day'.[200] As well as assuming responsibilities Schiff seems clear of his right to assume commensurate powers, particularly concerning decision-making in the family. The domination of one masculinity by another, however, whilst damaging to the father, reaffirms in the son the argument that the ghetto was able to provide the required conditions for the practice of masculinity.

Also seeming to assert masculinity through a comparison based upon age, Zelkowicz describes Rumkowski preparing to give his 'give me your children' speech, noting,

> [i]t is immediately, startlingly evident that this man has undergone a transformation in the past few days or hours. His head is stooped, as if he can hardly hold it atop his shoulders; his gaze is lifeless and opaque. We behold a frail old man who can barely put one foot in front of the other – an old man, like the old men who have gathered in this square.[201]

Finally, Władysław Szpilman shows the competition of age in masculinity, when he comments of traders in the Warsaw ghetto, '[o]ld Jews, emaciated beyond recognition, tried to draw your attention to some sort of rags from which they hoped to make money. Young men traded in gold and notes, fighting bitter and rancorous battles over battered watch-cases, the ends of chains, or worn and dirty dollar bills.'[202] That such a comparative approach to gender strengthened the masculine identity of its author is unsurprising if we again consider the role of comparison in male gender identity; however we have no proof of this having adversely affected the masculinities of older men who, on the contrary, seem, in different ways, to assert their own masculine identities through masculinism as successfully as their detractors.

* * *

Writing about life in the ghettos, Lancman noted that '[d]uring this time the will to live was extremely strong and far more intense than normal. While physical strength ebbed, the mind daily conquered death. Hope overcame despair. Illusion blotted out the bitter truth.'[203] Exactly as this comment suggests, something to do with the circumstances of the ghettos allowed some Jewish men to reassert their masculinities, even if only in part or for periods of time. Clearly this reassertion was not universal; moreover, it is more likely to have occurred for Jews in certain circumstances than others, dependent upon, amongst other things, the work they undertook and their responsibilities as providers. Nevertheless, in cases where men were able to find stability, even in the extreme conditions of the ghettos, this stability enabled them more closely to conform to the normative identities toward which they had previously oriented themselves, and, in doing so, successfully to practise their masculinity. Through access to provision, protection and status, even with limitations and restrictions unimaginable before the war, men were able to ignore compromising individual elements of masculine identities and instead, relying on an environment gendered male, assert strong male gender identities.

Where the deconstruction damaged masculinities, both in extreme and more manageable circumstances, simply on the basis of the persistent nature of deconstruction, enclosure enabled Jewish men to reassert strong masculinities, largely regardless of the severity of conditions, based on the reverse: stability. For most men, this stability came in the form of ghetto life, still largely lived within family units, in a daily pattern which partially reflected 'normal' life, and within a Jewish community. Whilst this is clearest in the ghettos, there is also evidence to suggest that where a similar stability could be found in the West, either in hiding or through involvement in certain resistance groups, a similar resurgence of masculine identities was possible through an identification with the same elements of normative masculinities, notably providing and protecting.

Of course many of these reasserted masculinities were not gender identities which would bear much comparison to that which had come before and they should not be understood as objectively strong or consistent gender identities. The strength of masculine identity found in this period was highly transitory, and a man who felt some sense of masculine pride in earning enough money to buy bread, finding that bread to buy and purchasing it, could still be crushed on returning home and finding that it was still nowhere near enough to feed his family. This should not, however, undermine the fact that, for whatever period of time, the circumstances of the ghetto enabled him to successfully perform his masculinity. Of course, the extent to which this masculinity was a product of complete despair must remain an outstanding question. We might imagine that the two were linked; however, very few men write about the connection, and certainly for many men survival was an active effort linked, they believed, to personal 'initiative, courage, taking risks, and disbelief in German promises',[204] rather than imminent collapse, and was something for which Bronowski at least showed a clear masculine pride.

That enclosure saw a short-lived revitalization of male gender identities should not for a minute lead one to underplay the extreme horror of life in the ghettos of German-controlled Poland or the very real threat to life that many, if not most, men faced on a daily basis. Nevertheless, although the Jews were starved, used for forced labour and killed during the period of ghettoization, to fixate on the ultimately hopeless nature of these circumstances would be to overlook the quotidian lives that many lived in the ghetto for months and years, the society they established, the confidence and strength it provided and the gender identities it supported.

4

Masculinity Upheld: Fatherhood and Filial Respect

In her memoirs, Miriam Don explains her survival thus: '[t]he fact that we succeeded in our great escape at all is solely due to the initiative, enterprise, optimism, fighting spirit and determination to succeed against all odds, of just one man: Benjamin Wolf Frankel; Wilek, my father'.[1] Henry Wermuth highlights the 'phenomenal willpower and physical durability of this extraordinary man – my father',[2] and Ben Helfgott repeatedly stresses his great respect for his father's courage 'and the way he simply did not accept defeatism at any time and was always a man of hope and a man of action'.[3] Henry Orenstein describes his father as 'unusually courageous',[4] and Marcel Liebman, on leaving Belgium for France on one of the last trains before the German invasion, notes,

> [t]he fact that we owed it to our father further reinforced the admiring trust which we placed in him at that time. For my part, I maintained this trust throughout the whole course of the war. Thus in my eyes my father embodied strength and wisdom; I never doubted the rightness of the decisions which he took upon himself without ever consulting any of us – my mother least of all.[5]

None of these descriptions of fathers, depicting them as strong, proactive, positive actors in the Holocaust, however, tally with the negative representation of Jewish fathers supplied by historians or even with my own conclusions which show patterns of masculine collapse and reassertion. It is to this contradiction that I turn finally, therefore, to understand what the available representations of fathers, largely written by children, might tell us about the impact of fatherhood on the masculine identities of both fathers and their sons. The image of fathers offered by historians is one which, at its most positive, can be summarized by Lawrence Langer's comment that 'I have found no evidence to suggest that mothers behaved or survived better than fathers',[6] but is rarely so generous. Instead, as with broader conclusions concerning the behaviour of Jewish men in the Holocaust, historians are more likely to follow Zoë Waxman, who tells us of Halina Birenbaum's 'disillusionment' with her father and relates the story of Vladka Meed's father's 'collapse' in the Warsaw ghetto,[7] or Nechama Tec who tells us the sensationalized and notorious story of David Sierakowiak's father stealing food from David and his sister.[8] Importantly, these approaches contrast sharply with representations of mothers who, even more than women in general, offer praise for the attempts women made to protect their children during this period, with Ofer and Weitzman referring to 'the ingenuity and adaptability of women to get food for children in Warsaw', as if fathers played no part in the sourcing of food for their families, or perhaps were simply not adaptable or ingenious in doing so.[9]

In order to illustrate the current historical approach to fatherhood in Jewish masculinity in this period, it is worth considering in some detail the case of David Sierakowiak. Born in Łódź in 1924, David, along with his parents and sister, Natalia, entered the ghetto in 1940. Whilst in the ghetto David continued to write almost daily in a journal documenting his life including his schooling, which continued after he entered the ghetto, work, political affiliations and ongoing conflicts with his family, notably his father. On numerous occasions, David used the journal to rail against his father's behaviour complaining on one occasion that his father was becoming 'greedier and more rapacious for every morsel, he cheats in a stupid, intricate way everywhere he can'. Specifically, he accuses his father of stealing food from him and his sister and causing the premature death of their mother from starvation.[10] Significantly, this and other similar quotations have been used by historians to support their representation of Jewish fathers and men in the Holocaust. One example of this tendency is Nechama Tec, who references the Sierakowiak case repeatedly and includes in her index an entry of 'fathers stealing food from children', as if it were a regular occurrence (which it may have been, but for which she provides no other evidence).[11]

In spite of some clearly reprehensible behaviour on the part of Sierakowiak Sr, however, any reading of this diary which uses it to reinforce the notion that Jewish fathers behaved in a weak or emasculated way during the Holocaust goes too far. Not only are these behaviours not representative of fathers in general, but more importantly I would suggest that Sierakowiak Sr is a perfect example of a father who, whilst experiencing moments of depression and poor parenting, also had periods of rejuvenation when he provided for and protected his children, acts for which he clearly received his son's grudging respect. This incident and others aside, the bulk of David Sierakowiak's diary catalogues his father's relatively successful attempts to find work and money to keep the family alive, both in and out of the ghetto.[12] According to his son, when Sierakowiak Sr was out of work, despite being 'suffocated' at home, he either spent time petitioning the council to allow him to sell family furniture to make money for food or was out looking for food and work for himself and his family. On 15 July 1941, David comments, 'Say what you will, you can't reproach him for laziness. He would be happy to do anything to provide bread for us.'[13] After the food-stealing episode David admitted that 'Neither his [his father's] willingness to wash my shirts nor his speed in buying all kinds of food rations and allocations are able to mollify me,'[14] suggesting that David's problems with his father existed somewhat separately from his daily performance as a father. For the most part, therefore, and in contrast to the historical record, David Sierakowiak acknowledged his father's role as patriarch of the family and his continued ability to provide for his family and fulfill his role as father and protector in extreme circumstances.

Finally, problematically, the approach to fatherhood and masculinity which condemns Sierakowiak Sr relies on the idea that only positive and unselfish behaviours can be understood as assertions of masculine or paternal identity. However, whilst stealing food surreptitiously is unlikely to make one feel masculine, the exercise of paternal power might – and those men who are given a larger share of rations than their wives or children, based either on their size, workload or simply upon their role within the family (and such men are much more commonly referenced in diaries than the stealing variety) – might well have used this confirmation of their status in the home to reinforce their masculine identities, abhorrent as the unfairness of the act might have been to their offspring. Outrageous as his son may have found it, Sierakowiak Sr may, we do not know, have considered it his right either as the head of the house, as the breadwinner or simply as a man to receive larger rations than his wife and children.

However, even the most optimistic analysis of masculine identity does not do justice to the extracts with which I began this chapter, and the question remains as to whether, leaving these quotations aside, the masculinities of fathers and fatherhood responded to the horrors of the Holocaust in the same way as broader male gender identities or whether an alternative trajectory for both behaviour and gender identity can be traced. Covering the same time periods and events as the previous two chapters and relying instead on the basic premise, already established, that the female gendered environment of the deconstruction and the male gendered environment of the ghettos and enclosure were as much a reality for fathers as for men more generally, this chapter will attempt to answer that question.

* * *

Fatherhood carries with it, however, some of its own theoretical concerns which impact on the answer to this question, key amongst which is an understanding of the particular practice of fatherhood in the period in question. Traditionally the early- to mid-twentieth century is seen as belonging to a pre-contemporary time when fathers were emotionally distant from their children and the sphere in which they resided, the home, and instead functioned largely in the public/work sphere, performing their duties as fathers through a relatively detached approach to provision and protection. Recently, however, debates amongst historians and sociologists, writing both about this period and earlier, have suggested that fathers might better be understood, allowing for large differences based on location, circumstances and employment, as being more closely involved in child-rearing and domestic life than previously thought.[15] To add complexity, Charlie Lewis has argued that a lack of longitudinal studies of fatherhood makes it hard to draw any firm conclusions about gendered parental behaviour at all,[16] whilst some sociologists have argued for a distinction to be made between different acts performed by fathers. Significantly, such an approach argues that whilst fathers may have been involved in the home for several decades, for example playing with children and helping with housework, these men were viewed as doing women's work.[17] This notion of the gendering of tasks then begs the question whether those men who were involved in the home might still have understood their gender identities as men and fathers to be entirely based around providing and protecting, even if the actuality of their fathering was much greater.[18]

Beyond these questions concerning the nature of twentieth-century fatherhood there are other concerns around sources. Since employment, sustenance and shelter were of central importance to survival in the ghetto, and therefore to delaying deportation and possibly thus surviving the camps, those fathers who were able to provide shelter and food for themselves and their children are necessarily more likely to have survived to record their stories than those fathers who were unable to provide such basic provisions. Similarly, Western European fathers who were unable to organize either successful hiding places or emigration opportunities are unlikely to have surviving children in a position to document their experiences. Consequently, that the majority of the available accounts involve men who continued to successfully perform elements of their roles as fathers during periods of the Holocaust is unsurprising.

Attempting to understand fatherhood, however, presents another problem, clearest in Poland where survival rates were highest amongst young men who were able to work for longest in the ghettos and camps. The age of these men means that their fathers were likely to have been relatively old during the Holocaust. In order, therefore, to have relevant testimonies relating to paternal behaviour it is necessary not only that the father was young enough to work during the Holocaust, and thereby to survive for any period, but also that his child was old enough to survive. This issue is further complicated by the fact that, once men became fathers themselves, they were very unlikely to write about or reference their own fathers, either positively or negatively. The older generations tend either not to be mentioned or to be viewed as irrelevant: depicted as slightly doddery or as a liability by their adult children and more positively, but as equally unimportant, by their grandchildren.[19] The bulk of the examples we have, therefore, are from men who were fathers of young children or from teenaged children of fathers in their fifties, a limited sample which necessarily restricts our ability to analyse and understand fatherhood.

Most problematic, however, is the nature of representations of the father by children and wives and the impact of these relationships upon masculine identities, any analysis of which should take seriously Lorna McKee and Margaret O'Brien's stress on the 'dialectical influence of parent on child and child on parent',[20] particularly in the maintenance of patriarchal roles in changing economic and cultural conditions. In particular, one should consider the ways in which children represent their fathers and whether any pattern in these representations might cast doubt on the reliability of their accounts as sources for study. The respect so obvious from children for their fathers during the Holocaust begins in most testimonies in the preceding period with children keen to stress their father's status within society during peace time. Testimonies refer to intelligence, as in the case of Marylou Ruhe who describes her father as 'very, very smart, he was my hero ... he was a genius',[21] to community standing, as with Orenstein who notes that his father ' was smart and energetic, and soon people began to take notice of the hard-driving young newcomer who often beat his competitors to the punch. It was not long before he won their respect and even admiration',[22] or, uncommonly, to physicality, as in Zuckerman's description of his father as 'a tall man with a small beard, and he held himself erect. I think it was Mordechai Tennenbaum who told me that if you had put a bucket of water on his head, not a single drop would have fallen to the ground.'[23] Many also mention the skill and intelligence of their fathers with particular reference to the First World War, most likely due to its significance to the circumstances in which they again found themselves. Liebman is one example of this, writing of his father's incarceration in a German camp in the First World War: '[w]ith his perfect knowledge of German, his considerable ingenuity, and a flair for organisation matched by a highly energetic sense of duty, he had become one of the camp leaders'.[24] Even amongst less than positive descriptions of fathers, in which stress is placed on a patriarchal or even dictatorial streak in fathers, the masculinities of the fathers do not seem to be in question.[25]

These largely positive descriptions of fathers and their masculinities continue into discussions of the Holocaust proper and most are keen to stress that, even where their fathers lost their factories or employment, they were able to make the most of the situation to provide financial support for the family; where firms were Aryanized, this tended to have been negotiated for the benefit of the family and many retained at home the means to continue making a living after they could no longer work officially.[26] Wermuth references his 'heroic father',[27] Ruszka Zar writes, '[a]s for my father he was bold, resourceful, daring, and already familiar with the intricacies of life as a fugitive',[28] and Helfgott describes in detail, and with great pride, his father smuggling flour into the ghetto, making money and protecting his family from the realities of ghetto life.[29]

The question remains, however, whether such praise can be accepted at face value, or should be understood as a tendency to lionize a dead parent.[30] And whilst there is no final answer to this question, it is significant that this degree of overt lionization seems less common in writing about mothers who died during the Holocaust than fathers, a distinction which perhaps indicates at least an element of truth in the picture of fathers painted by these sources. Ultimately, to dismiss widespread appreciation of men as unwarranted hero worship, whilst using positive comments concerning women at the same time to prove their resilience and gendered strength during the Holocaust, as historians have been happy to do, would be to apply a problematic double standard.

Understanding this evidence is further complicated by the interplay between mothers and fathers, both in their own accounts and in those written by children. One example of this is the tendency amongst fathers to play down the actions of their wives in the care of their children and, although our capacity to corroborate these sources is very limited, in the case of Martin Parker, already mentioned briefly, we can do exactly that. Throughout his lengthy testimony, Parker stresses his wife's weakness and his own action in supporting the family during this time,[31] recounting an occasion on which the entire family was called to the *Umschlagplatz* in the Warsaw ghetto. Whilst Halina particularly relates her mother's role in keeping her alive on this occasion, Parker hardly mentions his wife, stressing instead his own role in saving Halina and in threatening a man who endangered her life. In her own testimony Halina also noted an occasion on which, during a period in hiding, her father requested that her mother buy him a German newspaper every day, something which she did, thereby risking her life on a daily basis. Halina goes on to note that she does not even think that her father considered the risk to his wife's life, suggesting a lack of connection between the parents as joint providers or protectors. In a similar way, Leon Greenman, a British-Dutch Jew living in Amsterdam with a Dutch wife, was held for some time in Westerbork[32] with his wife, child and father, before being deported; however in accounts he hardly mentions his wife or her role in their lives at this time. There is no way to corroborate or question Leon Greenman's testimony, and certainly the loss of his wife and child in Auschwitz should be factored into his reasons for not discussing them in detail; nonetheless it is worth considering how this account might look had anyone else lived to tell their story.[33]

Also significant to understanding the representation of parents is the fact that children have a tendency to elevate the importance of one parent over the other, almost as if in recording their testimonies they feel forced to choose a dominant parent in the fact of their survival. Ben Helfgott talks at length about his father before realizing that he has omitted to mention his mother and specifically noting that she too was wonderful, but that his father's struggle was more a 'part of the whole struggle and survival'. Helfgott clearly feels bad about his dismissal of his mother, but does not feel he can do justice to both parents.[34] Likewise, Nicole David makes a direct comparison between her feelings about her mother's disappearance – she just didn't think about it – and her occasional visits to see her father to whom she was particularly attached.[35] Lea Goodman reacts similarly, talking at length about the way in which she was affected by the lack of a father – how she missed him and envied other girls who had fathers. In contrast she speaks very little of her mother who was with her in hiding but who suffered a mental breakdown during the period.[36] Finally, Marcel Hipszman records surprise that although until her deportation in the Vel d'Hiv round-up he spent most of his life with his mother in Paris – his father being away for many months at a time working as a logger to avoid detection by the French or German governments – he has almost no memories of her but retains strong memories of his father from various stages of his childhood.[37] Of course there is no simple explanation for this different presentation of fathers and mothers, but it is worth considering in attempting to grapple with questions of fatherhood and the practice of masculinity.

Finally, one should consider the dialectic relationships between children, particularly sons, and their fathers and the impact of this dialectic on male gender identities, since, notably, accounts written by children predominantly tell us about the way in which the author perceives their father's masculinity, rather than the direct impact of events on the masculinity of their father. If we agree with McKee and O'Brien about the dialectic relationship, then we might argue that the very fact of a son's clear respect for his father's masculine performance in the Holocaust would have affirmed the masculinity of his father by providing him with status and respect, and in itself tells us something about the gender identity of his father. It is on this basis that I shall use such sources, carefully, as a way of understanding the impact of the Holocaust on the masculine identities of fathers. I shall seek, however, to ascertain whether the impact of the dialectic relationship is the same for all elements of masculinity, normative or individual, or whether the respect of a child is only significant where it is matched by some other influence contributing to paternal, masculine, self-respect.

* * *

It is the loss of fathers which provokes some of the most keenly felt emotional responses in diaries from the wartime and shows the ongoing importance of these male figures in the lives of children and young men. Yitzchak Rudashevski, talking of his friend Gabik's loss of his father, a respected and learned man, commented, 'Gabik no longer has a father. I sensed how much misfortune inheres in this world. How will Gabik see it through, he who is so gay, so frivolous?'[38] Gabik seems to be in his late teens and is employed and yet Rudashevski seems to question his capacity to function without a father, such was the importance of this relationship. In another case David Rubinowicz refers to children of a neighbouring family as orphans and questions their ability to survive, although they still have a mother, such is the importance he places on the role played by fathers in the ghetto in the protection and survival of children.[39] Julius Feldman's final words in his diary before being deported, although he has lost many other family members, are indicative of this particular reliance on the father: '[h]ow terribly I feel the lack of my beloved father, whom everyone knew'[40]. This line is interrupted and it is highly unlikely that he knew he was to be deported and meant it as the final words it became, nonetheless it clearly highlights the central role his father played in his life. In very similar circumstances, the final line of Vladka Meed's diary has the same focus and, despite hardly mentioning her father throughout the diary, since he had died of pneumonia soon after entering the ghetto, she writes, '[n]othing. Nothing was left me of my past, of my life in the ghetto – not even the grave of my father.'[41] This chapter seeks to understand whether this pride, love and respect for fathers and for their masculinities that we see in the testimonies and diaries of so many children can be found reflected in the masculinities of their fathers during the Holocaust and how this ties to our understanding of Jewish masculinities in the Holocaust more generally.

Normative masculinities

Protection took any number of forms during the Holocaust, but one of the most fundamental was the advice given by fathers to their children and to which many children directly attributed their survival. Particular to fathers – I can find not a single example relating to mothers – diaries and testimonies from the Holocaust are littered with pieces of advice offered by fathers that children used to protect themselves. Jan Hartman remembers, '[m]y father, who was a hunter, told me, "[y]ou remember how a hare can survive when the chain of hunters comes. If the hare jumps and runs zigzag they will get him; but if the hare stays in his little hole, it will survive. You remember that".'[42] Hartman later comments, '[t]hat was the rule that helped my brother and me survive: never volunteer for anything.'[43] Similarly Checinski, following a fight, relates how his father suggested he avoid antisemitism, '[y]our best protection is never to show the slightest weakness, either physical or spiritual'. Showing the ongoing significance of this lesson Checinski goes on to comment, '[m]aybe, this is why I managed to survive the darkest days in the history of mankind.'[44] Again in almost identical circumstances, Zar recounts how, whilst posing as a gentile, several people guessed that she was a Jew. After one such encounter she noted 'I laughed and thought of my father's words: "[n]ever show fear to your enemies, because if they think you are afraid of them, they are absolutely merciless. Instead, attack your attacker. Always do the unexpected." Once again he was right. For the second time I owed him my life.'[45] The first time is recorded in the title and frontispiece of Zar's book and reads, '*If you're ever on the run and have to hide, the best place is right in the mouth of the wolf.* Herman Guterman's advice to his daughter Ruszka'.

Also recording the words of his father in the title of his book, Wermuth wrote *Breathe Deeply My Son*, whose title he later explained when writing about his arrival in Auschwitz:

> [i]nto this onslaught of unstoppable, alternating interplay of visions and fear I heard my father's voice. He sounded so dispassionate, so naturally cool as if he were offering me advice on how to behave at a dinner table. He then uttered the unforgettable words which I have chosen as the title to this book: '[s]hould we be gassed, breathe deeply, my son, breathe deeply, to get it over with quickly.'[46]

Unlike the other examples, Wermuth Sr is not attempting here to save his son's life and yet he is very clearly still trying to protect him, even if the only remaining way to do that is to afford him a better death. Last is the case of Benno Benima, where the exact words of advice are not recorded, and yet their impact is much the same as if they had been. In his testimony Benima repeatedly describes a single occasion in Amsterdam, some time after the German invasion, when he wished to go out in the evening with friends. Without clearly explaining why, Benima's father refused to let him go out, keeping him in the house for the entire evening. They found out the next day that on the evening before 200 young men had been rounded up in the streets and deported to labour camps. None of them were ever to return. In his recounting Benima makes it very clear that he believes had he gone out that night he would also now be dead, and very clearly attributes his survival to his father's wisdom.[47]

Each of the cases described is recounted by a child who seems clearly to value, rather than question, their father's role in their protection and survival. It is harder to be clear about the extent to which this attribution of survival to paternal advice was significant to the masculinity of fathers, but it is worth noting that not only was this advice seen as protective by children but also in most cases the advice was clearly delivered with the intention of offering protection. For some, we can speculate, therefore, that simply the act of offering protective advice would have reinforced their normative masculine identity, and for those who were able to see their children apply such advice or use it to survive, this might have been far stronger.

For many more, although advice was not so clearly imparted to protect, it remained a key element of the mental, and sometimes physical, survival of, overwhelmingly, male children in the Holocaust. Stanley Faull attributes his survival to his father's decision not to emigrate before the war but to remain in their home commenting,

> 'look we are going through a difficult period but that is going to end and there is going to be normality', my father said. And he was the only person I looked up to and what my father said this must be right, this is the way I was brought up. So therefore it was an inbuilt thing, well I've got to survive because dad said so.[48]

Also stressing the importance of the advice of a father, Oskar Rosenfeld comments, '[w]hen my father appears in my dream, it means something good is going to happen. Therefore, the danger of being deported now has passed. I can feel it, I know it',[49] whilst Frank quotes his father from early in the Holocaust when the family is lined up for deportation: '[m]y son, I'm sure you'll be the one that'll survive and you'll tell the world what really happened with us. I don't know what will happen with us, if we are going to live or we're going to die, but I can tell you, I had the feeling that you will be there, you will survive, and you will tell the world what really happened to us, to the Jews'.[50] In contrast to these cases, Rubinowicz makes the importance of fatherly advice clear when he mourns the absence of his own father on going to pray at Whitsun.[51] Noting that most young men were there with their fathers and so could ask if they forgot the words to the prayer, he asks 'who is there to tell me?'[52] These comments cannot be directly related to the masculinities of the fathers to whom they refer, since in many cases the father could not have understood their comments as advice giving, and yet they are perhaps relevant in relation to the father–son dialectic. The appreciation and respect these men, then boys, would have shown for their fathers and their advice might well have had an impact upon the masculinities of their fathers.

For the most part, however, paternal protection and provision, particularly, but not exclusively, in the ghettos, were achievable and achieved through traditional methods. Fathers organized housing, found hiding places and provided food and protection for their families through working, smuggling and sustained negotiation and effort. One of very few such clear examples from the West, Otto Berets records his own experiences in Holland during the Holocaust whilst in hiding and supporting his wife and two children. In his interview, when speaking of his struggle to educate his daughter satisfactorily at home, Berets is asked in what ways he could be a father during the period. Without hesitating Berets responds, 'I was not a father, I was a protector.' He then expands on this, explaining that his fathering was almost entirely channelled into protection, something at which he considered himself extremely successful.[53] More often, however, these accounts of fatherhood come from children, as when George Weiss writes of his wartime experiences as a child, largely spent in Belgium often without his father who was interned as a German national. At one point Weiss describes his flight to Abbeville with his mother who was subsequently badly wounded in a bombing raid and hospitalized. These events left Weiss alone and homeless until his father came and found him, something which Weiss describes with some awe as 'a miracle', and returned the family to Belgium. Weiss's father later found hiding for the whole family and Weiss notes of the period in general, 'people didn't have food, but with my father there was always food to eat'.[54]

Similarly, writing of the events of the deconstruction, Wermuth describes his father being unemployed, having recently been released from jail, and his mother losing her bread round. Money was extremely tight and so Henry stole some food from their hosts in order to help his family. He then comments: 'I had not, however, reckoned with the resilience of my dear father. Somehow, for the next few months, we ate; not opulently, hardly ever a piece of meat, but we did not starve.'[55] Despite his father's provision of food, however, Henry is clear to note that this did not mean his father did not experience pain and upset, commenting that '[f]ear of penury, hunger, homelessness was gnawing at every parent's heart'.[56] Similarly Ruhe acknowledged the damage their situation was causing her father: '[p]hysically, he was going down somewhat. Mentally, of course he wasn't quite the same as he had been before.' And yet she still lauded his masculinism commenting, 'but he kept up his spirits, he was very protective of me, very, very protective. We were very close together. Father had a watch and sold bits of it to make money'. Even fathers who were not necessarily expected to perform well in such conditions are praised for their efforts – Meir Bakalchuk in the Dereczin Memorial book records how his father saved the town priest from the Communists noting, 'I knew my father as a scholar, who always had learning on his mind. I never saw a hero in him. Every disturbance filled him with fear. It was therefore a wonderment to me, as to where he got so much courage in those difficult months of the Dereczin community'.[57]

For many fathers, as with all men, simply going to work, a clear act of provision, seems to have been key to the masculine assertion of fathers. Raymond-Raoul Lambert discussed his own work, reinforcing his career choices by asserting that his ultimate aim was protection of, and provision for, his family and linking career advancement directly to his role in the family in his comment that '[b]efore all this happened I had the greatest reward of my social work career, which allows me to envisage a future of maximum security for my wife, my children, and myself'.[58] Even in cases where fathers did not need to work, employment seems to have been a positive option. For example, Moshe Flinker's father returned to work ultimately because it was agreed that the activity would be positive for the whole family, even though it was in no way a financial requirement.[59] Finally, in considering attempts to provide and protect we must include efforts which, although potentially damaging in hindsight, would, at the time, have fed into the masculinity of the man involved, through his ability to perform his normative identity. One example of this is Kaplan's recording of a man who removed his son's name from a list of Jews designated for emigration, believing that the greatest danger was for his son's name to be on any list in the hands of the Nazis.[60] We do not know the outcome of this choice but the act itself, regardless of its outcome, might well have contributed to the reinforcement of his masculinity. Similarly, Lambert made a very clear, active decision that his children would not be separated from him. In describing this choice, he noted, '[m]y instinct is to have absolute faith in the future, and duty compels me to be the last to leave the ship. My wife and children are not to be separated from me',[61] clearly associating the decision with his role as a patriarch and thereby showing the connection between the protective decision and his gender identity.

One example both of protecting and of providing in the ghettos, particular to fathers, can be seen in those who needed their children to work, either to help support the family or because they felt that being a worker would better protect their child. In such cases it was not uncommon for men to find work placements for their sons in their own organizations, something which links to ideas of inheritance and descent, but also placed fathers in a position to continue protecting their sons. Rudashevski noted that his friend Gabik, whose father had recently died, inherited his father's job in the library[62] – something which Gabik's father had established for him by employing him in a lower job in the library during his life. Julius Feldman's father organized work for his son in the municipal garden in the ghetto, an achievement which would have reinforced his masculinity not only by finding work for his son but in the protection he afforded his son by finding him a relatively untaxing, safe and pleasant job.[63] Wermuth's father found work for himself and his son in a sign-painting workshop (although this was later, once they were in the camp Klaj)[64] and Ben Helfgott's father, at his son's request, used his influence to find his son work in a glass factory despite his own misgivings and the fact that he had already made other plans for the family to leave the ghetto.[65] As Helfgott tells the story, someone suggested that the factory was no longer recruiting so he demanded that his father get him the work in order to 'prove to them what a marvellous man my father is'. His father initially refused but Helfgott replied, 'I have already told my friends that you can fix it and you are not going to let me down' and so the work was found. Later when the work proved too hard and Helfgott was beaten his father arranged a bribe to ensure him an easier position in the same factory.[66]

Many of these examples, but particularly the work that Helfgott Sr found for his son, overlap with the third element of masculinism, status, the loss of which through humiliation was as common to fathers as to other men, particularly for those humiliated in front of their children, as in the case of Barbara Stimler's father who was made to dance and then beaten.[67] Stimler notes the humiliation of this event not only for her father but for herself and her mother, with the assault on her father representing an assault on the pride of the entire family. But in the case of Helfgott particularly we also see the capacity of fathers to reassert their status through reference to their children. Not only is Ben Helfgott's boast about his father's ability to get him work in the glass factory beneficial to his own masculinity but it reinforces that of his father.[68] That his father had already made other plans for the whole family which he put on hold to fulfil his son's request, and thereby prove his own power, shows the importance of such reassurance for his own identity.

The importance of children in the establishment of male status is apparent in the way in which children write about their fathers and we repeatedly see children noting the power and status of their fathers, particularly within the ghetto, as a source of pride. Rena Zabielak describes how, in collaboration with the Order Service, her father opened a sweet shop in the Warsaw ghetto. Through this shop he was able to earn enough money to keep the family in some luxury for a period during the war. In recording this story, however, Zabielak is keen to note how her father's wealth enabled him to support others in their building and to hand out sweets to starving children on his way home from work, thus asserting his status and his position within the community.[69] Sara Zyskind also writes proudly of her father's status within the ghetto as she was saved from deportation by the Chief of Police who knew her father.[70] For Elie Wiesel, whose relationship with his father was more strained than most, his father's status, not only in the wider family, but more broadly in the community and later in the ghetto, was a key point of pride. Wiesel bore a grudging respect for this side of his father, and those aspects of his father's character which he considered problematic do more to assert his father's strong masculinity than to question it.[71]

For a few like Wiesel and Efrat-Feldman, writing in the Dereczin Memorial book, the status of fathers within the ghetto community impacted clearly on masculine identities, and Efrat-Feldman notes, '[d]uring the first days of the Nazi occupation, my father once again proved adept at protecting the interests of the Jewish community'.[72] These assertions were most common once inside the ghettos, and for some, a previously absent masculinity based on status could even be created in the ghetto. Lancman writes with some surprise of his father's plan in the ghetto to march typhoid sufferers toward the main gate, writing '[w]hatever we may think of his plan today, the seed of rebellion was planted and the idea itself was something new and heartening'.[73]

I have written elsewhere about the importance of descent, particularly to those men with culturally Jewish normative masculinities, however, in relation to fathers there is a notable shift in emphasis from descent as a historical phenomenon (i.e. the focus on one's forebears) to a focus on the future and the extent to which, through having children, one has become part of history. Not only is this emphasis clear in the examples of life-saving advice discussed above, where the advice and guidance offered by fathers become an integral part of the survival and future of their families, effectively securing for them a place in posterity, but also through parting words, comforting ideas and discussion that appear repeatedly in the sources. Several parents, when they believe they may be parted from their children, offer words of advice, directly linked to religious heritage. David Kahane records passing advice to his three-year-old daughter, a gift of heritage which matters a great deal to Kahane, particularly since he is a rabbi and she is going into hiding with a Christian family, writing, '[l]ook well, my little girl, let this sight be etched deeply into your memory. Do not forget you are a daughter of Israel, the daughter of Holy people'.[74] Similarly, in a poem addressed to a daughter, Simcha Bunim Shayevitsh wrote,

> The evil day has arrived.
> The evil hour has arrived,
> When I must teach you, a little girl,
> The terrible *parshe* of *Lekh Lekho*.
> The poem goes on,
> And not understand that in our blood
> Flows the power of our forefathers
> Who in all generations
> Performed all kinds of sacrifices.[75]

Finally, practical acts of descent where a father passes to his son responsibility for the family are rare but important. In the case of Michael Diment this was decision-making responsibility whilst his father was in jail,[76] whereas for Marcel Liebman it involved assuming a protective role over his brothers whilst continuing to report to his father in the form of letters.[77]

Whilst this sense amongst fathers of establishing the past in the future, a continuity relevant to their own masculine identities and that of their sons, is particularly clear amongst those men likely to have oriented themselves strongly, if not uniquely, toward a Jewish normative masculinity, it is also apparent to a lesser degree amongst those with more assimilated lives. Notable amongst these is Rosenfeld, who, whilst involved in the Jewish community before the war, lived a relatively assimilated life in Austria, drew on discussions of generations, descent and children in writing, '[s]hould we want to be smarter than our ancestors? They went into the fire. For us, for us who are alive today. And our children here won't want to be smarter than us, their fathers ... This is how it will go generation to generation.'[78] Equally, Perechodnik, a secular Jew with a disdain for religious Judaism, stressed the importance of descent and heritage, this time particularly of a male child, when his brother-in-law died and Perechodnik noted his own envy that he died with a son since 'he does not wholly die'.[79]

This infiltration of the particularly Jewish emphasis on heritage and descent into other normative masculinities suggests the possibility of a fourth normative masculine identity – paternal masculinity – an idea reinforced by John Tosh who argues for understanding the relevance of personal, non-financial inheritance in the masculine identities of both fathers and their sons. Specifically, Tosh argues, the passing on of a heritage of family achievement, in whatever form, acts to establish a son's masculinity whilst the act of establishing a son's masculinity both reinforces that of the father, as a creator of men, in the present and establishes it for the future, as a patriarch.[80] In this way, descent and heritage become not only relevant but also central to the masculinities of all fathers in a way that is not significant to childless men, and suggests the existence of a separate normative identity.

This suggestion is reinforced by the behaviour of fathers who found themselves without their children during the Holocaust. Sources show that many such men, in spite of the absence of their own children, found themselves continuing to perform as fathers, since that role was central to their identities. Describing this phenomenon Ringelblum cites the example of Gepner, who was highly placed in the Warsaw ghetto administration, and who behaved in a fatherly way to many children in the ghetto, although his own had escaped, noting, '[t]he policies of Gepner's Food Supply Agency are scandalous and deserve special treatment. But Gepner, who is now childless (his children have left the country), pours out all his fatherly feelings on other children. He has become the great patron of children in the ghetto'.[81] Ringelblum also writes of the 'tragedy of families: thousands of men without wives, men who have remained alive and don't know what they are living for',[82] hinting at the idea that once one has become a parent one's identity changes and cannot be reversed. Moreover, numerous sources speak of men who when no longer able to protect their own children risked their lives to save those of family or friends and there is a clear sense that once a man has children that fact becomes key to his identity. Notably, such men are rarely described without a reference to the number of children they have as in Ringelblum's comment, 'three Jews were killed ... one of them a refugee who was the father of eight children'.[83] Martin Parker offers another clear example of the permanent impact of being a parent and as he repeatedly makes it clear that the existence of his daughter, that is, his role as a father, was significant in increasing his desire to struggle and survive.[84]

As having children changes the masculine identity toward which a man orients himself, so it also changes his practised masculinity. For some fathers, protection and provision were a reflex rather than a choice and such behaviours were instinctive rather than selective. Corni translated the anonymous diary of a young girl in the Łódź ghetto which describes a father sharing his rations with his child; she notes: '[d]espite everything a father is a father. He … gets two soups there and he gives one to me'.[85] Similarly, Zyskind, who lives alone with her father for some time after her mother's death, records numerous examples of her father's instinctive parenting and the pride she feels in it. Not only does her father give her most of his own food, telling her that it only makes him more hungry; however, when she goes to him, very ill in hospital, to explain that she is being deported, he demands his clothes, dresses and leaves with her for deportation. It is clear that there is little that he can do, but his need to protect nonetheless compels him to accompany her.[86]

Individual elements of masculinities

It is, however, the individual elements of masculine identity which offer the most interesting insight into the masculinities of both fathers and their sons during the Holocaust. Outside of normative masculine identities and formed by a host of factors – ranging from the individual's early experiences to the form of their body – these individual elements, which seem to be of as limited relevance to the masculinities of fathers as I have shown them to be to the masculinities of all Jewish men in this period, are nevertheless significant to children. This is particularly the case where fathers became less able to perform the normative elements of their masculinities during the Holocaust, since these individual elements nevertheless allowed children to sustain respect for their fathers and their gender identities. Chief amongst these individual elements, general advice, knowledge and support by fathers were all used by children to reinforce their belief in, adherence to, and respect for their fathers.

Beyond the role of life-saving advice in the sustaining of gender identities, however, separate attention must be paid to the display of knowledge, whether in the form of facts or in the form of advice about almost any subject, through which sons displayed their respect for their fathers. Wells records his father's words early on in the deconstruction when he asks for advice:

> [h]e did not wish to advise me. 'Whatever I suggest may bring about your misfortune. I should reproach myself bitterly all my life were I to give you some advice that would prove to your disadvantage. In such times as ours one cannot listen to anyone's advice; not even to one's own father or mother. Rely on your own sense as up to now. Trust in God as you have done so far, and all will end well'.[87]

Although it does not display any particular element of masculinity on the part of his father – on the contrary, the refusal to engage with his son's request for clear parenting might be considered a failure of a fatherly masculinity – Wells credits the response in some way with the making of his own masculinity and highlights the wisdom of his father. Likewise, Zar records much of what her father says in direct quotation marks, in contrast to the lack of comments she notes from her mother, clearly viewing his words with particular significance, even if she gives no suggestion that they were equally beneficial to her father.

Another example of the passing on of wisdom or knowledge as reinforcing the esteem in which children held their fathers, is the case of Alex Meijer, who spent much of his time, whilst hiding on a Dutch farm, bonding with his father by learning skills including how to milk a cow. In this sustained practice and the way in which he speaks about this time spent with his father, Meijer offers a clear example of the transmission of knowledge benefitting the developing masculinity of a son and his appreciation of his father.[88] The frequency with which these exchanges are mentioned in Alex's diaries is of particular significance and underlines both their importance to Alex and the power of his father's patriarchal presence in his development. In a similar fashion, Otto Frank acted as a point of wisdom and knowledge for his children once in hiding, assuming a patriarchal role, organizing rotas and choosing study topics for the children in order to increase their learning and avoid boredom. Significantly, in the case of Frank, we can see that such a transfer of knowledge directly impacted on the masculinity of the father since, as discussed already, hiding seemed to offer Otto Frank a strength, calm and purpose that he had lacked before the family went into hiding.[89] The fact that the knowledge transmitted is not advice directly pertaining to the Holocaust, in contrast to most examples in the ghettos, is explained in these cases since the families, both in hiding in the West, whilst being in constant danger, do not seem to have felt the same imminent threat that was clear to those in the ghettos. This limited security then provided the time and space available for a broader education and development of masculinity than was possible for those in the ghettos.

The notion of fathers being respected for their wisdom extends beyond this life advice, to include more factual ideas of knowledge. Respect for paternal opinion can be found particularly in relation to the war effort, on which subject sons often cite their fathers in a display of clearly gendered respect and pride. This is of significance since, in many cases, knowledge would have been gathered from illegal radios to which the whole family were listening; its attribution almost uniquely to fathers, therefore, is indicative of the power with which the father remains imbued in the eyes of his children. Meijer is again a clear example of this phenomenon as, throughout his years in hiding, he listens to the radio in the cupboard, as do other members of the family; however, he cites only, and regularly, his father's opinion regarding the progress of the war.[90] Moreover, where knowledge about the war effort is attributed to fathers its impact is twofold, since not only is the father's masculinity confirmed by his knowledge and intellect but he is the bearer of news which, at several points, had the effect of lightening the mood for Jewish families.[91] As bearers of such 'truth', fathers, far from being depressed figures, were given the power of supplying optimism and positivity. When asked if his father had lost hope during their time in the ghetto, Helfgott said that his father and his father's friends were, on the contrary, armchair politicians convinced that the Germans would lose the war.[92] Notable here is, once again, not only the knowledge attached to his father but also the positive connotations that his father's opinions therefore carried. Another example of this can be seen in the case of Diment, who keenly notes that it is his father's knowledge which allows them to build a mill to grind wheat in the ghetto and thereby make flour.[93] This development is significant not only for the survival of his family but of many others and Diment notes the rage of the Germans on finding the mill as a matter of pride.

Even in the case of sons who question their father's authority and character, a respect for power and knowledge can be found. Flinker shows his respect for his father by speaking through his father when he wishes to assert something. Reflecting exactly this, when Flinker disagrees with his mother he notes, '[m]y father gave her a similar answer whenever she broached the subject to him'.[94] Feldman, showing the power of his father's words, quotes his father even when the subject is distasteful to him, regardless of content. In attempting to understand his own descent and patriarchal heritage he comments, 'Why? Because I was a Jew. "Because", as my father put it, "a Jewish mother gave birth to me".'[95] Whilst his father seems almost to have been negating his own role in his son's descent and current predicament, it is notable that his son still chooses to impart this 'wisdom' through his father and does not do so with any bitterness or anger.

Such identification with the words of their fathers can also be seen in the writing of female children in this period. Notable in this regard are the writings of Etty Hillesum, a well-educated Dutch Jew, in her mid-twenties by the time of the German invasion, who recorded her experiences during the Holocaust in a series of diaries, noting particularly the intensification of anti-Jewish measures and her corresponding interest in religious matters. Hillesum's diaries show an increasing respect for her father and his behaviour as the Holocaust progresses, detailing how, prior to the outbreak of war, she had found both her parents extremely trying, but following the German invasion she saw a change in her father. One example of this can be seen in Hillesum's recording of her father as saying, '[o]ne should be thankful, nowadays, each day the sun shines and one is still at large. At least that's what I tell other people all the time'.[96] Whilst she prefaces this by referring to him as 'my poor father' the 'poor' is not pity that he has misunderstood something, but more pity that he has understood it so well. This is, after all, quite akin to her own philosophy for managing events. Hillesum's respect for her father seems to grow in light of the way in which he managed his experiences in the Holocaust, and this wry but honest aphorism can be seen as proof of a respect for him and, as in other cases, a note of her father as a source of wisdom or truth. This is reinforced by a later account of a conversation with her father in which she relates that '[l]ast time I saw my father, we went for a walk in the dusty, sandy wasteland: he is so sweet and wonderfully resigned … We may suffer, but we must not succumb'.[97] Although she sees him as resigned, this is not a negative quality for Hillesum. Rather the comment, 'We may suffer, but we must not succumb' is effectively a homily that she has learnt from her father.[98]

In a very different way, many children found respect for fathers and their masculinity through paternal displays of love and devotion, although for the fathers in question these can be damaging as much as they are positive and there is no clear link between them and paternal masculine identities. Writing in the Dereczin Memorial Book, Mina Liebreider notes that '[t]he Germans killed my brother-in-law Jonathan in Slonim. He possibly could have saved himself, since the partisans proposed to him that he go with them, but without the children. He did not want to leave the children alone'.[99] However it remains unclear how this impacted upon his brother-in-law and we have no evidence to suggest that such act of self-sacrifice was masculinizing for the actor. Similarly, Abraham Lewin documents the case of a father who hands himself over to the Germans because his family has been taken. 'I feel a great compassion and admiration for this straightforward person. Strong in mind as well as strong in body.'[100] Clearly in Lewin's eyes this man's actions confirmed his masculinity as a father in stark contrast to Lewin's feelings about his own failure to do likewise when his wife is taken; but again we do not know the impact of this action on the masculinity of the man in question. Also writing in the Dereczin Memorial Book, Kaminetsky-Friedman's final paragraph describes her leave-taking from her father noting his paternal devotion and the 'blessings he bestowed upon us in connection with our flight into the forest, and the tears with which he bestowed those blessings'.[101]

Similarly lauding paternal love as masculinizing, Ringelblum makes a point of noting that men as well as women wrapped up their children in an attempt to smuggle them out of the ghettos in the hope of finding them some means of surviving. Each of these cases is a display of sacrifice and pain for reasons of love, which are accompanied by a strong degree of respect toward the father in question, and whilst we have no evidence to suggest that it is equally sustaining for the men involved, the fact that they are recounted by men who are themselves fathers (Ringelblum, Lewin and Liebreider) indicates the potential of such acts to strengthen paternal masculine identities.

Depression and power within the home are also significant elements of individual masculinities which show diverse and complex responses to the same events for fathers and their children. These elements of masculinities are overstated amongst Jewish fathers, just as for Jewish men more generally,[102] since, far from showing apathy, numerous sources from this period point to fathers, in spite of emotional turmoil, using their connections to exploit Aryanization to their own benefit – Martin Parker received no financial remuneration for his business, but credited the Aryan family who took it over with later saving his family's lives[103] and Michael Etkind's father stalled the Aryanization of his business long enough to take home fabric from his factory so that he might continue to work and earn money.[104] Equally, in this period, decision-making remained clearly within the domain of fathers – Flinker's father was instrumental in moving the family within Holland before ultimately finding them a hiding place.[105] And despite Flinker regularly noting his father and mother arguing about the family's movements, in every case it is his father who prevails.[106] Similarly, Meijer's family went into hiding organized entirely by his father and Alex was, he noted, 'spurred on by papa' – returning to education at the behest of his father – a man who was not only the decision maker, but actively sought solutions and behaved very much as a strong patriarch throughout the war.[107] Equally, Knoller's father makes the decision that his son should leave Austria and arranges his passage to Belgium, even though he and his wife were not able or willing to go with him.[108]

Beyond these examples, there is even evidence that, where fathers were imprisoned or absent for a period of time, both fathers and sons record them as maintaining their role as decision makers and actors in the family. Rubinowicz's father notably continued to send instructions concerning how the family should act even after he had been arrested and put in a nearby work camp and despite having little knowledge of the circumstances of the family since he was not receiving their mail.[109] That he wrote with instructions is not on its own evidence of his position or power, but Rubinowicz clearly notes that the family obeyed these instructions where at all possible and Rubinowicz still clearly counts his father as the patriarch of the family, despite his prolonged absence. In one letter Rubinowicz Sr writes, 'Dear children, obey your mother',[110] a command which, although it represents a transfer of authority, was still a clear display of patriarchal power since, in insisting that his children obey their mother, Rubinowicz Sr shows first that he holds power which might be transferred and, second, suggests that he believed such a command would be obeyed by his family – which it indeed was.

The respect that children had for their fathers, however, does not seem to have diminished, even where there was depression and apathy, and Liebman wrote of his father, '[t]his feeling of disquiet insinuated itself into each one of us. My father lost his self-confidence. Until the day he died, thirty years later, he would never really recover it'.[111] Instead, emotional outpourings seem to have had little impact on the way in which children perceived the masculinity of their fathers. Where fathers cried it was very rarely accompanied by any other physical signs of distress or loss of control, making it easier to sustain respect for their masculine identity, something which is reflected in accounts written by children who clearly justify such actions. One example of this is Halina Sands, who noted her father returning from a day at the *Umschlagplatz* and weeping, but clearly continued to see him as a figure of power and protection,[112] whilst Eli Wiesel reported his father's tears but continued to acknowledge his father's role as family patriarch, noting his plans for moving the family into hiding (although this did not ultimately come to pass) and later as a community leader in the ghetto.[113] Later in the Holocaust, as they arrive in the camp, Wiesel Sr takes Elie's hand to protect him; a protection he is only still able to offer because, for Elie, his masculinity and patriarchal role are still intact. Similarly, Rudashevski details his father being beaten, but the way in which he writes about his father's behaviour or his role within the family does not change at all. Rather, it is Rudashevski himself who seems to suffer from his father's beating.[114]

Even when a father's depression led indirectly to his own death, as in the case of Sarah Wachler-Ogulnick who jumps from a deportation train to save her own life but whose father would not follow, there is little sign of decreased respect or adherence to her patriarch. On the contrary, in response to this Wachler-Ogulnick notes, '[m]y father (ז״ל) never even gave thought to running from the Germans and death. He was certain that all was lost. The Germans had reached the gates of Moscow, all the Jews will be slaughtered, and therefore it was appropriate to go with the community and share in the fate of the entirety of our people.'[115] In writing thus she certainly has no reproach for her father and instead praises him for his behaviour toward his community and his people as a display of patriarchal responsibility. The majority of such sources, however, also suggest that neither sustained action and productivity amongst fathers nor the clear respect of their children were able to impact on depression once a father had succumbed.

Case study of Roman Halter[116]

Roman Halter has written a book, recorded an extensive interview with the Imperial War Museum and I have interviewed him myself. Between these different records it has been possible to piece together a quite developed understanding of his history and, particularly, that of his father, Mordechai, and what emerges is a case which successfully illustrates many of the dominant themes of fatherhood found in this book. The key to much of this is the age of Halter and his father during the Holocaust: at its end Roman was 17 and had strong memories of his father both before and during the Holocaust. Moreover, Roman and his father had spent all of the deconstruction and their time in the Łódź ghetto together, allowing Roman to comment on the ways in which his father reacted and behaved as the Holocaust progressed with great clarity.

It is noteworthy that Halter's discussion of the pre-war period is very detailed and includes a long explanation of his father's youth and early experiences. Clearly a point of significant pride for his family in general and Roman in particular, Mordechai survived being called for service in the Russian army – generally considered a death sentence – and returned to his family significantly wealthier than he left. Mordechai was then sent to England where he was in a financial position to assist one of his brothers in setting up a business and another in emigrating to Canada. Roman relates these stories deliberately and repeatedly in an attempt to show his father's strength and the respect felt for him in the family. In a very different way, Roman also reinforces the transmission of history and tradition as a key element of masculinity when he recounts a single moment of tenderness sat on his father's knee reading the Haggadah. In contrast to this praise, Roman also clearly relates what he saw as examples of his father's limitations as a parent, depicting him as having failed to be a 'modern' father. Nevertheless, in spite of, or perhaps the more so because of, this condemnation, it is clear that Roman's principal understanding of Mordechai is as a strong patriarch in control of his family who, despite a leaning to extreme authoritarianism, was highly respected within the family.

When the war began, Mordechai, as a respected elder, made decisions for various members of the family, including sending Roman's sister to Warsaw, where she remained until her death during the war, and taking the decision that the family not try to leave Poland – although his wife did briefly look into obtaining exit visas. According to Roman, this decision was largely based on his father's age, 62 at the time of the German invasion, Mordechai felt he was too old to attempt to start again. However, if we look closely at his refusal to emigrate it does not seem to be as negative as Roman initially suggests – rather Mordechai knew of family members who had moved to Palestine and found the life there extremely hard. Moreover, a well-connected *volksdeutsch*[117] friend in the town had told him that there was no need to leave, that he would protect them. In this light the decision to stay in a place where he had friends, status and connections, rather than move to Palestine where his brother-in-law had died, seemed like a sensible, logical defence of the family. That it did not turn out to be such should not change the nature of the decision – a proactive one made by a family patriarch.[118]

Later, whilst still in their home town of Chodecz, but after the German invasion, and having lost their house and Mordechai's factory, one of Roman's elder brothers was executed by the SS. This led to Mordechai falling into a deep depression. When questioned on this Roman believes that Mordechai realized that he had failed his family and that he should have been more proactive in organizing emigration and marshalling various family members to organize the escape of the others. Roman also notes that until his own death Mordechai talked about the death of this son, clearly a loss which affected him deeply. Exactly as before, whilst Mordechai, despite the loss of his business and home, had been continuing to provide for and protect his family this had been enough to sustain him and his masculine identity. It was only on the murder of his son that his inability to protect was so clearly demonstrated and he became depressed. Several elements of this depression are important, however, and reflect ideas of masculinity in fatherhood found throughout this chapter: according to Roman, Mordechai's mood improved greatly in two circumstances: the first whenever Roman shaved his father and the second when they entered the Łódź ghetto.

In the first case, when Roman shaved his father, he would ask his father for advice about such things as how to feed geese – whilst imparting such knowledge Mordechai would come back to life for a few minutes seeming to completely regain his former vigour and showing the masculine impact of transmission of knowledge and advice. The second time Mordechai came out of his depression it was permanent and was a product of reaching the ghetto – part of a convoy of 360 from Chodecz with only 120 places available in the Łódź ghetto. It was not clear what would happen to those who did not get in (they were in fact murdered nearby), and, according to Roman, Mordechai realized that he had to do everything in his power to gain entry for his family. By bribing various people and selling valuables Mordechai was able to gain entry for all six members of his family, a clear act of both providing and protecting which was enough to bring him out of his depression. Once in the ghetto it was agreed that Mordechai and his wife's father should enter an old people's home since there they would receive extra rations, some of which they might then be able to save for Roman and his mother. This they did for some time with Roman and his mother visiting his father often and sharing potatoes from his rations. When asked if he took over as the 'man of the house' at this point, Roman is clear that he did not. Although he worked at various stages in the ghetto, so too did his mother, and Roman at no point assumed his father's role as carer. Rather, his father continued to make decisions for the family where necessary and to hold what remained of the family valuables. Notably, when another sister reached Łódź and needed help to gain entry into the ghetto for herself and her children, Roman went to his father for advice and was given items to sell in an attempt to save them.

Although the situation in the ghetto deteriorated rapidly and there was little that anyone could do to help the family, Mordechai did make a series of final gestures which seem both to reaffirm his role as a father and his strong masculine identity. The day before his death, Mordechai visited Roman and his mother and explained several things to Roman: he passed on the address of an aunt in Switzerland who might help him after the war; he told Roman the location of a buried chest of tea and soap in Chodecz which he might retrieve after the war and use to make money; and he told Roman that when he, Mordechai, died, Roman should take his coat to a specific tailor and have it altered to make a winter coat for himself. These pieces of information were Roman's examples of the life-saving advice that many fathers gave their children. Roman used all three to protect himself in the ghetto and to thrive once the war ended and their passing on had great significance for his father in a final display of masculine provision and protection. Revealing the existence of items buried some years earlier, Mordechai also shows that he had been involved in proactive fathering at a time when he appeared to be in a deep depression. Further, it later transpires that Mordechai had left furs and clothing with two different sets of family friends in Chodecz which Roman was able to claim after the war.

Mordechai Halter's story reinforces many of the conclusions drawn about paternal masculinity in this chapter. Although he did sink into depression, he also briefly came out of it in the ghetto when he was better able to perform as a father again, even if only in limited circumstances. He passed on advice and items to help Roman survive, important both on his deathbed and during his depression when the act of giving advice seems to temporarily revive him. Finally, throughout the account we can see Roman's deep respect for his father, particularly his masculinity, and a wish not to attempt to take his father's place in the family even as he grows into manhood working in the ghetto and his father weakens. There is nonetheless also a defensive tone in Roman's account of his father's masculinity which does not seem to denote his own questions concerning his fathering, but may represent those of others in the family or of his father himself. Notably, after the war in a discussion with old family friends concerning his family, a friend comments that his grandfather was a wise and good man. Halter comments, to himself, but considers it important enough to note in his book *Roman's Journey*, 'Father was clever too.'[119]

* * *

Exactly as with Jewish men and their masculinities more broadly, Jewish fathers in this period were only able to practise strong masculinities at those times in the Holocaust when they were able to successfully perform elements of their normative identities. The successful practice of individual elements of their masculinities, in contrast, failed to offer a basis firm enough to reinforce their gender identities. That this was the case even when their children clearly found those same individual elements to be definitively masculine shows the strength and primacy of normative gender identities amongst Jewish men in this period. One particular difference between broader male gender identities and the identities of fathers, however, is clear: Jewish fathers from a range of backgrounds relied heavily on descent and the transmission of heritage in the practice of their normative identities, so much so that it perhaps became an element of all normative identities – effectively, that fathers all practised the normative identity of fathers (rather than the dominant, subordinate and independent masculinities previously considered), with the masculinism of providing, protecting and status often channelled through their children. It is also clear that, because of the centrality of this new element of masculinity, through the parent–child dialectic, children were able to respond to the masculinity they saw in their fathers and, in doing so, potentially create a sense of paternal masculinity in their fathers. This is not to suggest that the Holocaust did not present major obstacles to the act of fathering, and that this was not often extremely damaging for the men involved;

however, what evidence there is leads one to reject the clarity and universality of the conclusion that 'despite their best efforts, men had to face the hard fact that they could no longer protect their families'.[120]

The more unexpected conclusion here, however, lies in what the evidence seems to tell us about the burgeoning masculinity of young men and even boys. Whilst Holocaust testimonies which reference the author's mother in the title are extremely rare, instances of books dedicated to fathers are not: Edward Gastfried entitled his work *My Father's Testament*, Checinski allows his father to narrate several chapters of *My Father's Watch* (although the watch in question is more of a bad omen than a positive association), Wermuth directly quotes his father in his title *Breathe Deeply My Son* and Ivan Singer called his book *My Father's Blessing*.[121] In strong contrast to current trends in historiography, these dedications further underline the respect in which many children in this period, particularly sons, held their fathers. In line with this, evidence shows that, in the eyes of a number of young men, the Holocaust did little to diminish the masculinities of their fathers. This is not to say that sons always found the behaviour of their fathers to be palatable, but even where it very overtly was not, we see children question the morality but not the masculinity of their fathers. On the contrary, sons clearly celebrated the masculinity of their fathers, their behaviour and their choices. That instances of role reversal between fathers and sons are so limited, something that Roman Halter asserts very clearly, further reinforces this point and underlines the respect which sons had for their fathers.

Perhaps even more interestingly, in the eyes of these children, not only were their fathers very clearly capable of performing acts key to their normative masculinities but they were lauded for their acts of individual masculinity which were as relevant to their children as the normative elements. One might even go on to speculate that this perhaps shows a greater flexibility amongst younger men in how they defined and understood masculinity and male gender identities than the older generations, with less reliance upon socially imposed normative gender identities and a greater capacity to acknowledge and respect individual, often less conformist, elements of those identities.

Conclusion

This work and its findings are for some, at best, counterintuitive and, at worst, disturbing. The thought that something like the ghettoization imposed on Jewish populations during the Holocaust could in any small way strengthen the damaged gender identities of those men who lived it is not comfortable. And yet, evidence shows that this is true – not because it overlooks the experiences of the Holocaust but because men's gender identities simply cannot be shown to reflect the daily realities of those men's lives, irrespective of their horrors, and because in some cases masculinities can even be seen to thrive on those negative experiences. Of course, this study has shown that there is no universal Holocaust experience; men in different countries from a variety of religious and assimilated backgrounds and living in a range of economic and social circumstances experienced the persecution, assault, humiliation and confinement of the Holocaust in myriad ways. Moreover, and confusing any attempt to understand the impact of persecution upon gender identities, these men did not all understand or perform their masculinities in the same way; instead the different masculine identities upon which the Holocaust impacted, themselves varied. And yet in spite of the numerous caveats laid out here and throughout this book, it is possible to draw several, clear conclusions.

Working from a theory of masculinity that acknowledges the relevance and impact of multiple, socially composed, normative gender identities, whilst also allowing for the experiences and background of the individual to equally weigh upon his masculinity, sources written by Jewish men and women who lived in Poland, Belgium, Holland and France between invasion and the end of enclosure, whether this came through death, liberation or deportation to the camps, overwhelmingly show trends in the way in which Jewish masculinities were affected by the Holocaust. This research shows a correlation, for many Jewish men, between a relatively stable capacity to provide and protect and a strengthened gender identity, and it suggests that basic instability, even in much less extreme circumstances, was fundamental to the collapse of masculine identities. More specifically, the period of instability and persecution which immediately followed invasion, and which for some did not end until the war also ended, was one characterized by a constant and incremental degradation in living standards and freedoms, in which the private and public lives of Jewish men were dismantled piece by piece, from unemployment to social exclusion. This deconstruction of lives often rendered it virtually impossible for Jewish men to practise strong masculine identities. However, whilst masculinities were damaged and derailed on a daily basis throughout the Holocaust by extreme acts of violence, degradation, humiliation and sorrow, in contrast to the emasculation of the constantly destabilizing changes inherent to the deconstruction, the, perhaps petrified, relative stability of enclosure (often in the form of ghettoization) seems to have offered, for many, the opportunity to practise strong masculine identities. Enclosure offered possibilities for men to restructure these eroded elements of their lives, through employment, socialization, leadership and comparative stability, not only in terms of opportunities but also through the reassurance of what many understood to be a unified, autonomous, Jewish society, which offered such a contrast to the constant shifting and erosion of the deconstruction. As a result, many men were able to re-form or reassert strong masculinities. Moreover, limited sources suggest that where Jews in Western Europe were able to find conditions of enclosure that mimicked the security that the ghettos appeared to offer, notably those who belonged to structured resistance organizations or who found relatively stable hiding places, they were equally able to re-establish strong gender identities.

The differences between these two periods that are significant for our understanding of these changes in masculinity are threefold, and between them speak not only to the practice of gender identities during the Holocaust, but perhaps also speak to the nature and formation of masculinity more generally. The broadest difference between the two periods was in the gendering of the environment and social expectations. During the deconstruction, men were encouraged not to act and instead to behave in a passive manner by hiding or fleeing, a behaviour tied up with complex ideas of diaspora and the place of Jews and Jewish communities in Western society. This approach effectively forced men into behaving in ways they understood to be feminine, and thereby into self-emasculation. In stark contrast, ghettoization forced men to act, to work and to struggle, and whilst this was often back-breaking and damaging in other ways, it tacitly encouraged behaviours understood as masculine and allowed men to perform key elements of their masculine identities.

The second, and perhaps the most significant, difference lay in the possibilities that men found for performing elements of the normative identities toward which they oriented themselves. The deconstruction left many Jewish men with no such possibilities, struggling to provide for or protect their families and often devoid of the trappings of status which underpinned these gender identities. Again, in contrast, enclosure, particularly in the form of ghettoization but also in some few cases in hiding, gave some men renewed access to their normative identities through a reestablishment of employment, provision and status.

Finally, third, and most specific to the individual, where the deconstruction saw relative stability regarding the individual elements of masculinity, enclosure was marked by the almost total collapse of many of these elements of masculinity, perhaps most clearly and starkly seen in the relationship men had with their own bodies – significantly the negative trajectory of these individual elements is in complete contrast to the positive trajectory of normative elements of masculine identities in the same period. Where the latter was tied to stability and therefore often improved with enclosure, the former responded more closely to changes in circumstance and therefore declined significantly during the same period. That the relative strength of the individual elements of masculinity during the deconstruction was nevertheless accompanied by overall collapse in many cases seems to suggest that, whilst individual elements of identity do form a part of broader masculine identities, they are alone not sufficient to sustain the performance of masculinity when not matched by strong normative practice.

My final chapter, in considering to what extent these conclusions could be applied specifically to the masculinities associated with fathers and fatherhood, makes two further assertions. First, that whilst the masculinities of fathers were equally reliant upon an ability to perform the normative masculinity toward which they oriented themselves, these norms stretched to encompass, regardless of the background of the fathers, questions of inheritance, heritage and ancestry, which are not always apparent in Jewish men who are not fathers and suggest a unifying of masculine practice amongst fathers during the Holocaust. The final finding of this research begins to consider the impact of age upon masculinity in this period. Using sources written by young men about their fathers, and considering the ways in which they show respect for, or pride in, the masculinities of their fathers, it becomes clear that whilst fathers may heavily rely upon elements of normative masculinities in the reinforcement of their gender identities, children are less selective, particularly in their analysis of the masculinities of their fathers. For young men writing about the masculinities of their fathers, and to a lesser extent forming their own gender identities, individual elements of their masculinity play a more central role in the practice of a strong masculinity than amongst older men. Specifically, sources show young men discussing the actions of their fathers as being overtly masculine through a discussion of individual elements of masculinity, even when the masculinities of their fathers are clearly diminished in relation to the key elements of normative identity. This is certainly not enough to conclude that younger men had less rigid notions of masculinity and were less dependent upon socially imposed markers of identity and more open to individual signifiers of gender than their elders, but it does offer a basis upon which to begin considering such questions.

* * *

But these findings are not conclusive. As much as they begin to sketch a way to understand the impact of the Holocaust on the gender identities of the Jewish men who lived through it, they leave any number of questions unanswered. Not only are the memories of one group of men, even when taken as the individual plural which Browning offers us, not evidence for the experiences of any other, but the testimonies, diaries and memoirs available by no means fairly represent a cross section of Jewry as it faced and endured the Holocaust. The essentially insurmountable problem is that two groups in particular, the ultra-orthodox (specifically those haredi Jewish men devoted to religious study) and those who succumbed to starvation soon after entering the ghettos, are barely present in this book. On the subject of the masculinity of these Jewish men I confess to silence. I regret that I have been unable to find sources to represent these men in even a limited way[1] – particularly the experiences of haredi men might have offered an extremely interesting contrast to the performances of masculinity more usually documented – and yet my decision to continue with writing this book which attempts to understand, nonetheless, the impact of the Holocaust on Jewish masculinities is based on the following quotation:

> [t]here are twenty thousand, perhaps thirty thousand, people who really have enough to eat; these are the social elite. They contrast with the quarter-of-a-million-strong mass of beggars and paupers who are only struggling to postpone death by starvation. … And in between these two is a group of about two hundred thousand 'ordinary people' who more or less manage, and retain some sort of human face. They are still clean, dressed, their stomachs are not swollen from starvation.[2]

Overlooking a slight numerical inaccuracy,[3] this statement presents an important truth: the only significant group available for historical study, and therefore the focus of this work, is the 'ordinary people'.

Equally, what came next is not in any way the domain of this book and my conclusions are not comprehensive in this respect. Jewish masculinities did not end with the enclosure: many Jews died in the ghettos, many more were deported to camps of labour and death and a very few escaped to join resistance groups or to hide for interminable periods. Equally those who were enclosed in hiding for longer periods left it because it became untenable, because they were betrayed and discovered or, for the very lucky few, because the war ended. How their masculine identities made these transitions and how the practice of masculinities functioned in the camp environment are not something I have considered. Many of those men who survived went on to join or form communities in Diaspora or in nascent Israel, and exactly how the impact of the Holocaust affected their existing masculinities as they rebuilt lives in the post-war period is a subject worthy of serious consideration by others. My work should, however, if I have done it correctly, support those historians by beginning to provide the background necessary to successfully understand how the masculinities of the Holocaust fed into everything that came after.

* * *

On the subject of establishing a printers' trust in the Warsaw ghetto, Alexander Donat wrote the following:

> [t]hough mine was only a tiny share in the business, with my earnings added to my wife's we were able to live better than we had since the outbreak of the war. Once again I was head of the family. I threw myself into my work, getting up at seven and coming home just before curfew; and since the job had nothing to do with either the Germans or the *Judenrat*, I enjoyed it. We all felt we were contributing to the economic survival of the ghetto.[4]

In these two sentences Donat neatly summarizes the collected memories of so many sources: that whilst the antisemitic persecution which began the Holocaust was damaging in the extreme to the masculinities of the Jewish men who experienced it, the period of the Holocaust in which Jews were enclosed offered to some the possibility of finding employment, of re-establishing social structures, and of reasserting status, and, in doing so, once again made it possible for many Jewish men to practise strong masculine identities. Of course, there remain questions without answers, exceptions and conundrums, but by overturning many of the existing orthodoxies in this field, we begin to understand the response of Jewish male gender identities to the Holocaust, with all the emotionally, mentally and physically scarring realities that included – and so begin to write the story of what has been, until now, the second sex of Holocaust gender history.

Notes

Introduction

1   Marion A. Kaplan, *Between Dignity and Despair: Jewish Life in Nazi Germany* (New York: Oxford University Press, 1998), p. 4.

2   Dalia Ofer and Lenore J. Weitzman, 'Introduction' in Dalia Ofer and Lenore J. Weitzman, eds., *Women in the Holocaust* (New Haven, CT: Yale University Press, 1998), p. 1.

3   Joan Ringelheim comments, '[c]urrent Holocaust literature focuses on the lives of men as written and perceived by men' (Joan M. Ringelheim, 'The Unethical and the Unspeakable: Women and the Holocaust', *Simon Wiesenthal Center Annual*, 1 (1984), p. 69), whilst Anna Hardman refers specifically to a 'masculinist perspective' (Anna Hardman, 'Women and the Holocaust', *Holocaust Educational Trust Research Papers*, 1:3 (1999–2000), p. 5).

4   In the first case, historians have found sources which discuss the equally negative results both of menstruation and of amenorrhea particularly in the camps, including the physical realities of menstruation without the necessary sanitary wear resulting in women being punished, both by Kapos and by Germans, for being unclean, and the shame and humiliation of not menstruating, often at a young age, combined with a very real fear that amenorrhea indicated permanent infertility (Brigitte Halbmayr, 'Sexualized Violence Against Women During Nazi "Racial" Persecution' in Sonja M. Hedgepeth and Rochelle G Saidel, eds., *Sexual Violence Against Jewish Women During the Holocaust* (Hanover, NH: Brandeis University Press, 2010), p. 34. In the case of sexual assault, which took numerous forms throughout the Holocaust, from attacks in the home during round-ups and searches to examinations and shaving on arrival in the camps and later rape and the establishment of brothels, the impacts on women were also multiple, from physical damage or pregnancy to severe emotional trauma (Halbmayr, 'Sexualized Violence Against Women', *passim*). Through a study of these, and other, gendered subjects, historians have not only increased our understanding of the realities of the Holocaust for women, itself a laudable end, but they have also uncovered complexities in the way we think about the Holocaust and gender. One example of this is the assault, or sexual coercion, of Jewish women by Jewish men. Previously largely unmentioned, such detail blurs the boundaries between victims and persecutors, forcing historians and survivors to reconsider the absolute victimhood

of Jewish men and highlighting a tendency to give primacy to Jewish actions seen as heroic. As Waxman notes, '[o]nce again, an exclusive, if understandable, emphasis on heroic resistance and Jewish solidarity has inadvertently silenced alternative voices' (Zoë Waxman, 'Rape and Sexual Abuse in Hiding' in Hedgepeth and Saidel, eds., *Sexual Violence Against Jewish Women During the Holocaust*, p. 131). Of equal significance are the reasons many women give for not recounting cases of sexual assault: whilst some suffered from ongoing shame and a wish neither to discuss such matters nor to have their children be aware of them, others also emphasise the relationship between their own testimony and those of other survivors. Something I shall consider later, the tendency of survivors not to recount issues that do not arise in other testimonies has pushed women into silence concerning experiences alien to men. Such gender history has forced the historian to reconsider the nature of testimonies and thus doubly impacted upon our understanding of the Holocaust.

5   Ringelheim, 'The Unethical and the Unspeakable', p. 72.

6   Jane Caplan, 'Gender and the Concentration Camps' in Jane Caplan and Nikolaus Wachsmann, eds., *Concentration Camps in Nazi Germany: The New Histories* (Oxford: Routledge, 2010), p. 84.

7   Ofer and Weitzman, 'Introduction', p. 1.

8   Joan M. Ringelheim, 'Women and the Holocaust: A Reconsideration of Research' in Carol Rittner and John K. Roth, eds., *Different Voices: Women and the Holocaust* (New York: Paragon House, 1993), p. 384.

9   Ringelheim, 'Women and the Holocaust', p. 386.

10 Zoë V. Waxman, 'Unheard Stories: Reading Women's Holocaust Testimonies', *The Jewish Quarterly*, 177 (2000), p. 53.

11 That said, it is not clear from Ringelheim's more recent work that the complications between historical study and gender politics have been overcome; nor, I think, would Ringelheim entirely wish them to be.

12 This is something I will consider further in Chapter 1 looking at the sociological underpinnings of definitions of masculinity.

13 Whilst not rejecting the dominant positive representation of the female gender role present in so much historical analysis, historians of women in the Holocaust are in the process of shifting their own focus away from studying women performing traditional female roles to studying those who conform less easily to stereotypes. The childless and those who acted as camp Kapos are two examples of women who did not necessarily fit caring, nurturing roles and, as a result, had been largely overlooked by historians until more recent research began to redress the balance with attempts to write a more nuanced view of women's behaviour (Waxman, 'Unheard Stories', p. 54). My own work largely attempts to avoid this concern by consciously addressing the idea that gender is not a unitary concept and that men, dependent on class, age and circumstances, have vastly differing ideas of what it is to be masculine.

14 I discuss this elsewhere, challenging the extent to which men stealing food from
    their children can be understood as a general problem in the ghettos.

15 In a possibly apocryphal story, during the war, Evelyn Waugh's wife obtained three
    bananas. Waugh ate all three himself in front of his children.

16 Dawid Sierakowiak, *The Diary of Dawid Sierakowiak* (London: Bloomsbury, 1996),
    p. 151 and elsewhere.

17 Sara Zyskind, *Stolen Years* (Minneapolis, MN: Lerner Publications Company, 1981).

18 This is particularly clear in the case of Judith Baumel's work *Double Jeopardy:
    Gender and the Holocaust* which, in spite of this ungendered title, notes in the
    introduction: 'Gender and the Holocaust complements the existing literature by
    presenting a volume of historical essays illuminating the factors which shaped
    the lives of Jewish women during and after the Holocaust.' Judith Tydor Baumel,
    Double Jeopardy: Gender and the Holocaust (London: Vallentine Mitchell, 1998).
    This problem is not particular to the Holocaust, but rather is only one example of
    a larger phenomenon in historical writing. As Peter Filene laconically comments,
    '[t]he vanguard of women's historians are looking toward gender history, but the
    gender includes only one sex' (Peter Filene, 'The Secrets of Men's History' in Harry
    Brod, ed., *The Making of Masculinities: The New Men's Studies* (Boston, MA: Allen &
    Unwin, 1987), p. 113).

19 Marlene E. Heinemann, *Gender and Destiny; Women Writers and the Holocaust*
    (New York: Greenwood, 1986).

20 This is particularly the case if we consider Sander Gilman's argument that 'the Jew
    at the *fin de siècle* is the male Jew', an elision of gender and sex which ensured that
    even seemingly ungendered antisemitism directed at the body was effectively an
    attack on men and their gender identities (Sander Gilman, *Franz Kafka. The Jewish
    Patient* (London: Routledge, 1995), p. 21). Whilst stereotypes of the Jewish female
    do exist, according to common characterization, 'The Jew' is inherently male, and
    yet since the gentile is manly, its antithesis, the Jew, is necessarily feminine. This
    meant that the Jewish male became unavoidably feminized. On this matter Ann
    Pellegrini writes, '[s]ignificantly, in the homology Jew-as-woman, the Jewish female
    body goes missing. All Jews are womanly; but no women are Jews' (Ann Pellegrini,
    Performance Anxieties: Staging Psychoanalysis, Staging Race (New York: Routledge,
    1997), p. 18).

21 Nechama Tec, *Resilience and Courage: Women, Men and the Holocaust* (New Haven,
    CT: Yale University Press, 2003), p. 75.

22 Raul Hilberg cited in Ringelheim, 'The Unethical and the Unspeakable', p. 72.

23 Emmanuel Ringelblum, *Notes from the Warsaw Ghetto: The Journal of Emmanuel
    Ringelblum*, ed. Jacob Sloan (New York: McGraw-Hill, 1958), p. 294.

24 Tec, *Resilience and Courage*, p. 73. It is not the conclusion here that I question;
    indeed with greater nuance this forms a part of one of my own conclusions. My
    question here is about the logical steps taken to reach this conclusion. Interestingly,

Sarah Horowitz, 'Gender, Genocide and Jewish Memory', *Prooftexts*, 20 (2000),
p. 13, discusses a precedent for such opinions in the Midrash discussing the idea
that, when in Egypt as slaves, the Jews were forced to perform the tasks of the
opposite gender. On this matter, Horowitz comments that in the Midrash the
men are weakened by this reversal whilst the women find it empowering. This
comparison does not appear in any other work I can find, but certainly presents
one interesting way of understanding the assumptions of authors writing about
gender in the Holocaust.

25 Some of these discussions I will go on to consider in detail in framing a theory of
masculinity on which to base my work.

26 Whilst specific national studies, for example Anna Hájková's work on Dutch Jews
in the Terezin Ghetto, add a great deal to our understanding of this period, it is not
my intention to look in this depth at one single element of Jewish identity. Rather,
as I shall go on to detail, my approach is to look collectively at the way in which the
various strands of identity – religious, national, social – overlap in the individual
to form and influence gender identities (Anna Hájková, 'Poor Devils of the Camps:
Dutch Jews in the Terezín Ghetto, 1943–1945', *YadVashem Studies* 34:1 (2015),
passim).

27 Amongst others Kim Wünschmann has written interestingly on this subject. Kim
Wünschmann, *Before Auschwitz: Jewish Prisoners in the Prewar Concentration
Camps* (London: Harvard University Press, 2015).

28 *Aliyah* was the word used by European Jews for the act of immigration to *Eretz
Israel*, and was a central pillar or Zionist teachings in the period prior to the
Holocaust.

29 *Oneg Shabbat* is the name that was given to the secret archive compiled in the
Warsaw ghetto and directed by the historian Emmanuel Ringelblum. Excerpts from
the archive can be found in numerous works including Joseph Kermish, *To Live
with Honor and Die with Honor!...: Selected Documents from the Warsaw Ghetto
Underground Archives 'O.S.'* (Jerusalem: Yad Vashem, 1986). The Chronicles of the
Łódź Ghetto was compiled in the ghetto by residents between 1942 and 1944 and
much of its text can be found in Lucjan Dobroszycki, ed., *The Chronicle of the Łódź
Ghetto, 1941-1944* (New Haven, CT: Yale University Press, 1984).

30 Jane Caplan and Nikolaus Wachsmann, 'Introduction' in Jane Caplan and Nikolaus
Wachsmann, eds., *Concentration Camps in Nazi Germany: The New Histories*
(Oxford: Routledge, 2010), p. 8.

31 A number of these discussions are indeed relevant to Holocaust studies more
generally and to the use of survivor testimony in particular and are not specific to
the study of masculinity. However, since the study of masculinity in this period
relies so heavily on testimony, and in most cases lacks any scope for sources to
be factually verified, it remains imperative to engage closely with these broader
debates and concerns before beginning my own substantive study.

32 Christopher Browning, *Collected Memories: Holocaust History and Postwar Testimony* (Madison, WI: The University of Wisconsin Press, 2003) p. 39.

33 Tony Kushner, 'Saul Friedländer, Holocaust Historiography and the Use of Testimony' in Christian Weise and Paul Betts, eds., *Years of Persecution, Years of Extermination: Saul Friedländer and the Future of Holocaust Studies* (London: Continuum, 2010), p. 71.

34 Art Spiegelman, *The Complete Maus* (London: Penguin, 2003).

35 There is a detailed historical and theoretical body of scholarship around these debates including the works of Alexandra Garberini, Saul Friedländer and Giorgio Agamben.

36 For a discussion of this editing process, see, amongst many, Nigel Caplan, 'Revisiting the Diary: Rereading Anne Frank's Rewriting' in Bloom, H., ed., *Bloom's Modern Critical Interpretations: The Diary of Anne Frank* (New York: Infobase Publishing, 2010), *passim*.

37 Dori Laub cited in Rachel F. Brenner, *Writing as Resistance: Four Women Confronting the Holocaust* (University Park, PA: Penn State Press, 1997), p. 4.

38 Annette Wieviorka, *Ils étaient juifs, résistants, communistes* (Paris: Stock, 1986), p. 133.

39 Saul Freidländer, *The Years of Extermination: Nazi Germany and the Jews, 1939–1945* (London: Weidenfeld & Nicholson, 2007), pp. xxv–xxvi.

40 Browning, *Collected Memories*, p. 84.

41 Christopher Browning, *Remembering Survival: Inside a Nazi Slave-Labor Camp* (New York: W.W. Norton & Co., 2011), p. 12.

42 The clearest example of this is *Oneg Shabbat*. Its founder and director was Emmanuel Ringelblum, already a noted historian before the war who intentionally embedded much of the academic rigour of his profession into the archive.

43 A comprehensive discussion of the lengthy, historical debate surrounding the use of post-war testimonies can be found in both James E. Young, *Writing and Rewriting the Holocaust: Narrative and Consequences of Interpretation* (Bloomington, IN: Indiana University Press, 1988), and Jeremy D. Popkin, 'Holocaust Memories, Historians' Memoirs: First-Person Narrative and the Memory of the Holocaust', *History & Memory*, 15:1 (2003), pp. 49–84.

44 Primo Levi, *The Drowned and the Saved* (London: Michael Joseph, 1988), p. 11.

45 Binjamin Wilkomirski was the name under which Bruno Dössekker published his book *Fragments: Memories of a Wartime Childhood* in which he claimed to have survived the Holocaust, including spending time in two concentration camps. His story was ultimately disproved in its entirety by the journalist Daniel Ganzfried in 1998.

46 Chaim A. Kaplan, *The Scroll of Agony. The Warsaw Diary of Chaim A Kaplan.* (London: Hamish Hamilton, 1965), p. 30. Kaplan was a Hebrew scholar and teacher born in 1880 in what is now Belorussia. He was already sixty when he entered the

ghetto where he continued to write his extensive diaries in Hebrew until his death in 1942, most likely in the Treblinka death camp. Kaplan went to great lengths to ensure that his diaries survived the Holocaust, something which he discusses on numerous occasions and which was clearly of great importance to him.

47 A Judenrat (pl. Judenräte) was a council of Jewish elders put in place by the occupying German forces to manage ghetto administration. This work, and the degree of collaboration between members of the *Judenrat* and the German authorities, varied significantly between the ghettos, but at its most controversial included compiling lists of ghetto inhabitants for deportation.

48 IWM – Roman Halter – 17183/17 and Roman Halter, *Roman's Journey* (London: Portobello Books, 2007).

49 IWM – Ben Helfgott – 9165/20.

50 IWM – Mala Tribich – 9121/4.

51 IWM – Martin Parker – 12597/9 and IWM – Halina Sand – 12526/7.

52 These problems of source veracity are not, however, unique to this study and methodologies already exist for managing the issues presented by post-war testimonies. This includes limiting oneself to writing micro-studies of a few, or even one, such testimony, enabling a reassuring level of confirmation concerning the 'truth' of the source. In the case of Helen 'Zippi' Spitzer Tichauer, Jürgen Matthäus and his fellow academics offer us as near to a cast-iron source as we will ever find, every moment of her multiple testimonies being checked and cross-checked, confirmed and corroborated. In particular Matthäus stresses the importance of relying, where possible, on the original testimony, oral or written, in its original language and by doing so avoiding errors of translation and truncation. Principally, however, whilst this approach offers insight into ways to analyse and understand a source, it cannot set a benchmark for future study, placing, as it does, historical impact secondary to theoretical impact. Jürgen Matthäus, ed., *Approaching an Auschwitz Survivor: Holocaust Testimony and Its Transformations* (Oxford: Oxford University Press, 2009).

53 Robert W. Connell, 'The Social Organization of Masculinity' in Stephen M. Whitehead and Frank Barrett, eds., *The Masculinities Reader* (Cambridge: Polity, 2001), p. 40.

54 Browning, *Collected Memories*, p. 39.

Chapter 1

1 Stephen M. Whitehead and Frank Barrett, 'Introduction, The Sociology of Masculinity' in Whitehead and Barrett, eds., *The Masculinities Reader*, p. 15.

2 Michael Roper and John Tosh, 'Introduction: Historians and the Politics of Masculinity' in Michael Roper, ed., *Manful Assertions* (London: Routledge, 1991), p. 19.

3   Joseph Pleck provides a good overview of these various theories and their failings
     (Joseph Pleck, *The Myth of Masculinity* (Cambridge, MA: MIT Press, 1981),
     passim; J. Pleck, 'The Theory of Male Sex-Role Identity: Its Rise and Fall, 1936 to
     the Present' in H. Brod, ed., The Making of Masculinities: The New Men's Studies
     (Boston, MA: Allen & Unwin, 1987), *passim*).

4   Michael S. Kimmel and Michael A. Messner, 'Introduction' in Michael S. Kimmel
     and Michael A. Messner, eds., *Men's Lives* (Boston, MA: Allyn & Bacon, 2001), p. xiv.

5   Kimmel and Messner, 'Introduction', p. xvi. Another example of this is Dawn
     Hadley's work which presents the idea of two competing dominant masculinities
     – those of medieval secular and ecclesiastical men (Dawn Hadley, 'Introduction:
     Medieval Masculinities' in Dawn Hadley, ed., *Masculinity in Medieval Europe*
     (London: Longman, 1999), *passim*).

6   Connell, 'The Social Organization of Masculinity', p. 38.

7   Connell, 'The Social Organization of Masculinity', p. 40.

8   Connell, 'The Social Organization of Masculinity', p. 40.

9   Alexandra Shepard, *Meanings of Manhood in Early Modern England* (Oxford:
     Oxford University Press, 2003), p. 251.

10   Early theories of gender identity clearly define *masculinity* as something classically
     normative, an imposed ideal of what it is to be masculine to which men attempt
     to conform. However, whilst historic examples of such overt gender imposition
     exist – one thinks principally of the widespread use of didactic texts in the Early
     Modern period, or of totalitarian regimes including Nazi Germany – such an
     approach has been largely rejected by historians and sociologists alike who argue
     against understanding masculinity simply as the 'acquisition and internalization of
     social norms'. Connell specifically rejects such an approach on the grounds that it
     suggests a clear top-down decision as to the masculinity to be promoted which is
     not evident in most societies.

11   Alan Petersen, *Unmasking the Masculine: 'Men' and 'Identity' in a Sceptical Age*
     (London: SAGE, 1998), p. 130.

12   This more psychological approach can particularly be seen in the work of
     Lynne Segal (Lynne Segal, *Slow Motion: Changing Masculinities, Changing Men*
     (Basingstoke: Palgrave Macmillan, 1997), p. 90.).

13   Segal, *Slow Motion*, p. 90.

14   Questions of change and continuity in gender identity will be further considered
     later in this chapter.

15   Whitehead and Barrett, 'Introduction', p. 20.

16   There is a large and developing body of work on the question of state manipulation
     of the body and its image at the turn of the twentieth century. Amongst many
     others see the various works of George Mosse, John Tosh and Joan Tumblety.

17   In this best selling work, Surén, formerly involved in the military, offered his
     thoughts on the physical and mental benefits of sports and nudity. The work

included a number of images depicting naked, young adults engaging joyfully in a range of outdoor sports. Hans Surén, *Der Mensch und die Sonne* (Stuttgart: Dieck and Co., 1924).

18 For further detail on the intricacies of these changes to masculinities, which responded to numerous political and social changes in the interwar period, see also Karen Hagemann, 'Home/Front: The Military, Violence and Gender Relations in the Age of the World Wars' in Hagemann and Schüler-Springorum, eds., *Home/Front: The Military, War and Gender in Twentieth-Century Germany*, p. 15.

19 Mosse writes a good deal about the background to this subject (George Mosse, *The Image of Man: The Creation of Modern Masculinity* (Oxford: Oxford University Press, 1996)). Similarly, Michael S. Kimmel (Michael S. Kimmel, 'The Contemporary "Crisis" of Masculinity in Historical Perspective' in Brod, ed., *The Making of Masculinities: The New Men's Studies* (Boston, MA: Allen & Unwin, 1987), p. 147) goes into detail on the topic.

20 Various historians have written about the impact on society of invalids returning from the First World War, amongst them Sabine Kienitz (Sabine Kienitz, 'Body Damage: War Disability and Constructions of Masculinity in Weimar Germany' in Karen Hagemann and Stefanie Schüler-Springorum, eds., *Home/Front: The Military, War and Gender in Twentieth-Century Germany* (Oxford: Berg, 2002)) and Deborah Cohen (Deborah Cohen, *The War Come Home: Disabled Veterans in Britain and Germany, 1914–1939* (Berkeley, CA: University of California Press, 2001).

21 Elizabeth Foyster, *Manhood in Early Modern England: Honour, Sex and Marriage* (London: Longman, 1999), p. 210 – 'Linking changes in the wider political, economic and social structure to those in personal relationship is not only extremely complex, it tends to subsume gender to those structures rather than seeing gender itself as a force for change in people's lives.'

22 John Tosh, 'The Old Adam and the New Man: Emerging themes in the History of English Masculinities, 1750–1850' in Tim Hitchcock and Michelle Cohen, eds., *English Masculinities, 1660–1800* (London: Longman, 1999), p. 218.

23 Foyster, *Manhood in Early Modern England, passim.*

24 C. Shawn McGuffey and B. Lindsay Rich, 'Playing in the Gender Transgression Zone: Race, Class and Hegemonic Masculinity in Middle Childhood' in Kimmel and Messner, eds., *Men's Lives*, p. 76.

25 Arthur Brittan, *Masculinity and Power* (Oxford: Wiley-Blackwell, 1989), p. 4. However, such a 'core' of masculinity might also be associated with Connell's 'hegemony' – the fundamental elements of masculinity which seem to sustain patriarchy.

26 David Gilmore discusses the exceptions which highlight these flaws (David D. Gilmore, *Manhood in the Making: Cultural Concepts of Masculinity* (London: Yale University Press, 1990), *passim*).

27 For detailed academic discussions concerning crises of masculinity, see, amongst others, the works of Georger Mosse, Michael Kimmel or Jason Crothamel.

28 This could be anything from playing skittles with his friends to carrying out his paid work or having sex.

29 Thomas I. Gerschick and Adam S. Miller, 'Coming to Terms: Masculinity and Physical Disability' in Kimmel and Messner, eds., *Men's Lives*, *passim*. This is something I will discuss in more detail when attempting to understand practical changes to Jewish masculine identity.

30 In a different context, similar conclusions are drawn by Timothy Nonn, 'Hitting Bottom: Homelessness, Poverty and Masculinity' in Kimmel and Messner, eds., *Men's Lives*, p. 247.

31 Segal, *Slow Motion,* p. xxiii.

32 Foyster, *Manhood in Early Modern England*, p. 1.

33 Tosh references Sinha's work on Bengal and Du Pisani's work on Afrikaners in John Tosh, 'Hegemonic Masculinity and the History of Gender' in Stefan Dudink, Karen Hagemann and John Tosh, eds., *Masculinities in Politics and War: Gendering Modern History* (Manchester: Manchester University Press, 2004), p. 53.

34 Tec, *Resilience and Courage,* p. 5. See also Lisa Pine, 'Gender and the Family' in Dan Stone, ed., *The Historiography of the Holocaust* (Basingstoke: Palgrave Macmillan, 2004), p. 370.

35 Ruth Bondy, 'Women in Theresienstadt and the Family Camp in Birkenau' in Ofer and Weitzman, eds., *Women in the Holocaust*, p. 323.

36 This is of course a generalization since tailors in this period were usually male. Nonetheless, the average woman would have been used to sewing in the home whilst men would not.

37 Leonore Davidoff and Catherine Hall, *Family Fortunes: Men and Women of the English Middle Class, 1780–1850* (London: Routledge, 2002), *passim*.

38 Yen Le Espiritu, 'All Men Are Not Created Equal: Asian Men in U.S. History' in Kimmel and Messner, eds., *Men's Lives*, p. 39, is one clear example of this.

39 Amanda Vickery, 'Golden Age to Separate Spheres? A Review of the Categories and Chronology of English Men's History' in Robert Shoemaker and Mary Vincent, eds., *Gender and History in Western Europe* (London: Arnold, 1998), *passim*.

40 Shepard, *Meanings of Manhood,* p. 2.

41 John Tosh, 'What Should Historians Do with Masculinity? Reflections on Nineteenth-Century Britain', *History Workshop Journal*, 38 (1994), *passim*.

42 Hadley, 'Introduction: Medieval Masculinities', p. 17.

43 Petersen, *Unmasking the Masculine*, p. 41.

44 Petersen, *Unmasking the Masculine*, p. 41.

45 Tosh, 'Hegemonic masculinity', p. 44.

46 Whitehead and Barrett, 'Introduction', p. 11.

47 It is impossible to analyse each individual on this basis. This approach must be, therefore, an analytical method applied to considerations of gender identity through the book rather than a way of understanding individual sources or voices.

48 This is discussed in detail in numerous works noted in note 19, but one might also consider the work of Perry Willson.

49 See, Marsha L. Rozenblit, 'European Jewry: 1800–1933' in Judith R. Baskin and Kenneth Seeskin, eds., *The Cambridge Guide to Jewish History, Religion and Culture* (Cambridge: Cambridge University Press, 2010), pp. 169–207.

50 Bart Wallet, 'Dutch National Identity and Jewish International Solidarity: An Impossible Combination? Dutch Jewry and the Significance of the Damascus Affair (1840)' in Yosef Kaplan, ed., *The Dutch Intersection: The Jews and the Netherlands in Modern History* (Leiden: Brill, 2008), p. 320.

51 Renée Poznanski, *Jews in France During World War II* (Hanover, MA: Brandeis University Press, 2001), p. 4.

52 Dan Michman, 'Research on the Holocaust in Belgium and in General: History and Context', in Dan Michman, ed., *Belgium and the Holocaust: Jews, Belgians, Germans* (Jerusalem: Yad Vashem, 1998), p. 30.

53 Esther Benbassa, *The Jews of France: A History from Antiquity to the Present* (Princeton, NJ: Princeton University Press, 1999), p. 166.

54 Michman, 'Research on the Holocaust', p. 30.

55 Poznanski, *Jews in France*, p. 2.

56 Poznanski, *Jews in France*, p. 4.

57 Antony Polonsky, *The Jews in Poland and Russia: Volume III, 1914–2008* (Portland, OR: The Littman Library of Jewish Civilisation, 2012), p. 121. The statistics that explain this diversity of voting habits are complex and lengthy; however, one good example is the 1938 local elections which saw the Zionists receive less than 25 per cent of the seats (as part of a bloc) in Warsaw, around 22 per cent in Łódź and all sixteen seats in the Lviv council.

58 Polonsky, *The Jews in Poland and Russia*, p. 126.

59 Polonsky, *The Jews in Poland and Russia*, p. 62.

60 This is discussed in various works but an overview can be found in Polonsky, *The Jews in Poland and Russia*, p. 204.

61 The theory of ideal types is closely associated with Max Weber and is detailed in numerous scholarly works including Max Weber, *The Methodology of the Social Sciences* (New York: Free Press, 1949), p. 90.

62 Mosse, *The Image of Man*, p. 5.

63 Mosse, *The Image of Man*, p. 105. Significantly even those men who actively opposed the First World War, Sassoon, Owen and Renn for example, did so largely on the grounds that it was an illegitimate war, rather than by opposing the concept of war entirely; so strong was the association of masculinity and warfare, p. 108.

64 Mosse, *The Image of Man*, p. 117.

65 Kienitz, 'Body Damage', *p. 182.*

66 Mosse, *The Image of Man,* p. 132.

67 Mosse, *The Image of Man,* p. 136.

68 One caveat here is worth noting. As already discussed, the Second World War was not unexpected and the 1930s, as a result, saw nations prepare themselves again for war. This included the sidelining of gentler ideas of male gender to be replaced with more overtly physical, militarized masculinity, a trajectory of changing gender identities which should be noted in writing about the eve of the Holocaust (Hagemann, 'Home/Front', p. 15).

69 Sander Gilman, *Jewish Self-Hatred: Antisemitism and the Hidden Language of the Jews* (Baltimore, MD: Johns Hopkins University Press, 1986), p. 2.

70 Gilman writes in detail about the shift in the negative image of the Jew, as seen by Jewish writers, from the eastern traditional Jew to the Western assimilated Jew at the same time as which the eastern stereotype became a positive image as it seemed to represent a more authentic, spiritual Jewish existence. Gilman, *Jewish Self-Hatred,* p. 270.

71 Gilman, *Jewish Self-Hatred,* p. 18.

72 The various elements of the Jewish male body targeted by antisemitism are detailed in Sander Gilman, *The Jew's Body* (London: Routledge, 1991), *passim.* However problematically, I would argue, these are very much seen from the perspective of the gentile, with little consideration of how a Jew might feel about specific elements of his own body.

73 Jay Geller, 'Freud, Blüher and the Secessio Inversa: Männerbünde, Homosexuality, and Freud's Theory of Cultural Formation' in Daniel Boyarin et al., eds., *Queer Theory and the Jewish Question* (New York: Columbia University Press, 2003), p. 106. This also links to Boyarin's ideas of a positively feminized Jewish male which I shall discuss later in this chapter.

74 Mosse, *The Image of Man,* p. 142.

75 Jonathan Boyarin and Daniel Boyarin, *Powers of Diaspora: Two Essays on the Relevance of Jewish Culture* (London: University of Minnesota Press, 2002), p. 45.

76 For example, the work included a number of direct comparisons – women and Jews 'sticking together' and 'sharing lack of character' – and the argument that Jewry was 'soaked in femaleness'. John M. Hoberman, 'Otto Weininger and the Critique of Jewish Masculinity' in N. Horowitz and B. Hyams, eds., *Jews and Gender: Responses to Otto Weininger* (Philadelphia, PA: Temple University Press, 1995) p. 142.

77 Hoberman, 'Otto Weininger and the Critique of Jewish Masculinity', p. 142.

78 Theodor Lessing, 'Jewish Self-Hatred' in Paul R. Mendes-Flohr and Jehuda Reinharz, eds., *The Jew in the Modern World: A Documentary History* (Oxford: Oxford University Press, 1995), p. 272.

79 Max Nordau, 'Jewry of Muscle'/'Muskeljudentum' from *Juedische Turnzeitung* (June 1903) in Mendes-Flohr and Reinharz, eds., *The Jew in the Modern World,* p. 435.

80   David Biale, 'Zionism as an Erotic Revolution' in H. Eilberg-Schwartz,ed., *People of the Body: Jews and Judaism from an Embodied Perspective* (Albany, NY: State Press of New York, 1992), p. 285.

81   John M. Efron, *Defenders of the Race: Jewish Doctors and Race Science in Fin-de-Siècle Europe* (New Haven, CT: Yale University Press, 1994), p. 177.

82   One reason the committee took so long to form, which goes to the heart of the ideological problems therein, was that scientists were uncomfortable with the idea of science being conducted in some sense in reverse: starting with the conclusion and then performing the science afterward. Paul Weindling, 'The Evolution of Jewish Identity: Ignaz Zollschan Between Jewish and Aryan Race Theories, 1910–45' in Cantor and Swetlitz, eds., *Jewish Tradition and the Challenge of Darwinism, passim.*

83   Efron, *Defenders of the Race,* p. 180.

84   This discussion is elucidated in both Boyarin and Boyarin, *Powers of Diaspora, passim,* and Daniel Boyarin, *Unheroic Conduct: The Rise of Heterosexuality and the Invention of the Jewish Man* (London: University of California Press, 1997), p. 11.

85   Boyarin and Boyarin, *Powers of Diaspora,* p. 45.

86   All of Boyarin's examples in this work are taken from ancient texts including the Babylonian Talmud and specifically the Haggadah.

87   Robin Judd, 'Moral, Clean Men of the Jewish Faith: Jewish Rituals and Their Male Practitioners, 1843–1914' in Ben Baader, Sharon Gillerman and Paul Lerner, eds., *Jewish Masculinities: German Jews, Gender, and History* (Bloomington, IN: Indiana University Press, 2012), *passim.* In Jewish societies *Mohelim* are those who perform circumcisions, whilst *Shochetim* are those trained and licensed to perform the ritual slaughter of animals.

88   Mitchell B. Hart, *The Healthy Jew: The Symbiosis of Judaism and Modern Medicine* (Cambridge: Cambridge University Press, 2007), p. 25.

89   Stefanie Schüler-Springorum, 'A Soft Hero: Male Jewish Identity in Imperial Germany Through the Autobiography of Aron Liebeck' in Baader, Gillerman and Lerner, eds., *Jewish Masculinities: German Jews, Gender, and History* (Bloomington, IN: Indiana University Press, 2012), pp. 90–113.

90   Schüler-Springorum, 'A Soft Hero', p. 103.

91   Amongst others, Gilman writes about this question in Gilman, *Franz Kafka. The Jewish Patient,* p. 22.

92   Hoberman, 'Otto Weininger and the Critique of Jewish Masculinity', p. 152. Significantly this concerns only the *image* of the Jewish father in Jewish and gentile discourse.

93   Isaac Bashevis Singer, *The Penguin Collected Stories of Isaac Bashevis Singer* (London: Penguin, 1984), *passim.*

94   Josef Katz, *One Who Came Back: The Diary of a Jewish Survivor* (Takoma Park, MD: Dryad Press, 2006), p. 8.

95 Huber was the German discus thrower at the beginning of Leni Riefenstahl's *Olympia*.
96 Sharon Gillerman, 'A Kinder Gentler Strongman? Siegmund Breitbart in Eastern
    Europe' in Baader, Gillerman and Lerner, eds., *Jewish Masculinities: German Jews,*
    Gender, and History, p. 199.

Chapter 2

1 Kaplan, *The Scroll of Agony*, p. 76.
2 The term 'deconstruction' used in this way is entirely my own.
3 'Aryanization' was the term used during this period to denote the removal of Jews
   from the world of business in countries under German occupation. For the most
   part, it entailed the transfer of Jewish businesses into the hands of 'Aryans' whom
   the regime deemed preferable.
4 Numerous historians discuss in detail the nature and impact of this process of
   deconstruction, amongst them Saul Friedländer, *Nazi Germany and the Jews: The*
   Years of Persecution: 1933–1939: Nazi Germany and the Jews 1933–1939: Years of
   Persecution, 1933–39 Vol 1 (London: Weidenfeld & Nicolson, 2007).
5 Some examples of this tendency to ignore, or only briefly consider, the
   deconstruction when writing accounts are Calel Perechodnik, *Am I a Murderer?*
   Testament of a Jewish ghetto Policeman (Boulder, CO: Westview Press, 1996), Julius
   Feldman, *The Krakow Diary of Julius Feldman* (Newark, NJ: Quill, 2002), David
   Kahane, *Lvov Ghetto Diary* (Amherst, MA: University of Massachusetts Press,
   1990), Alex Meijer, *Alex's Diary, 1942–45* (Israel: Biblio Books, 2005) and Roman
   Frister, *The Cap or the Price of a Life* (London: Weidenfeld & Nicolson, 1999).
   Vladka Meed (Vladka Meed, *On Both Sides of the Wall* (Tel Aviv: Beit Lohamei
   Haghettaot, 1977)) only begins her account after entering the ghetto, a trend which
   can also be found in recorded accounts in the Imperial War Museum including
   Ben Helfgott (IWM – Ben Helfgott – 9165/20), who records only one reel of twenty
   on the period and Roman Halter (IWM – Roman Halter – 17183/17) who records
   only one of seventeen. This tendency, however, is also linked to the questions they
   are asked, which diminishes our ability to discuss the accounts themselves as proof
   of the deconstruction but again suggests a problematic approach to the period by
   historians. For Sara Zyskind, this period is one of extreme activity and turmoil,
   including the relocation of the entire family, her father's assault and the loss of all of
   their belongings, and yet only sixteen pages detail the events from September 1939
   to the closure of the ghetto in May 1940. In stark contrast, the time spent in the
   ghetto is meticulously detailed (Zyskind, *Stolen Years*).
6 The German campaign in Poland is well researched and can be found discussed
   in the works of Alexander Rossino and Jochen Böhler amongst others. Operation

Barbarossa was the name given to the Nazi campaign to invade the Soviet Union which began in 1941.

7 The UGIF was the administrative body established by the Nazis in 1941 to formally represent the Jews of occupied and 'free' France. Despite the internment and deportation or a number of its key officials in 1943, the organization continued to work beyond the liberation to support Jews still remaining in France.

8 Yehuda Bauer, *A History of the Holocaust* (New York: Franklin Watts, 2001), p. 253.

9 Contradicting this, some might argue that in Jewish families where women commonly worked with, or occasionally even in lieu of, their husbands, this might not be the case. However, Hyman has convincingly shown that many Jewish families, even in the more traditional east, were, by this time, aspiring to bourgeois formations of the family, with male breadwinners and decision makers and increasingly passive, child-oriented women, even where realities continued to dictate that both parents work to support the family. Paula E. Hyman, 'Gender and the Jewish Family in Modern Europe' in Ofer and Weitzman, eds., *Women in the Holocaust*, p. 27.

10 Helen Kotlar, *We Live in a Grave* (New York: Shengold, 1980), p. 33.

11 Kotlar, *We Live in a Grave*, p. 17.

12 Mark Lewis and Jacob Frank, *Himmler's Jewish Tailor: The Story of the Holocaust Survivor Jacob Frank* (Syracuse, NY: Syracuse University Press, 2000), p. 28. Similarly, Rena Zabielak looked after her father, hiding him or protesting that he was ill when the Germans came to their home. The family assumption that women were safe and men were not seems, in this case, to have been sustained since she was not hurt (that we know of) and her father remained safe (IWM – Rena Zabielak – 17369–4).

13 Alexander Donat, *The Holocaust Kingdom* (New York: The Holocaust Library, 1978), p. 4.

14 Fania Freich quoted in David Boder, *I Did Not Interview the Dead* (Urbana, IL: University of Illinois Press, 1949), p. 64.

15 'We had also heard that in Metz the Germans had been arresting women and children, but not everybody could bring themselves to believe it.' Albert Hipszman brother of Marcel in Marcel Hipszman, *Souvenirs d'enfance de Marcel: Un enfant dans la guerre* (unpublished, 2003), p. 10, shown to me by the author in Paris, September 2010.

16 Bernstein is one very clear example of this (Sholom-Abner Bernstein, 'I Was a Refugee in Oppressed Dereczin' in Jacob Berger, ed., *The Dereczin Memorial Book: A Book of Remembrances Honoring the Communities of Dereczin, Halinka, Kolonia-Sinaiska* (Mahwah, NJ: Jacob Berger, 2000)).

17 Dalia Ofer, 'Gender Issues in Diaries and Testimonies of the Ghetto: The Case of Warsaw' in Ofer and Weitzman, eds., *Women in the Holocaust*, p. 147.

18 Marcel Liebman, *Born Jewish: A Childhood in Occupied Europe* (London: Verso, 2005), p. 13.

19 Levi, *The Drowned and the Saved*, p. 58. Levi particularly writes about shame emanating from a failure to act, in this case to help a friend, but rarely from actions, even ones which damaged others – such as stealing bread. He also describes how gentile prisoners were able to escape this shame because the power they held within the camp structure more commonly enabled them to act.

20 Emphasis my own. Levi, *The Drowned and the Saved*, p. 54.

21 Abe Mohnblum in Boder, *I Did Not Interview the Dead*, p. 109.

22 Saul Friedländer, *When Memory Comes* (New York: Farrar, Straus, Giroux, 1979), p. 55.

23 Amongst many, see note 73 for several examples of this.

24 Yitzhak Katznelson, *Vittel Diary* (Tel Aviv: Ghetto Fighters' House/Beit Lohamei Haghetaot, 1972), p. 17. Katznelson's revitalization after the establishment of the Warsaw ghetto is something I shall go on to discuss in the next chapter.

25 Levi, *The Drowned and the Saved*, p. 56.

26 Moshe Flinker, *Young Moshe's Diary. The Spiritual Torment of a Jewish Boy in Nazi Europe* (Jerusalem: Yad Vashem, 1971), p. 24.

27 Flinker, *Young Moshe's Diary*, p. 88.

28 Raymond Raoul Lambert, *Diary of a Witness 1940–1943* (Chicago, IL: Ivan R Dee, 2005), p. 79.

29 Lambert, *Diary of a Witness 1940–1943*, p. 93.

30 Liebman, *Born Jewish*, p. 44.

31 Polonsky, *The Jews in Poland and Russia*, p. 62.

32 Johanna-Ruth Dobschiner, *Selected to Live* (London: Hodder and Stoughton, 2000), p. 17.

33 Abram Lancman, *Youth in the Time of the Holocaust* (Warsaw: Rytm, 2005), p. 35.

34 Examples of this are numerous but include the fathers of Roman Halter (IWM – Roman Halter – 17183/17), Ben Helfgott (IWM – Ben Helfgott – 9165/20) and Lili Pohlmann (IWM – Lili Pohlmann – 17340/18).

35 Liebman, *Born Jewish*, p. 13.

36 I will go on to discuss examples of this in more detail throughout this study.

37 In the case of Barbara Stimler, when the SS came to the family home, her father fled, her mother was then beaten and she was sexually assaulted (IWM – Barbara Stimler – 17475/5).

38 Katznelson is one clear example of this. He fled to Warsaw from Łódź because his wife begged him to do so (Katznelson, *Vittel Diary*, p. 15).

39 Lewis and Frank, *Himmler's Jewish Tailor*, p. 28

40 Lewis and Frank, *Himmler's Jewish Tailor*, p. 28.

41 Whilst this massive displacement of Polish and Jewish-Polish men has been written about by numerous historians, it has most commonly been analysed from the perspective of those women left behind. Historians of gender have tended to argue

that this movement of people shows the transfer of responsibility for caring and protection from men onto women, regularly ignoring, however, the impact of such a move, often made unwillingly, upon the men themselves. Many of these men struggled hard to establish new, safer lives, the only aim of which was to bring their families out of danger. One example of this is Kruk who fled Warsaw for Vilnius where he received a visa to go to the United States; however, he refused to leave until his wife could join him, by which time it was too late to leave and they both died in the Holocaust (Herman Kruk, *The Last Days of the Jerusalem of Lithuania. Chronicles from the Vilna Ghetto and the Camps, 1939–44* (New Haven, CT: Yale University Press, 2002)).

42 Alexander Bronowski, *They Were Few* (New York: Lang, 1991), p. 4.

43 Lewis and Frank, *Himmler's Jewish Tailor*, p. 33.

44 Donat, *Holocaust Kingdom*, p. 5.

45 Leon Wells, *The Janowska Road* (New York: Holocaust Library, 1978), p. 39.

46 Aleksandra Kroh, *Lucien's Story: A Memoir* (Evanston, IL: Northwestern University Press, 1993), p. 2.

47 Liebman, *Born Jewish*, p. 47.

48 Liebman, *Born Jewish*, p. 94.

49 Liebman, *Born Jewish*, p. 113.

50 Sam Pivnik, *Survivor: Auschwitz, the Death March and My Fight for Freedom* (London: Hodder, 2013), p. 8.

51 Shoah Foundation interview with Samuel Schryver (found at sfi.usc.edu and viewed repeatedly between 1 January 2013 and 20 December 2013).

52 Kaplan, *Between Dignity and Despair*, p. 5.

53 Katz, *One Who Came Back*, p. 86. Both of these quotations are taken from individuals writing about Poland, but reflect similar, although sometimes less overt, comments about experiences in other countries.

54 Ringelblum, *Notes from the Warsaw Ghetto*, p. 69.

55 Yitzhak Zuckerman, *A Surplus of Memory: Chronicle of the Warsaw Ghetto Uprising* (Berkeley, CA: University of California Press, 1993), p. 18.

56 Exactly how this affected different Jewish men depended on their levels of assimilation and exclusion from society and is something I will consider later in the chapter.

57 Mary Berg, *The Diary of Mary Berg: Growing Up in the Warsaw Ghetto* (Oxford: Oneworld, 2006), p. 2.

58 Perechodnik, *Am I a Murderer?*, p. 1.

59 These are memorial books published after the Holocaust by surviving members of communities to remember the people, places and lives that had been lost.

60 Dr. Asher Heller, 'The Destruction of the Jewish Community of Rzeszow' in Moshe Yari-Wald, ed., *Rzeszów Jews Memorial Book* (Tel Aviv: Rzeszower Societies in Israel and U.S.A, 1967), p. 74.

61 Bernstein, 'I Was a Refugee', p. 213.

62 Motl Eisenberg, 'Running from Death' in Berl Kagan, ed., *Szydłowiec Memorial Book* (New York: Shidlowtzer Benevolent Association, 1989), p. 166.

63 Ringelblum, *Notes from the Warsaw Ghetto*, p. 108.

64 Kaplan, *The Scroll of Agony*, p. 2.

65 Lancman, *Youth in the Time of the Holocaust*, p. 22.

66 Perechodnik (Perechodnik, *Am I a Murderer?*, p. 108) notes several stories about Jewish heroism during the struggle to stop the German invasion, suggesting that when all the other soldiers in a group would flee only the Jews would stay on to fight.

67 Julian Castle Stanford, *Reflections: The Diary of a German-Jew in Hiding* (Oakland, OR: Institute for the Righteous Acts of the Judah L. Magnes Memorial Museum, 1965), p. 32.

68 Berg, *The Diary of Mary Berg*, p. 5.

69 Kaplan, *The Scroll of Agony*, p. 33.

70 Zyskind, *Stolen Years*, p. 27.

71 Kaplan, *The Scroll of Agony*, p. 135.

72 Ringelblum, *Notes from the Warsaw Ghetto*, p. 39.

73 'My father avoided this problem by never wearing a hat, not even on the coldest days of those terrible Polish winters. "Why give them the pleasure?" he would say when people called him a *meshoogene* (crazy man) for not wearing a hat.' Thomas Buergenthal, *A Lucky Child* (London: Profile Books, 2009), p. 43. Likewise Susan Sinclair comments on the embarrassment of her father leaving the house without his hat on (Lyn Smith, *Forgotten Voices of the Holocaust* (London: Ebury Press, 2005), p. 54).

74 Michael Zylberberg, *A Warsaw Diary, 1939–1945* (London: Vallentine Mitchell, 1969), p. 21.

75 Władysław Szpilman, *The Pianist. The Extraordinary Story of One Man's Survival in Warsaw, 1939–1945* (London: Phoenix, 2003), p. 49.

76 Evidence suggests that a similar sense of humiliation was invoked by the use of 'Du' rather than 'Sie' by Germans when speaking to Jewish men. For many, this would have been seen as a rejection by the, often young, German soldiers of the status and respect they felt they had earned. This slur would have been understood by Yiddish-speaking Jews in any country; nevertheless, for linguistic reasons it is a phenomenon largely recorded by those living in Germany during the Holocaust.

77 For example, Chaim Kaplan (*The Scroll of Agony*, p. 36).

78 Ringelblum, *Notes from the Warsaw Ghetto*, p. 32.

79 Zyskind, *Stolen Years*, p. 31.

80 Kaplan, *The Scroll of Agony*, p. 53.

81 Kahane, *Lvov Ghetto Diary*, p. 9. The wearing of the star was introduced in western Poland in 1939 and eastern Poland in 1941, but did not reach the other countries under study until April–November 1942.

82 Shoah Foundation interview with Maurice White (found at sfi.usc.edu and viewed repeatedly between 1 January 2013 and 20 December 2013).

83 And, importantly, less easily identified as Jewish if questioned.

84 Here we need to consider arguments made by Ringelheim (Joan M. Ringelheim, 'The Split between Gender and the Holocaust' in Ofer and Weitzman, eds., *Women in the Holocaust*, p. 343) and Waxman (Z. Waxman, *Writing the Holocaust: Identity, Testimony, Representation* (Oxford: Oxford University Press, 2008), p. 138) that women only mention those events that seem important in the light of subsequent events (i.e. assault seems irrelevant when placed next to mass murder and the horror of the ghettos). Both argue that what these women consider important is strongly influenced by a gendered discourse concerning the history of the Holocaust, which is to say that women tend not to write about things which only affect women since there is little precedent for it in the historiography as constructed predominantly by men. If this is the case, however, male writings which regularly reference humiliations of status as discussed in this chapter would give women permission to do likewise, and yet they do not, reinforcing the impression that such occurrences were more common in the lives of men than women.

85 Kruk, *The Last Days of the Jerusalem of Lithuania*, p. 28.

86 Bernstein, 'I Was a Refugee', p. 219.

87 Zuckerman, *A Surplus of Memory*, p. 27.

88 This was particularly the case in the Baltic states, which are outside the scope of this book, but varied significantly between different European countries and cities.

89 Castle Stanford, *Reflections*, p. 74.

90 Katz, *One Who Came Back*, p. 7.

91 Dalia Ofer, 'The Community and the Individual: The Different Narratives of Early and Late Testimonies and Their Significance for Historians' in David Bankier and Dan Michman, eds., *Holocaust Historiography in Context. Emergence, Challenges, Polemics and Achievements* (Jerusalem: Yad Vashem, 2008), *passim*.

92 One example of this is Abraham Zwirek who references his father banning him from attending football matches before the German invasion because of antisemitism (IWM – Abraham Zwirek – 9192/6). However, plenty of other examples appear, particularly in audio accounts where interviewees are asked directly about such matters. (One question arises here concerning the extent to which these men were prompted to discuss such events by their interviewer, but still when asked they do make a link between pre-war assaults and the early humiliations of the deconstruction.)

93 Ringelblum, *Notes from the Warsaw Ghetto*, p. 82.

94 Laura Jockusch, *Collect and Record! Jewish Holocaust Documentation in Early Postwar Europe* (Oxford: Oxford University Press, 2012), p. 37.

95 Joseph Schupack, *The Dead Years* (New York: Holocaust Library, 1986), p. 37.

96 Bernstein, 'I Was a Refugee', p. 230, Masha and Abraham Kulakowski, 'Two Years in the Partisan Forces' in Berger, ed., *The Dereczin Memorial Book*, p. 273 and Shmuel Borenstien, 'With the Dereczin Fighters in the Forest' in Berger, ed., *The Dereczin Memorial Book*, p. 283.

97 Gerschick and Miller, 'Coming to Terms', p. 313.

98 This is at least partially a question of sources – those men who were starving in the very early period were often very poor and had extremely limited resources. These were, therefore, some of the first men to die and consequently they very rarely managed to live to record their experiences. As is generally true of my research, those who survived to record their stories, given that the Holocaust lasted over five years, had some resources which allowed them to endure the early years in limited comfort.

99 The loss of personal space, when it came, features more rarely in men's accounts than the expropriation of businesses and loss of work, and the real damage in such cases seems to have been to women who, enduring any number of other losses, were unable to bear the loss of the home. This conclusion, borne out in the testimonies, reinforces the suggestion that women's gendered identities were more closely formed in the home, whilst men relied more heavily on their role in public for gender affirmation.

100 Kaplan, *Between Dignity and Despair,* p. 32.

101 Szpilman, *The Pianist,* p. 31.

102 'They [G & G] emphasise the close identification of women with their bodies, and the consequent fact that "violations of the body are defacements of identity, and so are investments of the body in others' modes of unifying self and other". They contrast women's embodiment with a male pattern of minimizing the "significance of intimates."' The exception to this lack of male embodiment, Langerwey argues, is the death of the father, something I shall consider in my final chapter (Mary Langerwey, *Reading Auschwitz* (Walnut Creek, CA: Alta Mira Press, 1998), p. 72).

103 See again, amongst others, the work of George Mosse, John Tosh and Joan Tumbelty, not to mention books like Surén, *Der Mensch und die Sonne* and the culture to which it was responding.

104 Fania Freich, quoted in Boder, *I Did Not Interview the Dead,* p. 86.

105 Kaplan, *The Scroll of Agony,* p. 56.

106 Kaplan, *The Scroll of Agony,* p. 15.

107 Katznelson, *Vittel Diary,* p. 17.

108 IWM – Roman Halter – 17183/17.

109 Friedländer, *When Memory Comes,* p. 55.

110 Pivnik, *Survivor,* p. 53.

111 On this question, Wells records an early bombardment during which women cry and hold onto their children whilst men 'try to look brave'. Wells, *The Janowska Road,* p. 24.

112 Adam Czerniakow, *The Warsaw Diary of Adam Czerniakow: Prelude to Doom* (New York: Stein and Day, 1979), p. 97.

113 Kaplan, *The Scroll of Agony,* p. 18.

114 Michael Diment, *The Lone Survivor: A Diary of the Lukacze Ghetto and Svyruukhy Ukraine* (New York: The Holocaust Library, 1992), p. 7.

115 IWM – Barbara Stimler – 17475/5.

116 There is a marked tendency for descriptions of emotional collapse in women to be relatively brief, often involving hysteria and brought on by a particular event. In contrast male emotional collapse is more usually described in terms of depression, likely to be long lived and less often a response to a particular event.

117 I have already discussed this debate in some detail in my introduction.

118 Donat, *Holocaust Kingdom,* p. 4.

119 IWM – Elisabeth Harrison – (8304/5).

120 It is important here to note that there are several cases in which men try to leave and women bring them back, either through fear of the unknown or because of children and family ties. One example of this is Zyskind whose father wished to flee but whose mother wanted to stay to protect her family (Zyskind, *Stolen Years,* p. 23).

121 Zuckerman, *A Surplus of Memory*, p. 28.

122 Jafa Wallach, *Bitter Freedom: Memoirs of a Holocaust Survivor* (Schuylkill Haven, PA: Hermitage Publishers, 2006), p. 10.

123 IWM – Sem Hartz – (12888/4).

124 One particularly good example is Moshe Flinker (Flinker, *Young Moshe's Diary,* p. 30).

125 IWM – Roman Halter – 17183/17.

126 Pivnik, *Survivor*, p. 58.

127 Katznelson, *Vittel Diary,* p. 18.

128 Edmund Kessler, *The Wartime Diary of Edmund Kessler. Lvov, Poland* (Boston, MA: Academic Studies Press, 2010), p. 45.

129 Elie Wiesel, *Night* (London: Penguin, 1981), p. 21.

130 Mihail Sebastian, *Journal, 1935–1944* (London: Heinemann, 2003) and Victor Klemperer, *I Shall Bear Witness: The Diaries of Victor Klemperer, 1933–1941* (London: Weidenfeld & Nicolson, 1998).

131 Philip Friedman, *Roads to Extinction: Essays on the Holocaust* (New York: Jewish Publication Society of America, 1980), p. 139.

132 Gerschick and Miller, 'Coming to Terms', *passim.*

133 Gerschick and Miller, 'Coming to Terms', p. 315.

134 Gerschick and Miller, 'Coming to Terms', p. 323.

Chapter 3

1 Again this periodization and labelling is entirely my own.

2 Irrespective of questions of masculinity, the realities of life in the ghetto – particularly the need to work in order to attempt to secure one's place in the ghetto – made it difficult to remain in the home, even should one wish it.

3   Gustavo Corni, *Hitler's Ghettos: Voices from a Beleaguered Society, 1939–1944* (London: Arnold, 2002), p. 134.

4   Michal Unger, 'The Status and Plight of Women in the Lodz Ghetto' in Ofer and Weitzman, eds., *Women in the Holocaust*, p. 127.

5   Whilst heart disease was listed as the main cause of death, we do not know how many of these were cases, which we know occurred often, in which deaths by starvation were listed as 'heart disease'. Nonetheless, nor does Unger, and the statistical reality of heart disease cases is something she completely ignores.

6   It is necessary throughout this work to write of the ghettos in the plural since to treat them on an individual basis is not achievable within its scope. Nevertheless it is important to note that the Nazi regime and its allies established over 1,100 ghettos across Europe in this period. Of these, many are out of geographical scope, but in Poland alone, there was still no single format for the ghettos, no universal rationale for their establishment and no plan for how they should be controlled. Whilst some lasted for several years, with Łódź the last to be liquidated the summer of 1944, others lasted only a matter of weeks or months. The only unifying feature of these spaces was, as Michman defines it, 'the forced concentration of Jews in a particular location' (p. xxii). Moreover, sources are scarce for many of the smaller ghettos, making any attempt to present a comprehensive study of ghetto life extremely complex. For the purposes of this work, therefore, 'ghettos' will, for the most part, be a reference to a small number of the larger ghettos, most obviously Warsaw, Łódź and Vilnius. Although where possible, sources will also be drawn from smaller ghettos and will largely bear out the conclusions I have drawn elsewhere. For a detailed discussion of the varied and complex nature of the ghettos, see Dan Michman, 'The Jewish Ghettos Under the Nazis and Their Allies' in Guy Miron and Shlomit Shulhani, eds., *The Yad Vashem Encyclopaedia of the Ghettos During the Holocaust* (Jerusalem: Yad Vashem, 2009).

7   Isaiah Trunk, *Łódź Ghetto: A History* (Bloomington, IN: Indiana University Press, 2006), p. 13.

8   Leni Yahil, *The Holocaust: The Fate of European Jewry* (New York: Oxford University Press, 1990), p. 167.

9   Amongst others, Roman Halter talks about this single-minded struggle for survival (Halter, *Roman's Journey*).

10 Not only were the earliest historians of the period keen to note what they considered the unlikely social and moral value retained by those in the ghettos (Gringauz discussed in Tim Cole, 'Ghettoization', in D. Stone, ed., *The Historiography of the Holocaust* (Basingstoke: Palgrave, 2006), p. 67), but more recently historians, notably David Cesarani, have written at length about the nature and impact of sustained cultural life in many of the ghettos of German-occupied Poland.

11 Exactly how this sense of unity overrode the reality of the ghettos is unclear; however, Jeremy Popkin perhaps offers one potential explanation in his analysis of

testimonies written by survivors who later became historians when he writes of a clear 'reaching back' for one's Judaism and community during this period. Popkin, 'Holocaust Memories, Historians' Memoirs', p. 63.

12 Donat, *Holocaust Kingdom*, p. 25.

13 Kruk, *The Last Days of the Jerusalem of Lithuania*, p. 101.

14 Meed, *On Both Sides of the Wall*, p. 132. Similarly Pinkus notes, 'there was a deceptive sense of strength, the illusion of safety created by the fact of living within an exclusively Jewish community' (Pinkus cited in Corni, *Hitler's Ghettos*, p. 51).

15 Stanislaw Adler, *In the Warsaw Ghetto* (Jerusalem: Yad Vashem, 1982), p. 220.

16 D. Feierstein, 'The Jewish Resistance Movements in the Ghettos of Eastern Europe: Reflections of the Relationships of Force' in Eric J. Sterling, ed., *Life in the Ghettos During the Holocaust* (Syracuse, New York: Syracuse University Press, 2005), p. 237.

17 Marek Web, *The Documents of the Lodz Ghetto: An Inventory of the Nachman Zonabend Collection* (New York: YIVO Institute for Jewish Research, 1988), p. 23.

18 Zuckerman, *A Surplus of Memory*, p. 124. The enterprise which he notes stemming from this autonomy was an increase in activities, including singing and teaching, which had been impossible before the ghettos were enclosed but which returned in the courtyards of the ghettos.

19 Kaplan, *The Scroll of Agony*, p. 207.

20 Perechodnik, *Am I a Murderer?*, p. 11. Likewise Adler noted,

> [w]ith the closure of the Quarter, the rummaging of German soldiers, the S.S., and the scoundrels working on their own account had stopped. The plundering had ceased and the unorganized stealing of furniture had become a rare occurrence. For the moment, the price of food had stopped rising. It is understandable, therefore, that we experienced a sense of relief in our part of the ghetto because living within an exclusively Jewish society, we were rid of the annoyance and degradation we had experienced in the Aryan Quarter.

Adler, *In the Warsaw Ghetto*, p. 53.

21 Sources pertaining to the wartime activities of the EIF are relatively limited but include Anny Latour, *La Résistance Juive en France* (1940–1944) (Paris: Stock, 1970) and Wieviorka, *Ils étaient juifs, résistants, communistes* as well as a number of documents and interviews held in *Le Centre de Documentation Juive Contemporaine* in Paris.

22 Shoah Foundation Interview with Hermann Bodner (found at sfi.usc.edu and viewed repeatedly between 1 January 2013 and 20 December 13).

23 Joseph Brenig is one clear example of this. Shoah Foundation Interview with Joseph Brenig (found at sfi.usc.edu and viewed repeatedly between 1 January 2013 and 20 December 13).

24 Sources suggest that in the period before they went into hiding in the annexe, Otto's behaviour was particularly erratic, and that he seemed to struggle with the conditions of the deconstruction, the loss of work and the fact that he was being

blackmailed by a gentile; unedited versions of Anne's diaries even suggest that on one occasion during the deconstruction Otto ran into the street with a knife, threatening to kill himself (Carol A. Lee, *The Hidden Life of Otto Frank* (London: Penguin, 2002) citing Anne's diaries from 7.5.44).

25 Lee, *The Hidden Life of Otto Frank*, p. 86.

26 E.H. (Dan) Kampelmacher, *Fighting for Survival* (Jerusalem: Yad Vashem, 2006), p. 104.

27 Meed, *On Both Sides of the Wall*, p. 199.

28 Of course, this is written through the eyes of his son; nevertheless the source clearly depicts the impact of instability on the father (Liebman, *Born Jewish*), *passim*.

29 Adler, *In the Warsaw Ghetto*, p. 11.

30 Simcha (Kazik) Rotem, *Memoirs of a Warsaw Ghetto Fighter: The Past Within Me* (New Haven, CT: Yale University Press, 1994), p. 2.

31 Leon Kruczkowski, 'The Warsaw Ghetto Uprising' in *Bleter far Geszichte*, Czasopismo Zydowskiego Instiytutu Historycznego w Polsce (1983), p. xlvi.

32 Draegerova in Corni, *Hitler's Ghettos*, p. 305.

33 The answers of S.Z. Stupnicki to a ghetto questionnaire cited in Kermish, *To Live with Honor*, p. 737.

34 Diment, *The Lone Survivor*, p. 89.

35 Kermish, *To Live with Honor*, p. 600.

36 One might also argue that this idea of an active ghetto environment feeds into broad readings of the term 'resistance' used to refute suggestions that Jews 'went like lambs to the slaughter', a phrase first attributed to Abba Kovner in the Vilnius Ghetto, but which appears throughout writings from the Holocaust.

37 Robert W. Connell, *Masculinities* (Cambridge: Polity Press, 1995), *passim*.

38 'Built like an athlete – tall and strong with a bull neck' and 'he was considered the most handsome and elegant officer of the Jewish police'. Ionas Turkov, *C'était ainsi: 1939–1943, la vie dans le ghetto de Varsovie* (Paris: Austral, 1995), p. 118.

39 Kermish, *To Live with Honor*, p. 302 – a description of the man who ran the cemetery.

40 Adler, *In the Warsaw Ghetto*, p. 21.

41 Kermish, *To Live with Honor*, p. 94.

42 This is most clearly seen in Dobroszycki, *The Chronicle of the Łódź Ghetto*, p. 163 and p. 167.

43 Taken from *Fun Letztn Hurbn, No,3,6* and cited in Dov Levin, 'The Fighting Leadership of the Judenräte in the Small Communities of Poland' in Yisrael Gutman and Cynthia J. Haft, eds., *Patterns of Jewish Leadership in Nazi Europe 1933–1945: Proceedings of the Third Yad Vashem International Historical Conference – April 1977* (Jerusalem: Yad Vashem, 1979), p. 146.

44 Another reading of this source might be that the author is praising Feinberg for placing his commitment to family and community over his own survival and

perhaps even commending a more feminized masculinity. Nevertheless, by tying his choice to a group of women and a rabbi, the author is clearly commenting on Feinberg's masculinity, regardless of exactly what that comment is, thereby proving, as I suggest above, that questions of masculinity and gender identity remained pertinent to ghetto discourse.

45 Abraham Lewin, *A Cup of Tears: A Diary of the Warsaw Ghetto* (Oxford: Blackwell, 1988), p. 177.

46 Dobroszycki, *The Chronicle of the Łódź Ghetto*, p. 164.

47 A number of notable Jewish men fled Poland before the Holocaust – a fact which became significant in the formation of the masculinities of younger men; nonetheless many remained and were involved in the establishment of the ghetto leadership.

48 Yosef Kermisz, 'The Judenrat in Warsaw' in Gutman and Haft, eds., *Patterns of Jewish Leadership in Nazi Europe 1933–1945*, p. 76.

49 Adler, *In the Warsaw Ghetto*, p. 228.

50 This was something that Kruk noted taking place in the Vilna ghetto (Kruk, *The Last Days of the Jerusalem of Lithuania*, p. 156). *Judenrat* is the singular form of the German word *Judenräte*, defined in note 47 of the Introduction.

51 Corni, *Hitler's Ghettos*, p. 153.

52 'Assume his position as a man.' This process is mentioned in several sources in the CDJC but particularly CDJC – CCXX – 45written on the 15 March 1942 attests to the fact that it continued throughout the war. This is one of a few instances in which I refer to French language sources. For the most part, however, I have restricted myself to those written in English. One reason for this is the reality of the linguistic skills that would be required in order to use all the languages in which sources from these countries were written, including Flemish, Dutch, French, Polish, Yiddish, Hebrew, Russian and German. Since this is impossible, without limiting the scope of the book, or biasing the German and French texts, more commonly used by more assimilated Jews, I have chosen instead, therefore, to read all sources in English. Necessarily this means that almost every source is a translation, whether the author's own, writing in a second or often third language, or an external translation. Once this is acknowledged as being the case, one can maintain historical integrity by applying the same care in using all sources, something which I have discussed in detail in relation to the analysis of testimony, and in this case stressing where possible the broader discussion of the individual's gender and the sense of their testimony rather than the meaning and use of individual words. The central benefit of this approach, however, is that English has already become a lingua franca for Holocaust testimony, resulting in many sources being published in English, regardless of their author's mother tongue. A decision to prioritize English language sources, therefore, responds to this tendency, allowing me to draw from the broadest possible range of sources

and acknowledges the important role played by language in the formation and transmission of Holocaust history. An interesting discussion of English-language Holocaust sources can be found in Simone Gigliotti, *The Train Journey: Transit, Captivity and Witnessing in the Holocaust* (Oxford: Berghahn Books, 2009), p. 19, whilst Alan Rosen, *Sounds of Defiance: The Holocaust, Multilingualism, and the Problem of English* (Lincoln, NE: University of Nebraska Press, 2008), offers a detailed consideration of many of the questions pertaining to the use of the English language in writing about the Holocaust more broadly.

53 CDJC – CDXXVII – 1 is a series of letters between Monsieur Eskenasy and F. Musnik, both of the EIF, detailing their internal power rivalry during 1942.

54 Shoah Foundation Interview with Samuel Schryver.

55 As already considered, the ghettos of German-occupied Poland were not homogenous. Christopher Browning, in discussions attempting to further understand the role of the ghettos in the escalation of the Nazi policy of genocide, has defined two central rationales behind the establishment of the ghettos. The 'productionist' agenda focused on the 'minimization of the burden of the ghettoized Jews on the Reich through the maximization of their economic potential. For them the ghettos were potential economic units whose labour could be rationally organized to make them self-sufficient or, even better, able to contribute to the German war economy'. In contrast, the goal of 'attritionists' was 'the decline, indeed even the "dying out", of the Jewish population' in which ghettos functioned as 'vast concentration camps facilitating the total extraction of Jewish wealth through the leverage of deliberate starvation'. Łódź is classically used as an example of the former, whilst Warsaw tends to be used as an example of the latter. Christopher Browning, *The Origins of the Final Solution: The Evolution of Nazi Jewish Policy September 1939–March 1942* (Jerusalem: Yad Vashem, 2004), p. 113.

56 Trunk, *Łódź Ghetto*, p. xli.

57 Kermish, *To Live with Honor*, p. 259.

58 In the case of doctors, this was a particularly large ration, showing how one's work could directly affect survival and provision.

59 Dobroszycki, *The Chronicle of the Łódź Ghetto*, p. 3.

60 Perechodnik, *Am I a Murderer?*, p. 92.

61 Ringelblum goes as far as to suggest that people only really existed in the ghettos if they possessed a work card (Ringelblum, *Notes from the Warsaw Ghetto*, p. 319).

62 Dobroszycki, *The Chronicle of the Łódź Ghetto*, p. 202.

63 Mordechai Chaim Rumkowski from a speech given in the Łódź ghetto on 17 January 1942 and cited in Alan Adelson and Robert Lapides, eds., *Lodz Ghetto: Inside a Community Under Siege* (London: Penguin, 1989), p. 209.

64 Perechodnik, *Am I a Murderer?*, p. 44. Although one should note that Perechodnik's own family were ultimately deported from the ghetto to Treblinka, where they died.

65 Zylberberg, *A Warsaw Diary*, p. 71.

66 Zylberberg, *A Warsaw Diary*, p. 90.

67 Ringelblum, *Notes from the Warsaw Ghetto*, p. 167.

68 Hurwitz cited in Adelson and Lapides, *Lodz Ghetto*, p. 95.

69 Yisrael Gutman, 'The Concept of Labor in Judenrat Policy' in Gutman and Haft, eds., *Patterns of Jewish Leadership in Nazi Europe 1933–1945*, p. 162.

70 Kessler, *The Wartime Diary of Edmund Kessler*, p. 46.

71 Browning, *The Origins of the Final Solution*, p. 125.

72 Gutman, 'The Concept of Labor in Judenrat Policy', p. 171.

73 Trunk, *Łódź Ghetto*, p. 401 – Trunk contrasts these examples of Warsaw and other ghettos with the situation in Łódź where, due to its particularly harsh administration, such self-determination was not possible. More closely managed than other ghettos and hermetically sealed, all but removing the possibility of smuggling, it has been suggested that decisions concerning work, and therefore provision, and ultimately life and death could only be made by Rumkowski himself. Whilst one might argue that this led men to feel less independent and powerful than in other ghettos, the success of Łódź's productionist aims may also have given added confidence to its inhabitants concerning their own survival as workers and that of their families as workers and, or, dependents. Moreover, if Trunk is correct in his suggestions that one key reason for establishing production in the Łódź ghetto was to bring money into the ghetto in order to allow workers to provide for their families, then it is not unreasonable to suggest that the inhabitants too might have appreciated this reasoning, flawed as it was.

74 Diane Plotkin, 'Smuggling in the Ghettos: Survivor Accounts from the Warsaw, Lodz, and Krakow Ghettos' in Sterling, ed., *Life in the Ghettos During the Holocaust*, p. 96.

75 Corni, *Hitler's Ghettos*, p. 137.

76 Unger, 'The Status and Plight of Women in the Lodz Ghetto', p. 135.

77 Donat, *Holocaust Kingdom*, p. 21.

78 Kermish, *To Live with Honor*, p. 361.

79 Whilst sources which involve men recording their own bravery are clearly questionable, still the nature of the record at least tells us something about the ability and desire to act in a masculine way as well as a general sense that such action was possible in the ghettos.

80 Used in this context to denote a holding area usually near a ghetto and a railway station where Jewish populations were assembled during the Holocaust prior to deportation to the camps. In this case, it is a reference to the square where Jews from the Warsaw ghetto were held before deportation.

81 Janine David, *A Square of Sky, a Touch of Earth: A Wartime Childhood in Poland* (Harmondsworth: Penguin, 1981), p. 189.

82 Zylberberg, *A Warsaw Diary*, p. 173.

83   Jakob Breitowicz, *Through Hell to Life* (New York: Shengold Publishers Inc., 1983), p. 39.

84   Shoah Foundation Interview with Hans Angress (found at sfi.usc.edu and viewed repeatedly between 1 January 2013 and 20 December 2013).

85   Benno Benninga, *In Hiding: Surviving an Abusive 'Protector' and the Nazi Occupation of Holland* (London: Vallentine Mitchell, 2007), p. 22.

86   Meijer, *Alex's Diary*, p. 2 and *passim* – Meijer notes that as his mother lived with them in the attic, she did the cooking. Had she been hidden elsewhere, as had originally been the plan, the men would have eaten with their hosts (p. 18).

87   Shoah Foundation Interview with Otto Berets (found at sfi.usc.edu and viewed repeatedly between 1 January 2013 and 20 December 2013).

88   Lee, *The Hidden Life of Otto Frank*, p. 86.

89   Shoah Foundation Interview with Joseph van West (found at sfi.usc.edu and viewed repeatedly between 1 January 2013 and 20 December 2013).

90   IWM – Sem Hartz – 12888/4 and Shoah Foundation Interview with Eric Baruch (found at sfi.usc.edu and viewed repeatedly between 1 January 2013 and 20 December 2013).

91   Kampelmacher, *Fighting for Survival*, p. 140.

92   Kampelmacher, *Fighting for Survival*, p. 106, Kampelmacher noted his clear satisfaction at being able to provide for himself and his host family with the money he earned working on farms.

93   Shoah Foundation Interview with Joseph Brenig.

94   Kurt Leuchter is one such example and is recorded by the Shoah Foundation as saying 'I learned how to handle weapons' (found at sfi.usc.edu and viewed repeatedly between 1 January 2013 and 20 December 2013).

95   Shoah Foundation Interview with Harry Alexander (found at sfi.usc.edu and viewed repeatedly between 1 January 2013 and 20 December 2013).

96   Shoah Foundation Interview with Samuel Schryver.

97   Sources for this powerlessness in the face of the Germans are myriad, but a clear example can be seen in Isaiah Trunk, 'The Typology of the Judenräte in Eastern Europe' in Gutman and Haft, eds., *Patterns of Jewish Leadership in Nazi Europe 1933–1945*, p. 20.

98   Trunk, *Łódź Ghetto*, p. 402.

99   Lichtenbaum succeeded Adam Czerniakow as head of the Warsaw ghetto *Judenrat* following the latter's suicide on the eve of a major deportation of Jews from the Warsaw ghetto to Treblinka death camp in July 1942.

100   Feierstein, 'The Jewish Resistance', p. 241.

101   For further discussion of the exact position of the ŻOB in the hierarchies of the Warsaw ghetto, see Israel Gutman, *The Jews of Warsaw, 1939–1943: Ghetto, Underground, Revolt* (Brighton: Harvester Press, 1982), pp. 228–249.

102   Feierstein, 'The Jewish Resistance', p. 238.

103 This is a point stressed by Kermisz who references a member of the *Judenrat* who resigned because he felt 'impotent'. If this has not been altered in translation, it is interesting here that he uses a language of masculinity, which suggests that even if his own masculinity is damaged, the discourse still exists and holds some power (Kermisz, 'The *Judenrat* in Warsaw', p. 86).

104 Corni, *Hitler's Ghettos*, p. 65.

105 Amongst these is Kaplan's diary (Kaplan, *The Scroll of Agony*) which refers to the members of the Judenräte as 'musclemen', a term which seems to value the masculinity of those it referred to, particularly if we consider discourses of the 'muscle Jew' prevalent in relation to Palestine in the pre-war period.

106 Adler, *In the Warsaw Ghetto*, p. 86.

107 Dobroszycki, *The Chronicle of the Łódź Ghetto*, p. 286. The late creation of women police confirms rather than challenges the point made above.

108 Corni, *Hitler's Ghettos*, p. 108.

109 'They saw this recently created institution as somewhere to build a career, earn some money and slake their thirst for power.' Turkov, *C'était ainsi*, p. 114.

110 Political parties and social groups also thrived on a similar military style esprit de corps, something which Sierakowiak records as does Trunk (*Łódź Ghetto*, p. 33).

111 Kaplan, *The Scroll of Agony*, p. 234.

112 Dan Michman, 'Jewish Leadership in Extremis' in Dan Stone, ed., *The Historiography of the Holocaust* (Basingstoke: Palgrave Macmillan, 2004), p. 325.

113 Levin, 'The Fighting Leadership of the Judenräte', p. 145.

114 Wacław Poterański, *The Warsaw Ghetto: On the 30th Anniversary of the Armed Uprising of 1943* (Warsaw: Interpress, 1973), p. 38.

115 Rotem, *Memoirs of a Warsaw Ghetto Fighter*, p. 22.

116 Numerous sources speak of the problems Jewish men faced in being fully assimilated into Western resistance organizations, most notably these include Eric Baruch (Shoah Foundation Interview) and David Lederman (Shoah Foundation Interview found at sfi.usc.edu and viewed repeatedly between 1 January 2013 and 20 December 13).

117 Berg, *The Diary of Mary Berg*, p. 52.

118 The masculinity of such organizations was reinforced by their composition, largely comprising young people, their leadership roles were often filled by men from working backgrounds including communal workers and trade unionists with strong traditional masculine identities. Kermish, *To Live with Honor*, p. 342.

119 Yahil, *The Holocaust*, p. 209.

120 Janina Bauman, *Beyond These Walls: Escaping the Warsaw Ghetto, a Young Girl's Story* (London: Virago, 2006), p. 62. Although several of these sources are written by women, they nevertheless describe action and labour, which for men would have directly impacted on their gender identities.

121 Shoah Foundation Interview with Joseph Brenig.

122 Poterański, *The Warsaw Ghetto*, p. 38.

123 IWM – Jonkje Grandia-Smits – (8635/6).

124 IWM – Freddie Knoller – (9092/13).

125 Shoah Foundation Interview with David Lederman.

126 Michael M. Checinski, *My Father's Watch* (Jerusalem: Gefen, 1994), p. 129.

127 Poterański, *The Warsaw Ghetto*, p. 35.

128 Meed, *On Both Sides of the Wall*, pp. 199–200.

129 Harold Werner, *Fighting Back: A Memoir of Jewish Resistance in World War II* (New York: Columbia University Press, 1992), p. 168.

130 CDJC – Survivors of the Shoah Series – Climaud.

131 'We Became Very Powerful.' CDJC – DLXI – 6 Maurice Bernsohn.

132 Adler, *In the Warsaw Ghetto*, p. 297.

133 Adler, *In the Warsaw Ghetto*, p. 328.

134 Czerniakow, *The Warsaw diary of Adam Czerniakow*, p. 376.

135 Lambert, *Diary of a Witness*, p. 153.

136 Werner, *Fighting Back*, p. 119.

137 Werner, *Fighting Back*, p. 121.

138 Werner, *Fighting Back*, p. 119.

139 Zuckerman, *A Surplus of Memory*, pp. 119–120.

140 Zylberberg, *A Warsaw Diary*, p. 34.

141 Yaffa Eliach, *Hasidic Tales of the Holocaust* (New York: Oxford University Press, 1982).

142 Eliach, *Hasidic Tales of the Holocaust*, p. 72.

143 Eliach, *Hasidic Tales of the Holocaust*, p. 11.

144 Kahane, *Lvov Ghetto Diary*, p. 48. The Arbeitsamt, in this context, was the work office, which assigned labour to those living inside the ghetto.

145 IWM – Freddie Knoller (9092/13).

146 Shoah Foundation Interview with Jacques Breitberg (found at sfi.usc.edu and viewed repeatedly between 1 January 2013 and 20 December 2013).

147 Shoah Foundation Interview with Joseph Brenig.

148 Oskar Rosenfeld, *In the Beginning Was the Ghetto* (Evanston, IL: Northwestern University Press, 2002), p. 16.

149 Rosenfeld, *In the Beginning Was the Ghetto*, p. 16.

150 David, *Square of Sky, a Touch of Earth*, p. 140.

151 Josef Zelkowicz, *In Those Terrible Days: Notes from the Lodz Ghetto* (Jerusalem: Yad Vashem, 2002), p. 48.

152 Wallach, *Bitter Freedom*, *passim*.

153 Bondy, 'Women in Theresienstadt and the Family Camp in Birkenau', p. 323.

154 Friedman, *Roads to Extinction*, p. 150.

155 Friedman, *Roads to Extinction*, p. 138. The men who filled this role varied between ghettos, depending on several factors including the position of assimilated men in

the ghetto administration. Nonetheless, even if the men change, the phenomenon remains very similar across the ghettos.

156 The Kehillot were a form of Jewish council used in many parts of Central Europe in the interwar period of the twentieth century, the rights and responsibilities of which varied from region to region.

157 Zelkowicz, *In Those Terrible Days*, p. 198.

158 Dobroszycki, *The Chronicle of the Łódź Ghetto*, p. 28.

159 Zuckerman, *A Surplus of Memory*, p. 117.

160 Corni, *Hitler's Ghettos*, p. 170. Whilst a few men were able to make the transition – Mary Berg's father goes from being an art dealer to a house janitor and earns people's respect (Berg, *The Diary of Mary Berg*, p. 74) – it was relatively rare.

161 Friedman, *Roads to Extinction*, p. 133.

162 Perechodnik, *Am I a Murderer?*, p. 95. Perechodnik records an example of a male visitor attempting to discuss literature. Perechodnik become annoyed since, in the circumstances, he sees intellectualism as trivial.

163 It is clear from numerous sources that, whatever prohibitions were in place, religion continued to be practised throughout the ghettos.

164 Lancman, *Youth in the Time of the Holocaust*, p. 60.

165 Pivnik, *Survivor*, p. 81.

166 Ringelblum, *Notes from the Warsaw Ghetto*, p. 82. Although some rabbis in the ghettos did lift the laws of Kashrut to enable people to eat whatever food was available to them, this does not diminish the struggle that many endured to remain kosher during this period, a struggle to which Pivnik clearly alludes.

167 Plotkin, 'Smuggling in the Ghettos', p. 105.

168 A German term sometimes used by the Nazis to denote the territory of the German Reich before the 1938 annexation of Austria. A number of Jews originally from this area were deported to ghettos further east during the early years of the 1940s.

169 Dobroszycki, *The Chronicle of the Łódź Ghetto*, p. 153.

170 Dobroszycki, *The Chronicle of the Łódź Ghetto*, p. 156.

171 Czerniakow, *The Warsaw diary of Adam Czerniakow*, p. 271 – that he also chooses to show them to others, and records doing so, enhances this impression.

172 Adler, *In the Warsaw Ghetto*, p. 50.

173 Lancman, *Youth in the Time of the Holocaust*, p. 60.

174 Pivnik, *Survivor*, p. 35.

175 Feierstein, 'The Jewish Resistance', p. 232.

176 Kermish, *To Live with Honor*, p. 755.

177 Kermish, *To Live with Honor*, p. 605.

178 David Shavit, *Hunger for the Printed Word: Books and Libraries in the Jewish Ghettos of Nazi-Occupied Europe* (Jefferson, NC: McFarland, 1997), p. 135.

179 Kaplan, *The Scroll of Agony*, p. 288.

180   Lancman, *Youth in the Time of Holocaust*, p. 83.

181   Kermish, *To Live with Honor*, p. 300.

182   Lancman, *Youth in the Time of Holocaust*, p. 83.

183   Rumkowski cited in Adelson and Lapides, *Lodz Ghetto*, p. 211.

184   Wallach, *Bitter Freedom*, p. 93.

185   Bronowski, *They Were Few*, p. 40.

186   On the gaining of knowledge Kaplan recorded, '[w]e listen to Reuters with great respect. Every word gives us courage; every small detail that points to any military weakness is carried through the length and breadth of the ghetto as though on eagles' wings' (Kaplan, *The Scroll of Agony*, p. 266) whilst great respect was also accorded to those involved in writing underground publications, of which there were more than thirty in the Warsaw ghetto alone between 1940 and 1942 (Poterański, *The Warsaw Ghetto*, p. 33).

187   Dobschiner, *Selected to Live*, p. 136.

188   Kampelmacher, *Fighting for Survival*, p. 111.

189   Kermish, *To Live with Honor*, p. 66.

190   Kaplan, *The Scroll of Agony*, p. 280.

191   Berg, *The Diary of Mary Berg*, p. 85.

192   Rumkowski cited in Adelson and Lapides, *Lodz Ghetto*, p. 212.

193   Zylberberg, *A Warsaw Diary*, p. 71 and p. 90.

194   Adler, *In the Warsaw Ghetto*, p. 309.

195   Sierakowiak, *The Diary of Dawid Sierakowiak*, passim.

196   Corni, *Hitler's Ghetto*, p. 56.

197   I. Trunk, *Jewish Responses to Nazi persecution: Collective and Individual Behavior in Extremis* (New York: Stein and Day, 1979), p. 32.

198   Kermish, *To Live with Honor*, p. 451.

199   Wells, *The Janowska Road*, p. 120.

200   Plotkin, 'Smuggling in the Ghettos', p. 114.

201   Zelkowicz, *In Those Terrible Days*, p. 276.

202   Szpilman, *The Pianist*, p. 67.

203   Lancman, *Youth in the Time of the Holocaust*, p. 61.

204   Bronowski, *They Were Few*, p. 41.

Chapter 4

1   Perla Frankel-Shalev and Miriam Don, *Memoir: A True Story of a Family's Escape* (Israel: Karen Dondushansky, 2006), p. 97.

2   Henry Wermuth, *Breathe Deeply My Son* (London: Vallentine Mitchell, 1993), p. 182.

3   IWM – Ben Helfgott – 9165/20. Notably Helfgott specifically refers to his father as a 'hero', as does Marylou Ruhe – 17753/4 – IWM, something I have never found in relation to mothers.

4   Henry Orenstein, *I Shall Live: Surviving the Holocaust 1939–1945* (Oxford: Oxford University Press, 1988), p. 14.

5   Liebman, *Born Jewish*, p. 13. Some time after the Holocaust Liebman comes to realize that this was extremely naïve and that his father was not what he had thought. This does not, however, change how he felt at the time or the impact this might have had on his own and his father's masculinity.

6   Lawrence Langer, *Preempting the Holocaust* (New Haven, CT: Yale University Press, 1998), p. 57.

7   Waxman, Z., 'Towards an Integrated History of the Holocaust: Masculinity, Femininity, and Genocide' in Christian Wiese and Paul Betts, eds., *Years of Persecution, Years of Extermination: Saul Friedländer and the Future of Holocaust Studies* (London: Continuum, 2010), p. 316.

8   Tec, *Resilience and Courage*, p. 62.

9   Ofer and Weitzman, 'Introduction', p. 9.

10   Sierakowiak, *The Diary of David Sierakowiak*, p. 196.

11   Tec, *Resilience and Courage*, pp. 62–63. Perhaps the only other example of this I can find is Donat, who tells the story of a man who steals bread and soup from his son in the camp. The son later dies as the camp is evacuated but we do not know exactly why (Donat, *Holocaust Kingdom*, p. 278).

12   'Successful' here is a relative term since ultimately the whole family perished; nonetheless for a period of time Sierakowiak Sr found work and provided food for his family.

13   Sierakowiak, *The Diary of David Sierakowiak*, p. 111.

14   Sierakowiak, *The Diary of David Sierakowiak*, p. 231.

15   Charlie Lewis, *Becoming a Father* (Milton Keynes: Open University Press, 1986), Introduction.

16   Lewis, *Becoming a Father*, p. 4.

17   Lewis, *Becoming a Father*, p. 7 – although this is certainly not a universally accepted position amongst historical sociologists.

18   Here, as elsewhere and for the same reasons, I intentionally exclude a discussion of those ultra-orthodox families in which men focused on their Torah studies even after marriage, and women acted as the main breadwinners.

19   This is certainly different for grandfathers who are often discussed with great pride and respect by grandchildren. However, I would argue that the expectations placed on a grandfather are so different to those placed on a father that the two cannot be usefully discussed in the same chapter. What is interesting in this case is the father–child relationship of support and dependence, rather than the grandfather–grandchild relationship of wisdom and care.

20 Lorna McKee and Margaret O'Brien, *The Father Figure* (London: Tavistock, 1982), p. 21.

21 IWM – Marylou Ruhe – 17753/4.

22 Orenstein, *I Shall Live*, p. 6.

23 Abraham Zuckerman, *A Voice in the Chorus: Life as a Teenager in the Holocaust* (Hoboken, NJ: KTAV Publishing House, 1991), p. 12.

24 Liebman, *Born Jewish*, p. 6.

25 The most obvious cases of this are Elie Wiesel (Wiesel, *Night*, p. 21) and Roman Halter (IWM – Roman Halter – 17183/17).

26 As discussed previously in detail.

27 Wermuth, *Breathe Deeply*, p. 135.

28 Ruszka Zar, *In the Mouth of the Wolf* (New York: The Jewish Publication Society of America, 1983), p. 11.

29 IWM – Ben Helfgott – 9165/20.

30 This problem is compounded by the accepted bias that sources contain toward presenting an idealized version of life before the Holocaust. Corni, *Hitler's Ghettos*, p. 5.

31 IWM – Martin Parker – 12597/9.

32 A transit camp in the north of the Netherlands where Jews were held prior to deportation to concentration and extermination camps.

33 IWM – Leon Greenman – 9274/23.

34 IWM – Ben Helfgott – 9165/20.

35 IWM – Nicole David – 15323/5.

36 IWM – Lea Goodman – 12536/6.

37 Hipszman, *Souvenirs d'enfance de Marcel*, p. 8.

38 Yitzchak Rudashevski, *The Diary of the Vilna Ghetto* (Tel Aviv: Ghetto Fighters' House/Beit Lohamei Haghetaot, 1973), p. 80.

39 David Rubinowicz, *The Diary of Dawid Rubinowicz* (Edinburgh: Blackwood, 1982), p. 60. However, the reverse cases also exist where children whose mother dies are called orphans (Kaplan, *The Scroll of Agony*, p. 307).

40 Feldman, *The Krakow Diary*, p. 80.

41 Meed, *On Both Sides of the Wall*, p. 335.

42 Smith, *Forgotten Voices of the Holocaust*, p. 150.

43 Smith, *Forgotten Voices of the Holocaust*, p. 150.

44 Checinski, *My Father's Watch*, p. 59.

45 Zar, *In the Mouth of the Wolf*, p. 27.

46 Wermuth, *Breathe Deeply*, p. 133. On a lighter note, Wermuth also notes carrying a spare pair of socks in his pockets to use as gloves on his father's advice. They came in handy, he notes, when he was made to dig in the snow by the Germans, again something for which he credits his father (p. 31).

47 Shoah Foundation interview with Benno Benima (found at sfi.usc.edu and viewed repeatedly between 1 January 2013 and 20 December 2013).

48 IWM – Stanley Faull – 18272/7.

49 Rosenfeld, *In the Beginning Was the Ghetto*, p. 55.

50 Lewis and Frank, *Himmler's Jewish Tailor*, p. 6.

51 The reference is to Whitsun although this is not a Jewish festival, and we must assume that the author or his editor has christianized the reference for the reader's ease. It is likely that he referring to Shavuot.

52 Rubinowicz, *The Diary*, p. 82.

53 Shoah Foundation interview with Otto Berets (found at sfi.usc.edu and viewed repeatedly between 1 January 2013 and 20 December 2013).

54 Shoah Foundation interview with George Weiss (found at sfi.usc.edu and viewed repeatedly between 1 January 2013 and 20 December 2013).

55 Wermuth, *Breathe Deeply*, p. 42.

56 Wermuth, *Breathe Deeply*, p. 36.

57 Meir Bakalchuk, 'Uprooted with the Maelstrom' in Berger, ed., *The Dereczin Memorial Book*, p. 325.

58 Lambert, *Diary of a Witness*, p. 153.

59 Flinker, *Young Moshe's Diary*, p. 54.

60 Kaplan, *The Scroll of Agony*, p. 281.

61 Lambert, *Diary of a Witness*, p. 153.

62 Rudashevski, *The Diary of the Vilna Ghetto*, p. 87.

63 Feldman, *The Krakow Diary*, p. 23.

64 Wermuth, *Breathe Deeply*, p. 63.

65 IWM – Ben Helfgott – 9165/20.

66 IWM – Ben Helfgott – 9165/20.

67 IWM – Barbara Stimler – 17475/5.

68 IWM – Ben Helfgott – 9165/20.

69 IWM – Rena Zabielak – 17369/4.

70 Zyskind, *Stolen Years*, p. 82.

71 Wiesel, *Night*, p. 14, p. 21 and p. 24 amongst others – this links to my earlier discussion about the amoral nature of masculinity. In the case of Wiesel, his objections to his father hinge on his being too powerful within the family and perhaps implacable. Whilst this is something Wiesel objects to, it is clear that he regards it as masculine.

72 Rachel Efrat-Feldman, 'The Fate of the Feldman Family' in Berger, ed., *The Dereczin Memorial Book*, p. 203.

73 Lancman, *Youth in the Time of the Holocaust*, p. 63.

74 Kahane, *Lvov Ghetto Diary*, p. 31 and p. 63.

75 Simcha Bunim Shayevitsh cited in Adelson and Lapides, *Lodz Ghetto*, p. 216.

76 Diment, *The Lone Survivor*, p. 18.

77 Liebman, *Born Jewish*, p. 126.

78 Rosenfeld, *In the Beginning Was the Ghetto*, p. 42.

79 Perechodnik, *Am I a Murderer?*, p. 7 – this is originally written in Latin by Perechodnik who uses the phrase, 'non omnis moriar'.

80 John Tosh, 'Authority and Nurture in Middle-Class Fatherhood', *Gender & History*, 8 (1996), p. 50. Tosh's work is based on nineteenth-century Britain; however, many of his ideas and the theoretical discussions of fatherhood can be readily transferred to other periods.

81 Ringelblum, *Notes from the Warsaw Ghetto*, p. 286.

82 Ringelblum, *Notes from the Warsaw Ghetto*, p. 321.

83 Ringelblum, *Notes from the Warsaw Ghetto*, p. 246.

84 It should be noted here that this answer is given as a response to a repeated direct question and as such should be treated with caution (IWM – Martin Parker – 12597/9).

85 Corni, *Hitler's Ghettos*, p. 136.

86 Zyskind, *Stolen Years*, p. 82 and p. 117.

87 Wells, *The Janowska Road*, p. 105.

88 Meijer, *Alex's Diary*, *passim*.

89 Lee, *The Hidden Life of Otto Frank*, p. 86.

90 Whilst this is certainly a product of life before the war when fathers would have had more access to knowledge concerning international situations and politics, nonetheless its continuity through wartime shows a continuity of this masculinity role of 'sage' and there is little evidence of this being limited in any way by the war (Meijer, *Alex's Diary*, p. 43 and p. 91 amongst others).

91 Most notably Mihail Sebastian (Sebastian, *Journal*, p. 150), but seen elsewhere.

92 IWM – Ben Helfgott – 9165/20.

93 Diment, *The Lone Survivor*, p. 58.

94 Flinker, *Young Moshe's Diary*, p. 36.

95 Feldman, *The Krakow Diary*, p. 12.

96 Etty Hillesum, *Etty: A Diary 1941–1943* (London: Jonathan Cape, 1983), p. 96.

97 Hillesum, *Etty: A Diary*, p. 198.

98 As has been discussed elsewhere, in this period notions of masculinity changed and were even reversed. Here Hillesum shows clear respect for her father's acknowledgement of the truth of their situation whilst remaining strong, whilst in different circumstances such resignation might not be seen as masculine or positive in any way.

99 Liebreider, M., 'The End of Halinka' in Berger, ed., *The Dereczin Memorial Book*, p. 247.

100 Lewin, *A Cup of Tears*, p. 179.

101 T. Kaminetsky-Friedman, 'The Bloody Tenth Day of *Ab*', in Berger, ed., *The Dereczin Memorial Book*, p. 235.

102 The case of Lili Pohlmann is interesting here. Although she described her father as 'completely lost' and is often quoted as discussing her father's collapse, her

testimony goes on to recount her father's rejuvenation, his employment as a carpenter which provided the work card which saved the whole family for some time, and his later decision to put Lili and her mother into hiding, an act which ultimately saved their lives (IWM – Lili Pohlmann – 17340/18).

103 IWM – Martin Parker – 12597/9.

104 IWM – Michael Etkind – 10406/24.

105 Flinker, *Young Moshe's Diary, passim.*

106 If this was indeed the case, it shows his father's power within the family, however, even if it is not the case that his father always won such arguments, the fact that the son only notes those where his father does win also says something about his representations of, and belief in, his father.

107 Meijer, *Alex's Diary*, p. 8.

108 Shoah Foundation interview with Freddie Knoller (found at sfi.usc.edu and viewed repeatedly between 1 January 2013 and 20 December 2013).

109 Rubinowicz, *The Diary of Dawid Rubinowicz*, p. 70.

110 Rubinowicz, *The Diary of Dawid Rubinowicz*, p. 74.

111 Liebman, *Born Jewish*, p. 93.

112 Smith, *Forgotten Voices of the Holocaust*, p. 127.

113 Wiesel, *Night*, p. 23.

114 Rubinowicz, *The Diary of Dawid Rubinowicz*, p. 16.

115 S. Wachler-Ogulnick, 'This Is How I Was Saved on the Day of Slaughter' in Berger, ed., *The Dereczin Memorial Book*, p. 245.

116 All references are taken either from Halter, *Roman's Journey*, from Roman Halter's interview with the Imperial War Museum, IWM – Roman Halter – 17183/17 or from a private interview with Roman Halter conducted by the author Anna-Madeleine Carey on 25 October 2010 at Roman's home.

117 A term used by the Nazis to signify those understood to be of German ethnicity, living outside Germany.

118 Roman later comments that his family were immediately starving upon entering the Łódź ghetto when others were not because they came from Chodecz rather than Łódź. This emphasis on location and being local would seem, at least partially, to confirm the importance of local knowledge in survival during this period and perhaps go further therefore to explain the actions of men like his father, Mordechai, IWM – Roman Halter – 17183/17.

119 Halter, *Roman's Journey*, p. 225.

120 Waxman, 'Towards an Integrated History of the Holocaust', p. 316.

121 Edward Gastfriend, *My Father's Testament: Memoirs of a Jewish Teenager 1938–1945* (Philadelphia, PA: Temple University Press, 2000), Checinski, *My Father's Watch*, Ivan Singer, *My Father's Blessing: My Salvation* (Sydney: Singer, 2004) and Wermuth, *Breathe Deeply*.

Conclusion

1   See my comments in the introduction on this subject.

2   Stefan Ernest cited in Barbara Engelking, *Holocaust and Memory. The Experience of the Holocaust and Its Consequences: An Investigation Based on Personal Narratives* (London: Leicester University Press, 2001), p. 104. Whilst the situation in Warsaw was not exactly mirrored in all other ghettos, I would argue that it is representative enough to underpin these conclusions.

3   At no point, it seems, were there half a million Jews in the Warsaw ghetto. At most, the ghetto held around 400,000 but sources vary.

4   Donat, *Holocaust Kingdom,* p. 49.

Bibliography

Archival sources

Testimonies of the Holocaust series

- IWM – Abraham Zwirek – 9192/6
- IWM – Barbara Stimler – 17475/5
- IWM – Ben Helfgott – 9165/20
- IWM – Elisabeth Harrison – 8304/5
- IWM – Freddie Knoller – 9092/13
- IWM – Halina Sand – 12526/7
- IWM – Jonkje Grandia-Smits – 8635/6
- IWM – Lea Goodman – 12536/6
- IWM – Leon Greenman – 9274/23
- IWM – Lili Pohlmann – 17340/18
- IWM – Mala Tribich (Helfgott) – 9121/4
- IWM – Martin Parker – 12597/9
- IWM – Marylou Ruhe – 17753/4
- IWM – Michael Etkind – 10406/24
- IWM – Nicole David – 15323/5
- IWM – Rena Zabielak – 17369–4
- IWM – Roman Halter – 17183/17
- IWM – Sem Hartz – 12888/4
- IWM – Stanley Faull – 18272/7
- IWM – Steven Frank – 22600/8

Shoah Foundation interviews

(All found at sfi.usc.edu and viewed repeatedly between 1 January 2013 and 20 December 2013.)
Benno Benima
David Lederman
Eric Baruch
Freddie Knoller
George Weiss

Hans Angress
Harry Alexander
Hermann Bodner
Jacques Breitberg
Joseph Brenig
Joseph Van West
Maurice White
Otto Berets
Samuel Schryver

Documents taken from *Le Centre de Documentation Juive Contemporaine* in Paris (CDJC)

- Survivors of the Shoah Series – Climaud
- DLXI – 6 Maurice Bernsohn
- CDXXVII – 1
- CCXX – 45

Printed primary sources

Adelson, A. and Lapides, R., eds., *Lodz Ghetto: Inside a Community Under Siege* (London: Penguin, 1989).

Adler, S., *In the Warsaw Ghetto* (Jerusalem: Yad Vashem, 1982).

Bakalchuk, M., 'Uprooted with the Maelstrom' in Berger, J., ed., *The Dereczin Memorial Book: A Book of Remembrances Honoring the Communities of Dereczin, Halinka, Kolonia-Sinaiska* (Mahwah, NJ: Jacob Berger, 2000) pp. 323–329.

Bashevis Singer, I., *The Penguin Collected Stories of Isaac Bashevis Singer* (London: Penguin, 1984).

Bauman, J., *Beyond These Walls: Escaping the Warsaw Ghetto, a Young Girl's Story* (London: Virago, 2006).

Benninga, B., *In Hiding: Surviving an Abusive 'Protector' and the Nazi Occupation of Holland* (London: Vallentine Mitchell, 2007).

Berg, M., *The Diary of Mary Berg: Growing Up in the Warsaw Ghetto* (Oxford: Oneworld, 2006).

Bernstein, S., 'I Was a Refugee in Oppressed Dereczin' in Berger, J., ed., *The Dereczin Memorial Book: A Book of Remembrances Honoring the Communities of Dereczin, Halinka, Kolonia-Sinaiska* (Mahwah, NJ: Jacob Berger, 2000) pp. 213–230.

Boder, D., *I Did Not Interview the Dead* (Urbana, IL: University of Illinois Press, 1949).

Borenstein, S., 'With the Dereczin Fighters in the Forest' in Berger, J., ed., *The Dereczin Memorial Book: A Book of Remembrances Honoring the Communities of Dereczin, Halinka, Kolonia-Sinaiska* (Mahwah, NJ: Jacob Berger, 2000) pp. 276–287.

Breitowicz, J., *Through Hell to Life* (New York: Shengold Publishers Inc., 1983).

Bronowski, A., *They Were Few* (New York: Lang, 1991).

Buergenthal, T., *A Lucky Child* (London: Profile Books, 2009).

Castle Stanford, J., *Reflections: The Diary of a German-Jew in Hiding* (Oakland, OR: Institute for the Righteous Acts of the Judah L. Magnes Memorial Museum, 1965).

Checinski, M., *My Father's Watch* (Jerusalem: Gefen, 1994).

Czerniakow, A., *The Warsaw Diary of Adam Czerniakow: Prelude to Doom* (New York: Stein and Day, 1979).

David, J., *A Square of Sky, a Touch of Earth: A Wartime Childhood in Poland* (Harmondsworth: Penguin, 1981).

Diment, M., *The Lone Survivor: A Diary of the Lukacze Ghetto and Svyruukhy Ukraine* (New York: The Holocaust Library, 1992).

Dobroszycki, L., ed., *The Chronicle of the Łódź Ghetto, 1941–1944* (New Haven, CT: Yale University Press, 1984).

Dobschiner, J., *Selected to Live* (London: Hodder and Stoughton, 2000).

Donat, A., *The Holocaust Kingdom* (New York: The Holocaust Library, 1978).

Efrat-Feldman, R., 'The Fate of the Feldman Family' in Berger, J., ed., *The Dereczin Memorial Book: A Book of Remembrances Honoring the Communities of Dereczin, Halinka, Kolonia-Sinaiska* (Mahwah, NJ: Jacob Berger, 2000) pp. 203–204.

Eisenberg, M., 'Running from Death' in Kagan, B., ed., *Szydłowiec Memorial Book* (New York: Shidlowtzer Benevolent Association, 1989) pp. 161–186.

Eliach, Y., *Hasidic Tales of the Holocaust* (New York: Oxford University Press, 1982).

Feldman, J., *The Krakow Diary of Julius Feldman* (Newark, NJ: Quill, 2002).

Flinker, M., *Young Moshe's Diary. The Spiritual Torment of a Jewish Boy in Nazi Europe* (Jerusalem: Yad Vashem, 1971).

Frankel-Shalev, P. and Don, M., *Memoir: A True Story of a Family's Escape* (Israel: Karen Dondushansky, 2006).

Friedländer, S., *When Memory Comes* (New York: Farrar, Straus, Giroux, 1979).

Frister, R., *The Cap or the Price of a Life* (London: Weidenfeld & Nicolson, 1999).

Gastfriend, E., *My Father's Testament: Memoirs of a Jewish Teenager 1938–1945* (Philadelphia, PA: Temple University Press, 2000).

Halter, R., *Roman's Journey* (London: Portobello Books, 2007).

Heller, A., 'The Destruction of the Jewish Community of Rzeszow' in Wald, M.Y., ed., *Rzeszów Jews Memorial Book* (Tel Aviv: Rzeszower Societies in Israel and U.S.A., 1967) pp. 74–94.

Hillesum, E., *Etty: A Diary 1941–1943* (London: Jonathan Cape, 1983).

Hipszman, M., *Souvenirs d'enfance de Marcel: Un enfant dans la guerre* (unpublished, 2003).

Kahane, D., *Lvov Ghetto Diary* (Amherst, MA: University of Massachusetts Press, 1990).

Kaminetsky-Friedman, T., 'The Bloody Tenth Day of Ab', in Berger, J., ed., *The Dereczin Memorial Book: A Book of Remembrances Honoring the Communities of Dereczin, Halinka, Kolonia-Sinaiska* (Mahwah, NJ: Jacob Berger, 2000) pp. 235–236.

Kampelmacher, E., *Fighting for Survival* (Jerusalem: Yad Vashem, 2006).

Kaplan, C., *The Scroll of Agony. The Warsaw Diary of Chaim A. Kaplan* (London: Hamish Hamilton, 1965).

Katz, J., *One Who Came Back: The Diary of a Jewish Survivor* (Takoma Park, MD: Dryad Press, 2006).

Katznelson, Y., *Vittel Diary* (Tel Aviv: Ghetto Fighters' House/Beit Lohamei Haghetaot, 1972).

Kermish, J., *To Live with Honor and Die with Honor!...: Selected Documents from the Warsaw Ghetto Underground Archives 'O.S.'* (Jerusalem: Yad Vashem, 1986).

Kessler, E., *The Wartime Diary of Edmund Kessler. Lvov, Poland* (Boston, MA: Academic Studies Press, 2010).

Klemperer, V., *I Shall Bear Witness: The Diaries of Victor Klemperer, 1933–1941* (London: Weidenfeld & Nicolson, 1998).

Kotlar, H., *We Live in a Grave* (New York: Shengold, 1980).

Kroh, A., *Lucien's Story: A Memoir* (Evanston, IL: Northwestern University Press, 1993).

Kruczkowski, L., 'The Warsaw Ghetto Uprising' in *Bleter far Geszichte*, Czasopismo Zydowskiego Instiytutu Historycznego w Polsce (1983) p. xlvi–xlviii.

Kruk, H., *The Last Days of the Jerusalem of Lithuania. Chronicles from the Vilna Ghetto and the Camps, 1939–44* (New Haven, CT: Yale University Press, 2002).

Kulakowski, M. and Kulakowski, A., 'Two Years in the Partisan Forces' in Berger, J., ed., *The Dereczin Memorial Book: A Book of Remembrances Honoring the Communities of Dereczin, Halinka, Kolonia-Sinaiska* (Mahwah, NJ: Jacob Berger, 2000) pp. 195–203.

Lambert, R., *Diary of a Witness 1940–1943* (Chicago, IL: Ivan R Dee, 2005).

Lancman, A., *Youth in the Time of the Holocaust* (Warsaw: Rytm, 2005).

Levi, P., *The Drowned and the Saved* (London: Michael Joseph, 1988).

Lewin, A., *A Cup of Tears: A Diary of the Warsaw Ghetto* (Oxford: Blackwell, 1988).

Lewis, M. and Frank, J., *Himmler's Jewish Tailor: The Story of the Holocaust Survivor Jacob Frank* (Syracuse, NY: Syracuse University Press, 2000).

Liebman, M., *Born Jewish: A Childhood in Occupied Europe* (London: Verso, 2005).

Liebreider, M., 'The End of Halinka' in Berger, J., ed., *The Dereczin Memorial Book: A Book of Remembrances Honoring the Communities of Dereczin, Halinka, Kolonia-Sinaiska* (Mahwah, NJ: Jacob Berger, 2000) pp. 247–248.

Meed, V., *On Both Sides of the Wall* (Tel Aviv: Ghetto Figher's House/Beit Lohamei Haghettaot, 1977).

Meiier, A., *Alex's Diary, 1942–45* (Israel: Biblio Books, 2005).

Nordau, M., 'Jewry of Muscle'/'Muskeljudentum' from *Juedische Turnzeitung* (June 1903) in Mendes-Flohr, P. and Reinharz, J., eds., *The Jew in the Modern World: A Documentary History* (Oxford: Oxford University Press, 1995) pp. 434–436.

Orenstein, H., *I Shall Live: Surviving the Holocaust 1939–1945* (Oxford: Oxford University Press, 1988).

Perechodnik, C., *Am I a Murderer? Testament of a Jewish Ghetto Policeman* (Boulder, CO: Westview Press, 1996).

Pivnik, S., *Survivor: Auschwitz, the Death March and My Fight for Freedom* (London: Hodder, 2013).

Poterański, W., *The Warsaw Ghetto: On the 30th Anniversary of the Armed Uprising of 1943* (Warsaw: Interpress, 1973).

Ringelblum, E., *Notes from the Warsaw Ghetto: The Journal of Emmanuel Ringleblum*, ed. Jacob Sloan (New York: McGraw-Hill, 1958).

Rosenfeld, O., *In the Beginning Was the Ghetto* (Evanston, IL: Northwestern University Press, 2002).

Rotem, S. (Kazik), *Memoirs of a Warsaw Ghetto Fighter: The Past Within Me* (New Haven, CT: Yale University Press, 1994).

Rubinowicz, D., *The Diary of Dawid Rubinowicz* (Edinburgh: Blackwood, 1982).

Rudashevski, Y., *The Diary of the Vilna Ghetto* (Tel Aviv: Ghetto Fighters' House/Beit Lohamei Haghetaot, 1973).

Schupack, J., *The Dead Years* (New York: Holocaust Library, 1986).

Sebastian, M., *Journal, 1935–1944* (London: Heinemann, 2003).

Sierakowiak, D., *The Diary of Dawid Sierakowiak* (London: Bloomsbury, 1996).

Singer, I., *My Father's Blessing: My Salvation* (Sydney: Singer, 2004).

Smith, L., *Forgotten Voices of the Holocaust* (London: Ebury Press, 2005).

Spiegelman, A., *The Complete Maus* (London: Penguin, 2003).

Szpilman, W., *The Pianist: The Extraordinary Story of One Man's Survival in Warsaw, 1939–1945* (London: Phoenix, 2003).

Turkov, I., *C'était ainsi: 1939–1943, la vie dans le ghetto de Varsovie* (Paris: Austral, 1995).

Wachler-Ogulnick, S., 'This Is How I Was Saved on the Day of Slaughter' in Berger, J., ed., *The Dereczin Memorial Book: A Book of Remembrances Honoring the Communities of Dereczin, Halinka, Kolonia-Sinaiska* (Mahwah, NJ: Jacob Berger, 2000) pp. 244–246.

Wallach, J., *Bitter Freedom: Memoirs of a Holocaust Survivor* (Schuylkill Haven, PA: Hermitage Publishers, 2006).

Wells, L., *The Janowska Road* (New York: Holocaust Library, 1978).

Wermuth, H., *Breathe Deeply My Son* (London: Vallentine Mitchell, 1993).

Werner, H., *Fighting Back: A Memoir of Jewish Resistance in World War II* (New York: Columbia University Press, 1992).

Wiesel, E., *Night* (London: Penguin, 1981).

Zar, R., *In the Mouth of the Wolf* (New York: The Jewish Publication Society of America, 1983).

Zelkowicz, J., *In Those Terrible Days: Notes from the Lodz Ghetto* (Jerusalem: Yad Vashem, 2002).

Zuckerman, A., *A Voice in the Chorus: Life as a Teenager in the Holocaust* (Hoboken, NJ: KTAV Publishing House, 1991).

Zuckerman, Y., *A Surplus of Memory: Chronicle of the Warsaw Ghetto Uprising* (Berkeley, CA: University of California Press, 1993).

Zylberberg, M., *A Warsaw Diary,1939–1945* (London: Vallentine Mitchell, 1969).

Zyskind, S., *Stolen Years* (Minneapolis, MN: Lerner Publications Company, 1981).

Secondary sources

Bauer, Y., *A History of the Holocaust* (New York: Franklin Watts, 2001).

Baumel, J., *Double Jeopardy: Gender and the Holocaust* (London: Vallentine Mitchell, 1998).

Benbassa, E., *The Jews of France: A History from Antiquity to the Present* (Princeton, NJ: Princeton University Press, 1999).

Biale, D., 'Zionism as an Erotic Revolution' in Eilberg-Schwarz, H., ed., *People of the Body: Jews and Judaism from an Embodied Perspective* (Albany, NY: State Press of New York, 1992) pp. 283–309.

Bondy, R., 'Women in Theresienstadt and the Family Camp in Birkenau' in Ofer, D. and Weitzman, L., eds., *Women in the Holocaust* (New Haven, CT: Yale University Press, 1998) pp. 310–326.

Boyarin, D., *Unheroic Conduct: The Rise of Heterosexuality and the Invention of the Jewish Man* (London: University of California Press, 1997).

Boyarin, J. and Boyarin, D., *Powers of Diaspora: Two Essays on the Relevance of Jewish Culture* (London: University of Minnesota Press, 2002).

Brenner, R. F., *Writing as Resistance: Four Women Confronting the Holocaust* (University Park, PA: Penn State Press, 1997).

Brittan, A., *Masculinity and Power* (Oxford: Wiley-Blackwell, 1989).

Browning, C., *Collected Memories: Holocaust History and Postwar Testimony* (Madison, WI: The University of Wisconsin Press, 2003).

Browning, C., *The Origins of the Final Solution* (Jerusalem: Yad Vashem, 2004).

Browning, C., *The Origins of the Final Solution: The Evolution of Nazi Jewish Policy September 1939–March 1942* (Jerusalem: Yad Vashem, 2004).

Browning, C., *Remembering Survival: Inside a Nazi Slave-Labor Camp* (New York: W.W. Norton and Co., 2011).

Caplan, J., 'Gender and the Concentration Camps', in Caplan, Jane and Wachsmann, Nikolaus, eds., *Concentration Camps in Nazi Germany: The New Histories* (Oxford: Routledge, 2010) pp. 82–107.

Caplan, J. and Wachsmann, N., 'Introduction', in Caplan, Jane and Wachsmann, Nikolaus, eds., *Concentration Camps in Nazi Germany: The New Histories* (Oxford: Routledge, 2010) pp. 1–16.

Caplan, N.A., 'Revisiting the Diary: Rereading Anne Frank's Rewriting' in Bloom, H., ed., *Bloom's Modern Critical Interpretations: The Diary of Anne Frank* (New York: Infobase Publishing, 2010).

Cohen, D., *The War Come Home: Disabled Veterans in Britain and Germany, 1914–1939* (Berkeley, CA: University of California Press, 2001).

Cole, T., 'Ghettoization' in Stone, D., ed., *The Historiography of the Holocaust* (Basingstoke: Palgrave, 2006) pp. 65–87.

Connell, R.W., *Masculinities* (Cambridge: Polity Press, 1995).

Connell, R.W., 'The Social Organization of Masculinity' in Whitehead, S. and Barrett, F., eds., *The Masculinities Reader* (Cambridge: Polity, 2001).

Corni, G., *Hitler's Ghettos: Voices from a Beleaguered Society, 1939–1944* (London: Arnold, 2002).

Davidoff, L. and Hall, C., *Family Fortunes: Men and Women of the English Middle Class, 1780–1850* (London: Routledge, 2002).

Dawidowicz, L., *A Holocaust Reader* (West Orange, NJ: Behrman House Inc., 1976).

Efron, J., *Defenders of the Race: Jewish Doctors and Race Science in Fin-de-Siècle Europe* (New Haven, CT: Yale University Press, 1994).

Eilberg-Schwartz, H., 'Introduction' in Eilberg-Schwarz, H., ed., *People of the Body: Jews and Judaism from an Embodied Perspective* (Albany, NY: State Press of New York, 1992) pp. 17–47.

Engelking, B., *Holocaust and Memory. The Experience of the Holocaust and Its Consequences: An Investigation Based on Personal Narratives* (London: Leicester University Press, 2001).

Falk, R., 'Zionism, Race, and Eugenics' in Cantor, G. and Swetlitz, M., eds., *Jewish Tradition and the Challenge of Darwinism* (London: University of Chicago Press, 2006) pp. 147–162.

Feierstein, D., 'The Jewish Resistance Movements in the Ghettos of Eastern Europe: Reflections of the Relationships of Force' in Sterling, E.J., ed., *Life in the Ghettos During the Holocaust* (Syracuse, NY: Syracuse University Press, 2005) pp. 220–257.

Filene, P., 'The Secrets of Men's History' in Brod, H., ed. *The Making of Masculinities: The New Men's Studies* (Boston, MA: Allen & Unwin, 1987) pp. 103–119.

Fletcher, A., *Gender, Sex and Subordination in England, 1500–1800* (New Haven, NJ: Yale University Press, 1995).

Foyster, E., *Manhood in Early Modern England: Honour, Sex and Marriage* (London: Longman, 1999).

Freidländer, S., *The Years of Extermination: Nazi Germany and the Jews, 1939–1945* (London: Weidenfeld & Nicholson, 2007).

Friedman, P., *Roads to Extinction: Essays on the Holocaust* (New York: Jewish Publication Society of America, 1980).

Geller, J., 'Freud, Blüher and the Secessio Inversa: Männerbünde, Homosexuality, and Freud's Theory of Cultural Formation' in Boyarin, D. et al., eds., *Queer Theory and the Jewish Question* (New York: Columbia University Press, 2003) pp. 90–121.

Gerschick, T. and Miller, A.S., 'Coming to Terms: Masculinity and Physical Disability' in Kimmel, M.S. and Messner, M.A., eds., *Men's Lives* (Boston, MA: Allyn & Bacon, 2001) pp. 313–326.

Gigliotti, S., *The Train Journey: Transit, Captivity and Witnessing in the Holocaust* (Oxford: Berghahn Books, 2009).

Gillerman, S., 'A Kinder Gentler Strongman? Siegmund Breitbart in Eastern Europe' in Baader, B., Gillerman, S. and Lerner, P., eds., *Jewish Masculinities: German Jews, Gender, and History* (Bloomington, IN: Indiana University Press, 2012) pp. 197–209.

Gilman, S., *Jewish Self-Hatred: Antisemitism and the Hidden Language of the Jews* (Baltimore, MD: Johns Hopkins University Press, 1986).

Gilman, S., *The Jew's Body* (London: Routledge, 1991).

Gilman, S., *Franz Kafka. The Jewish Patient* (London: Routledge, 1995).

Gilmore, D., *Manhood in the Making: Cultural Concepts of Masculinity* (London: Yale University Press, 1990).

Gutman, Y., 'The Concept of Labor in Judenrat Policy' in Gutman, Y. and Haft, C., eds., *Patterns of Jewish Leadership in Nazi Europe 1933–1945: Proceedings of the Third Yad Vashem International Historical Conference – April 1977* (Jerusalem: Yad Vashem, 1979) pp. 151–180.

Hadley, D., 'Introduction: Medieval Masculinities' in Hadley, D., ed., *Masculinity in Medieval Europe* (London: Longman, 1999).

Hagemann, K., 'Home/Front: The Military, Violence and Gender Relations in the Age of the World Wars' in Hagemann, K. and Schüler-Springorum, S., eds., *Home/Front: The Military, War and Gender in Twentieth-Century Germany* (Oxford: Berg, 2002) pp. 1–42.

Hájková, A., 'Poor Devils of the Camps: Dutch Jews in the Terezín Ghetto, 1943–1945', *YadVashem Studies* 34:1 (2015), pp. 77–111.

Halbmayr, B., 'Sexualized Violence Against Women During Nazi "Racial" Persecution' in Hedgepeth, S. and Saidel, R., eds., *Sexual Violence Against Jewish Women During the Holocaust* (Hanover, NH: Brandeis University Press, 2010) pp. 29–44.

Hardman, A., 'Women and the Holocaust', *Holocaust Educational Trust Research Papers* 1:3 (1999–2000).

Hart, M., *The Healthy Jew: The Symbiosis of Judaism and Modern Medicine* (Cambridge: Cambridge University Press, 2007).

Heinemann, M.E., *Gender and Destiny; Women Writers and the Holocaust* (New York: Greenwood, 1986).

Hoberman, J., 'Otto Weininger and the Critique of Jewish Masculinity' in Horowitz, N. and Hyams, B., eds., *Jews and Gender: Responses to Otto Weininger* (Philadelphia, PA: Temple University Press, 1995) pp. 140–155.

Horowitz, S., 'Gender, Genocide and Jewish Memory', *Prooftexts* 20 (2000), pp. 158–191.

Hyman, P., 'Gender and the Jewish Family in Modern Europe' in Ofer, D. and Weitzman, L., eds., *Women in the Holocaust* (New Haven, CT: Yale University Press, 1998) pp. 25–39.

Jockusch, L., *Collect and Record! Jewish Holocaust Documentation in Early Postwar Europe* (Oxford: Oxford University Press, 2012).

Judd, R., 'Moral, Clean Men of the Jewish Faith: Jewish Rituals and Their Male Practitioners, 1843–1914' in Baader, B., Gillerman, S. and Lerner, P., eds., *Jewish Masculinities: German Jews, Gender, and History* (Bloomington, IN: Indiana University Press, 2012) pp. 72–89.

Kaplan, M.A., *Between Dignity and Despair: Jewish Life in Nazi Germany* (Oxford: Oxford University Press, 1998).

Kermisz, Y., 'The Judenrat in Warsaw' in Gutman, Y. and Haft, C., eds., *Patterns of Jewish Leadership in Nazi Europe 1933–1945: Proceedings of the Third Yad Vashem International Historical Conference – April 1977* (Jerusalem: Yad Vashem, 1979) pp. 75–90.

Kienitz, S., 'Body Damage: War Disability and Constructions of Masculinity in Weimar Germany' in Hagemann, K. and Schüler-Springorum, S., eds., *Home/Front: The Military, War and Gender in Twentieth-Century Germany* (Oxford: Berg, 2002) pp. 181–204.

Kimmel, M.S., 'The Contemporary "Crisis" of Masculinity in Historical Perspective' in Brod, H., ed., *The Making of Masculinities: The New Men's Studies* (Boston, MA: Allen & Unwin, 1987) pp. 121–153.

Kimmel, M.S. and Messner, M.A., 'Introduction' in Kimmel, M.S. and Messner, M.A., eds., *Men's Lives* (Boston, MA: Allyn & Bacon, 2001) pp. ix–xvii.

Kushner, T., 'Saul Friedländer, Holocaust Historiography and the Use of Testimony' in Weise, C. and Betts, P., eds., *Years of Persecution, Years of Extermination: Saul Friedländer and the Future of Holocaust Studies* (London: Continuum, 2010) pp. 67–81.

Langer, L., *Preempting the Holocaust* (New Haven, CT: Yale University Press, 1998).

Langerwey, M., *Reading Auschwitz* (Walnut Creek, CA: Alta Mira Press, 1998).

Latour, A., *La Résistance Juive en France (1940–1944)* (Paris: Stock, 1970).

Le Espiritu, Y., 'All Men Are Not Created Equal: Asian Men in U.S. History' in Kimmel, M.S. and Messner, M.A., eds., *Men's Lives* (Boston, MA: Allyn & Bacon, 2001) pp. 33–41.

Lee, C., *The Hidden Life of Otto Frank* (London: Penguin, 2002).

Lessing, T., 'Jewish Self-Hatred' in Mendes-Flohr, P. and Reinharz, J., eds., *The Jew in the Modern World: A Documentary History* (Oxford: Oxford University Press, 1995) pp. 237–239.

Levin, D., 'The Fighting Leadership of the Judenräte in the Small Communities of Poland' in Gutman, Y. and Haft, C., eds., *Patterns of Jewish Leadership in Nazi Europe 1933–1945: Proceedings of the Third Yad Vashem International Historical Conference – April 1977* (Jerusalem: Yad Vashem, 1979) pp. 133–149.

Lewis, C., *Becoming a Father* (Milton Keynes: Open University Press, 1986).

Matthäus, J., ed., *Approaching an Auschwitz Survivor: Holocaust Testimony and Its Transformations* (Oxford: Oxford University Press, 2009).

McGuffey, C.S. and Rich, B.L., 'Playing in the Gender Transgression Zone: Race, Class and Hegemonic Masculinity in Middle Childhood' in Kimmel, M.S. and Messner, M.A., eds., *Men's Lives* (Boston, MA: Allyn & Bacon, 2001) pp. 73–87.

McKee, L. and O'Brien, M., *The Father Figure* (London: Tavistock, 1982).

Michman, D., 'Research on the Holocaust in Belgium and in General: History and Context' in Michman, D., ed., *Belgium and the Holocaust: Jews. Belgians. Germans* (Jerusalem: Yad Vashem, 1998).

Michman, D., 'Jewish Leadership in Extremis' in Stone, D., ed., *The Historiography of the Holocaust* (Basingstoke: Palgrave Macmillan, 2004) pp. 319–340.

Michman, D., 'The Jewish Ghettos Under the Nazis and Their Allies' in Miron, G., and Shulhani, S., eds., *The Yad Vashem Encyclopaedia of the Ghettos During the Holocaust* (Jerusalem: Yad Vashem, 2009).

Mosse, G., *The Image of Man: The Creation of Modern Masculinity* (Oxford: Oxford University Press, 1996).

Nonn, T., 'Hitting Bottom: Homelessness, Poverty and Masculinity' in Kimmel, M.S. and
    Messner, M.A., eds., *Men's Lives* (Boston, MA: Allyn & Bacon, 2001) pp. 242–251.

Ofer, D., 'Gender Issues in Dairies and Testimonies of the Ghetto: The Case of Warsaw'
    in Ofer, D. and Weitzman, L., eds., *Women in the Holocaust* (New Haven, CT: Yale
    University Press, 1998) pp. 143–168.

Ofer, D., 'The Community and the Individual: The Different Narratives of Early and
    Late Testimonies and Their Significance for Historians' in Bankier, D. and Michman,
    D., eds., *Holocaust Historiography in Context. Emergence, Challenges, Polemics and
    Achievements* (Jerusalem: Yad Vashem, 2008) pp. 519–535.

Ofer, D., and Weitzman, L., 'Introduction' in Ofer, D. and Weitzman, L., eds., *Women in
    the Holocaust* (New Haven, CT: Yale University Press, 1998) pp. 1–18.

Pellegrini, A., *Performance Anxieties: Staging Psychoanalysis, Staging Race* (New York:
    Routledge, 1997).

Petersen, A., *Unmasking the Masculine: 'Men' and 'Identity' in a Sceptical Age* (London:
    SAGE, 1998).

Pine, L., 'Gender and the Family' in Stone, D., ed., *The Historiography of the Holocaust*
    (Basingstoke: Palgrave Macmillan, 2004) pp. 364–382.

Pleck, J., *The Myth of Masculinity* (Cambridge, MA: MIT Press, 1981).

Pleck, J., 'The Theory of Male Sex-Role Identity: Its Rise and Fall, 1936 to the Present'
    in Brod, H., ed., *The Making of Masculinities: The New Men's Studies* (Boston, MA:
    Allen & Unwin, 1987) pp. 21–38.

Plotkin, D., 'Smuggling in the Ghettos: Survivor Accounts from the Warsaw, Lodz,
    and Krakow Ghettos' in Sterling, E.J., ed., *Life in the Ghettos During the Holocaust*
    (Syracuse, NY: Syracuse University Press, 2005) pp. 85–119.

Polonsky, A., *The Jews in Poland and Russia: Volume III, 1914–2008* (Portland, OR: The
    Littman Library of Jewish Civilisation, 2012).

Popkin, Jeremy D., 'Holocaust Memories, Historians' Memoirs: First-Person Narrative
    and the Memory of the Holocaust', *History & Memory* 15:1 (2003), pp. 49–84.

Poznanski, R., *Jews in France During World War II* (Hanover, MA: Brandeis University
    Press, 2001).

Ringelheim, J., 'Women and the Holocaust: A Reconsideration of Research' in Rittner,
    C. and Roth, J.K., eds., *Different Voices: Women and the Holocaust* (New York:
    Paragon House, 1993) pp. 373–405.

Ringelheim, J., 'The Split Between Gender and the Holocaust' in Ofer, D. and Weitzman,
    L., eds., *Women in the Holocaust* (New Haven, CT: Yale University Press, 1998)
    pp. 340–351.

Ringelheim, J.M., 'The Unethical and the Unspeakable: Women and the Holocaust',
    Simon Wiesenthal Center Annual 1 (1984), pp. 69–88.

Roper, M. and Tosh, J., 'Introduction: Historians and the Politics of Masculinity' in
    Roper, M., ed., *Manful Assertions* (London: Routledge, 1991) pp. 1–24.

Rosen, A., *Sounds of Defiance: The Holocaust, Multilingualism, and the Problem of
    English* (Lincoln, NE: University of Nebraska Press, 2008).

Rossino, A., *Hitler Strikes Poland: Blitzkrieg, Ideology and Atrocity* (Lawrence, KS: University Press of Kansas, 2003).

Rozenblit, M., 'European Jewry: 1800–1933' in Baskin, J., and Seeskin, K., eds., *The Cambridge Guide to Jewish History, Religion and Culture* (Cambridge: Cambridge University Press, 2010) pp. 169–207.

Schüler-Springorum, S., 'A Soft Hero: Male Jewish Identity in Imperial Germany Through the Autobiography of Aron Liebeck' in Baader, B., Gillerman, S. and Lerner, P., eds., *Jewish Masculinities: German Jews, Gender, and History* (Bloomington, IN: Indiana University Press, 2012) pp. 90–113.

Segal, L., *Slow Motion: Changing Masculinities, Changing Men* (Basingstoke: Palgrave Macmillan, 1997).

Shavit, D., *Hunger for the Printed Word: Books and Libraries in the Jewish Ghettos of Nazi-Occupied Europe* (Jefferson, NC: McFarland, 1997).

Shepard, A., *Meanings of Manhood in Early Modern England* (Oxford: Oxford University Press, 2003).

Surén, H., *Der Mensch und die Sonne* (Stuttgart: Dieck and Co., 1923).

Tec, N., *Resilience and Courage: Women, Men and the Holocaust* (New Haven, CT: Yale University Press, 2003).

Tosh, J., 'What Should Historians Do with Masculinity? Reflections on Nineteenth-Century Britain', *History Workshop Journal* 38 (1994), pp. 179–202.

Tosh, J., 'Authority and Nurture in Middle-Class Fatherhood', *Gender & History* 8 (1996), pp. 48–64.

Tosh, J., 'The Old Adam and the New Man: Emerging Themes in the History of English Masculinities, 1750–1850' in Hitchcock, T. and Cohen, M., eds., *English Masculinities, 1660–1800* (London: Longman, 1999) pp. 217–238.

Tosh, J., 'Hegemonic Masculinity and the History of Gender' in Dudink, S., Hagemann, K. and Tosh, J., eds., *Masculinities in Politics and War: Gendering Modern History* (Manchester: Manchester University Press, 2004) pp. 41–58

Trunk, I., 'The Typology of the Judenräte in Eastern Europe' in Gutman, Y. and Haft, C., eds., *Patterns of Jewish Leadership in Nazi Europe 1933–1945: Proceedings of the Third Yad Vashem International Historical Conference – April 1977* (Jerusalem: Yad Vashem, 1979) pp. 17–30.

Trunk, I., *Łódź Ghetto: A History* (Bloomington, IN: Indiana University Press, 2006).

Unger, M., 'The Status and Plight of Women in the Lodz Ghetto' in Ofer, D. and Weitzman, L., eds., *Women in the Holocaust* (New Haven, CT: Yale University Press, 1998) pp. 123–143.

Vickery, A., 'Golden Age to Separate Spheres? A Review of the Categories and Chronology of English Men's History' in Shoemaker, R. and Vincent, M., eds., *Gender and History in Western Europe* (London: Arnold, 1998) pp. 197–225.

Walker, K., "'I'm Not Friends the Way She's Friends": Ideological and Behavioural Constructions of Masculinity in Men's Friendships' in Kimmel, M.S. and Messner, M.A., eds., *Men's Lives* (Boston, MA: Allyn & Bacon, 2001) pp. 367–379.

Wallet, B., 'Dutch National Identity and Jewish International Solidarity: An Impossible Combination? Dutch Jewry and the Significance of the Damascus Affair (1840)' in Kaplan, Y., ed., *The Dutch Intersection: The Jews and the Netherlands in Modern History* (Leiden: Brill, 2008) pp. 319–330.

Wardi, D., *Memorial Candles: Children of the Holocaust* (London: Routledge, 1992).

Waxman, Z., 'Unheard Stories: Reading Women's Holocaust Testimonies', *The Jewish Quarterly* 177 (2000), pp. 53–58.

Waxman, Z., 'Rape and Sexual Abuse in Hiding' in Hedgepeth, S. and Saidel, R., eds., *Sexual Violence Against Jewish Women During the Holocaust* (Hanover, NH: Brandeis University Press, 2010) pp. 124–136.

Waxman, Z., 'Towards an Integrated History of the Holocaust: Masculinity, Femininity, and Genocide' in Wiese, C. and Betts, P., eds., *Years of Persecution, Years of Extermination: Saul Friedländer and the Future of Holocaust Studies* (London: Continuum, 2010) pp. 311–323.

Web, M., *The Documents of the Lodz Ghetto: An Inventory of the Nachman Zonabend Collection* (New York: YIVO Institute for Jewish Research, 1988).

Weber, M., *The Methodology of the Social Sciences* (New York: Free Press, 1949).

Weindling, P., 'The Evolution of Jewish Identity: Ignaz Zollschan Between Jewish and Aryan Race Theories, 1910–45' in Cantor, G. and Swetlitz, M., eds., *Jewish Tradition and the Challenge of Darwinism* (Chicago, IL: University of Chicago Press, 2006) pp. 116–136.

Whitehead, S. and Barrett, F., 'Introduction, The Sociology of Masculinity' in Whitehead, S. and Barrett, F., eds., *The Masculinities Reader* (Oxford: Polity, 2001) pp. 1–26.

Wieviorka, A., *Ils étaient juifs, résistants, communistes* (Paris: Stock, 1986).

Wünschmann, K., *Before Auschwitz: Jewish Prisoners in the Prewar Concentration Camps* (London: Harvard University Press, 2015).

Yahil, L., *The Holocaust: The Fate of European Jewry* (New York: Oxford University Press, 1990).

Index